A RESTATEMENT OF RABBINIC CIVIL LAW

A RESTATEMENT OF RABBINIC CIVIL LAW

VOLUME VIII

LAWS OF LOST AND FOUND OBJECTS
LAWS OF INHERITANCE
LAWS OF THE UNPAID BAILEE

Emanuel Quint

Jerusalem Institute of Jewish Law

Jason Aronson Inc.
Northvale, New Jersey
Jerusalem

This book was set in 11 pt. Cheltenham by Alabama Book Composition of Deatsville, Alabama.

10 9 8 7 6 5 4 3 2 1

Library of Congress Cataloging-in-Publication Data
(Revised for vol. 8)

Quint, Emanuel B.
A restatement of rabbinic civil law.
Adaptation of: Hoshen mishpat / Joseph ben Ephraim Karo.
Includes bibliographical references and indexes.
Contents: v. 1. Laws of judges, laws of evidence—v. 2. Laws of loans—[etc.]—v. 8. Laws of lost and found objects, laws of inheritance, laws of the unpaid bailee.
1. Jewish law. I. Karo, Joseph ben Ephraim, 1488–1575. Hoshen mishpat. II. Title.
LAW 340.5′25694 89-18546

ISBN 0-87668-765-6 (set)
ISBN 0-87668-799-0 (v. 1)
ISBN 0-87668-678-1 (v. 2)
ISBN 0-87668-396-0 (v. 3)
ISBN 0-87668-197-6 (v. 4)
ISBN 1-56821-167-8 (v. 5)
ISBN 1-56821-319-0 (v. 6)
ISBN 1-56821-907-5 (v. 7)
ISBN 0-7657-9969-3 (v. 8)

Manufactured in the United States of America. Jason Aronson Inc. offers books and cassettes. For information and catalog write to Jason Aronson Inc., 230 Livingston Street, Northvale, New Jersey 07647.

To my wife Rena

And He brought forth His people
with joy (b'Rena),
His chosen ones with singing.
Psalm 105:43

CONTENTS

Chapter 260
SPYING AN OBJECT THAT WAS DELIBERATELY PLACED THERE

Chapter 261
OBJECTS THAT MAY BE KEPT BY THE FINDER

Chapter 262
HOW A FOUND OBJECT IS ACQUIRED

Chapter 263
LOST OBJECTS OF GENTILES OR OF SINNERS

Chapter 264
THE DIGNITY OF THE FINDER

Chapter 265
PRIORITY IN PICKING UP LOST OBJECTS

Chapter 266
THE CARE TO BE GIVEN TO A FOUND OBJECT

Chapter 267
THE ANNOUNCEMENT AND THE RESTORING OF THE FOUND OBJECT

Chapter 268
NOT TO TAKE COMPENSATION FOR RESTORING A LOST OBJECT

Chapter 269
PICKING UP A LOST OBJECT FOR OR WITH ANOTHER PERSON

Chapter 270
OBJECTS FOUND BY A DEAF-MUTE, A MENTALLY DEFICIENT, OR A MINOR

Chapter 271
OBJECTS FOUND BY CLOSE RELATIVES OR BY AN EMPLOYEE

Chapter 272
HELPING TO LOAD, UNLOAD, AND RELOAD ANIMALS: RIGHT OF WAY OF PASSAGE

Chapter 273
OWNERLESS PROPERTY

Chapter 274
THE TEN DECREES OF JOSHUA

Chapter 275
PROPERTY OF A PROSELYTE WHO DIES WITHOUT HEIRS

Part II
LAWS OF INHERITANCE

Chapter 276
LAWS OF INTESTACY

Chapter 277
LAWS OF PRIMOGENITURE

Chapter 278
OBJECTS NOT INCLUDED IN THE PRIMOGENITURE PORTION

Chapter 279
DECLARING WHO ARE AND WHO ARE NOT HIS HEIRS

Chapter 280
DOUBTFUL HEIRS

Chapter 281
DEVIATIONS IN NAMING BENEFICIARIES

Chapter 290
GUARDIANS

Part III
LAWS OF THE UNPAID BAILEE

Chapter 291
THE RESPONSIBILITIES OF THE UNPAID BAILEE

Chapter 292
UNAUTHORIZED USE OF THE OBJECT BY THE BAILEE

Chapter 293
THE RETURN OF THE ENTRUSTED OBJECT

Chapter 294
THE BAILEE DENIES LIABILITY

Chapter 295
BAILEE DESIRES TO PAY RATHER THAN TAKE AN OATH

Chapter 296
MISCELLANEOUS PLEAS OF THE OWNER AND THE BAILEE

Chapter 297
BAILEE'S DENIAL OF HAVING THE ENTRUSTED OBJECT IN HIS POSSESSION

Chapter 298
THE BAILEE PLEADS THAT HE IS NOT AWARE OF THE VALUE OF THE OBJECT

Chapter 299
TWO OWNERS ENTRUSTING ONE OBJECT WITH THE BAILEE

Chapter 300
TWO CLAIMS MADE AGAINST THE BAILEE, ONE OBVIOUSLY FALSE

Chapter 301
MATTERS NOT INCLUDED IN THE LAWS OF BAILEES

Chapter 302
PERSONS INCLUDED IN THE LAWS OF BAILEES

PUBLISHER'S NOTE

The series of volumes entitled *A Restatement of Rabbinic Civil Law*, by Rabbi Emanuel Quint, of which this book is the eighth, is a restatement of the fourth part of R. Yosef Karo's *Shulhan Aruch*. This fourth part, called *Hoshen haMishpat* ("Breastplate of Judgment"), codifies such laws as court procedure, torts, contract law, agency, inheritance, theft, destruction of property, and labor. Volume I covered Laws of Judges and Laws of Evidence; Volume II covered Laws of Loans; Volume III covered Laws of Pleading; Volume IV covered Laws of Collection of Debts, Laws of Collections from Heirs, Laws of Mortgages, Laws of Agency, Laws of Guarantee, and Laws of Presumption of Ownership of Personality; Volume V covered Laws of Presumption of Ownership of Realty, Laws of Injury to Neighbors, Laws of Joint Ownership of Realty, and Laws of Partition of Realty; Volume VI covered Laws of Partnership, Laws of Agents, Laws of Sales, and Acquisition of Personality; Volume VII covered Discrepancies in Sales, Gifts of a Healthy Person, and Gifts *Causa Mortis;* and this Volume covers Laws of Lost and Found Objects, Laws of Inheritance, and Laws of the Unpaid Bailee. Subsequent volumes in this series follow chapter by chapter through *Hoshen haMishpat*, and the series includes all 427 chapters of Part Four of R. Karo's work.

The Jewish code of civil law is at once one of the most difficult fields of study for the expert and one of the most compelling for the layperson. Based on Biblical injunction, reinforced by Rabbinic enactments and by thousands of Rabbinic court rulings, Jewish civil law is a sophisticated legal system, built upon meticulous moral standards.

The Jerusalem Institute of Jewish Law, founded by Rabbis Adin Steinsaltz and Emanuel Quint, is dedicated to the study of Jewish civil law through two of Judaism's seminal legal texts, the Talmud and the *Shulhan Aruch*. While other portions of the *Shulhan Aruch* have been greatly explicated and popularized, *Hoshen haMishpat*, the section dealing with civil law, has been regarded as a closed book to all but the most scholarly. Yet, especially in today's complex commercial environment, the study of Jewish business ethics should be an urgent reminder that Jewish law governs all areas of life.

In order to clarify and simplify the law and render it more certain, the first step must be the preparation of an orderly restatement of the common law, including in that term not only the law developed solely by judicial decision but also the law that has grown from the application by the courts of generally and long-adopted statutes and codes.

The function of the courts is to decide the controversies brought before them. The function of the Jerusalem Institute of Jewish Law is to state, clearly and precisely in the light of the decisions, the principles and rules of common law. The sections of the Restatement express the result of a careful analysis of the subject and a thorough examination and discussion of pertinent cases.

PREFACE

This is the eighth volume of *A Restatement of Rabbinic Civil Law*, a restatement of *Shulhan Aruch, Hoshen haMishpat*, written by Rabbi Yosef Karo in the middle of the sixteenth century.

This volume commences with the Laws of Lost and Found Objects, Laws of Inheritance, (which are bound up with the topics of Gifts *Causa Mortis* and the Laws of Wills) and Laws of the Unpaid Bailee.

The first topic is one that causes many observant Jews problems. What if money is found in the synagogue, or some other place where a finder's conscience suddenly calls out to the finder whether he can keep the money.

What if a person dies without a will, or his will is invalid? Who are his *halachik* heirs? What are the laws of primogeniture (the first born if he is a male)? What if a person turns up and claims to be an heir of the decedent? Another topic that many people think about, especially young people who have young children, who should be a guardian of the children? These topics are covered in this volume.

This last topic is the opening of related topics dealing with bailees and is continued throughout Volume IX, where are discussed laws of the Paid Bailee, Laws of Renters, and Laws of Borrowers. The topic of an unpaid bailee is not alien to most people. Very often a person is in an airport and must leave his seat to go to a restroom and cannot take his bags with him. He asks someone, whom he may have known from before or just met, to watch his valise. What are the responsibilities of the watchman?

ACKNOWLEDGEMENT

Let them praise the Name of the Lord,
For His Name alone is exalted;
His glory is above earth and heaven.
Psalm 148:13

It is once again my great pleasure to thank the following:

My dear friend Marvin Klitsner, Esq., whose many suggestions and penetrating questions resulted in a better manuscript.

Arthur Kurzweil, a great publisher, Steve Palmé, a great production editor, and Pamela Roth. They once again turned my manuscript into a book.

Leah Globe, artist, author, community activist, and a great mother, mother-in-law, grandmother, and great-grandmother.

My children and grandchildren, who continue to bring Rena and myself so much happiness:

Menucha, Ezra, Odeliyah, Moriyah, Eliyana, Chamutal, Carmi, Yinon Yitzchak, Hephzibah, Netta, and Eden Chwat

Naomi Rachel, Reuven, Eliyahu Yaakov, Shoshana, Michal Sara, and Boaz Yehudah Silverman

Jodi Miriam, Daniel, Elad Yisroel, and Roni Yosef Patt

Rachel, David Michael, Zipporah, Yosef Avraham, and Yisroel Yitzchak Quint.

Part I

LAWS OF LOST AND FOUND OBJECTS

Chapter 259

OBJECTS THAT MUST BE PICKED UP, ANNOUNCED, AND RESTORED

INTRODUCTION

Beginning with this chapter and continuing through chapter 271, Rabbi Yosef Karo discusses the laws of lost and found objects, and the responsibility of the finder to the owner of the lost object.

As is usual in the Talmud and the codes, including the *Shulhan Aruch*, many of the topics are intertwined. I have slightly rearranged the topics and chapters to simplify the order of the topics. In addition to the rearrangement, I have classified all of the laws of lost and found objects so as to fall into one of the following three categories: (1) Chapter 259, the finder *must* pick up the object and restore the object to its owner, if certain stated criteria are all present; (2) Chapter 260, the finder *may not* pick up the object because the circumstances indicate that it is not a lost object but rather was deliberately left there by the owner; and (3) Chapter 261, the finder *may* retain the object for himself, because one or more of the criteria required for category (1) to be operative are not present nor do the circumstances indicate that the object was deliberately placed there to fall under category (2). Under category (3) the finder has the option to pick up the found object or leave it where it lies. Very often only a slight change in the facts will take the object from category (1) (or category (2)) and place it into category (3). Thus what *seems to be the same* law will appear in

Chapter 259 (or Chapter 260) and also in Chapter 261. The facts, however, will be different, sometimes only slightly different. There are cross-references from one chapter to the other in such instances.

The topics as they appear in the *Shulhan Aruch* are:

Chapter 259, Restoring lost objects; from which places is the finder obligated to restore the object?

Chapter 260, One finds an object that was obviously placed there.

Chapter 261, One finds an object in a place where it is obvious that it is not lost.

Chapter 262, Which objects must be announced [that they were found], and which objects may be retained [by the finder]?

Chapter 263, One finds an object that he is embarrassed to restore.

Chapter 264, His lost object has precedence over the lost object of any other person; the lost object of his rabbi [Torah teacher] and the lost object of his father, which has precedence?

Chapter 265, Not to take compensation for [restoring] a lost object.

Chapter 266, The laws concerning the lost objects of sinners.

Chapter 267, How is the announcement made? The care to be taken of the lost object while it is yet in his possession.

Chapter 268, The law of acquiring ownership of the lost object by his courtyard or his four cubits.

Chapter 269, Picking up a lost object for another person; if it was so picked up by a deaf-mute or a normal person.

Chapter 270, The finds of: a deaf-mute, a mentally deficient, and a minor; his son and his daughter; his slave and maid servant; his wife; and his employee.

Chapter 271, Finding an animal, a *get* [bill of divorce], a note of indebtedness; and a receipt.

I have rearranged the chapters as follows.

Chapter 259, Objects that must be picked up, announced, and restored.

Chapter 260, Objects that may not be picked up.

Chapter 261, Objects that may be retained by the finder.

Chapter 262, How a found object is acquired.

Chapter 263, Lost Objects of Gentiles[1] and sinners.

1. The role of the Gentile in the lost and found process is discussed in Chapter 263. See note 25 below.

Chapter 264, The dignity of the finder.

Chapter 265, Priority in picking up found objects.

Chapter 266, The care to be given to a found object.

Chapter 267, The announcement and the restoring of the found object.

Chapter 268, Not to take compensation for restoring a lost object.

Chapter 269, Picking up a lost object for another person.

Chapter 270, Objects found by a deaf-mute, a mentally deficient, or a minor.

Chapter 271, Objects found by close relatives or by an employee.

Chapters 259, 260, and 261 are treated as a unit and the laws that appear in *Shulhan Aruch* in any of these three chapters are now placed in the chapter that best fits the legal category of the found objects involved. Each of these three chapters will commence with a general statement of the laws of that chapter. In Chapters 260 and 261 the statements of the law are followed by sections dealing with individual examples of the laws of that chapter; Chapter 261 concludes with a section in the nature of an omnibus section collecting many other examples not discussed in the individual sections. In this chapter (259), the statements of the law is also followed by an omnibus section dealing with examples.

The first topics discussed in this chapter are the Torah commands: (1) for a person not to turn aside when he spies a lost object, but to pick it up; and (2) to restore it to its owner. When are these commandments applicable? If the finder turns aside and does not pick up the object, what are his transgressions? If one picks up the object with the intent not to restore it to its owner, what are his transgressions?

There follows a restated list of criteria that have to be present before the finder is obligated not to turn away from the found object, but rather to pick it up and to restore it to its owner. As is seen throughout these chapters, the obligation on the finder to pick up the object is not always present; there are times that he must pick it up, there are times when he may not pick it up, and there are times when he may or may not pick it up. Whether or not there is an obligation to pick up the object may depend upon the object or upon the place where the object is found, or other criteria. There are persons who are not under the obligation to pick up lost objects. There are objects that are not worth picking up. It may be an object that will belong to whoever picks it up and the finder does not want the object.

The criteria for imposing the obligation on the finder to pick up the object are discussed in the sequence in which they appear on the list of criteria. One criterion deals with whether the owner is deemed to have abandoned hope to have the lost object found and restored to him; an example is losing an object by *force majeure*, such as a raging river. In this latter case the object is not technically lost since the owner sees the object being swept away but he cannot do anything about it.

The thing that was lost and then found is designated as "the object." The person who lost the object, usually the owner of the object, is designated herein as the "owner" or "Ruven"; the person who finds the object is designated herein as the "finder" or "Shimon." The term "restore" means to deliver the found object to its rightful owner.[2] The term "retain" means that the finder may by picking it up acquire the object for himself and treat it as his own for all purposes. In this last situation the finder need not pick it up at all and may leave it where it is. The term "abandoned hope" means that the owner abandons hope of the object being restored to him by the finder of the object.[3]

TEXT

The commandment not to turn aside from a lost object

The Torah requires every Jew, man or woman, who sees an object lost by a fellow Jew in a public place, to stop, to pick up the object, to care for it until it is restored to the owner, and to restore it to its rightful owner. These Torah requirements are only present when all of the

2. I have not used the term "return" since it might be thought to mean that the person (the finder) who is delivering the object to its owner took it from the owner in the first place.

3. The term "has *not* abandoned hope" means that the owner has not abandoned hope of the object being found and restored to him by the finder of the object.

criteria listed below are present. The Torah command appears as follows:[4]

> You shall not see the ox of your brother or his sheep or goat cast off, and hide yourself from them; you shall surely return them to your brother. If your brother is not near you and you do not know him, then gather it inside your house, and it shall remain with you until your brother inquires after it, and you shall return it to him. So shall you do for his donkey, so shall you do for his garment, and so shall you do for any lost article of your brother that may become lost from him and you find it; you shall not hide yourself.

What emerges from these verses are two commandments: (1) the negative commandment "not to turn aside" when one sees a lost object, and (2) the positive commandment to restore the lost object to its rightful owner.[5] There are also circumstances under which the additional transgression of "not to rob" may be present. The laws that follow assume that all of the criteria are present.[6]

The mere turning aside and not bothering to pick up the lost object is a transgression of the negative commandment of not to turn aside, and also a transgression of the positive commandment to restore the found object to its owner. Thus if one sees a lost object, and the criteria listed below are met, he cannot ignore the object; he must pick it up and then seek out the owner and restore it him.[7]

Assume the finder picks up the object with the intent of not restoring it to the owner.[8] The finder transgresses the positive command "to restore the object," and two negative commandments: "not to

4. Deuteronomy 22:1–3.

5. See Maimonides, *Book of Commandments*, Positive Commandment 204 and Negative Commandment 269.

6. The codes mention the fact that the finder will transgress the Torah commands only if he finds the object before the owner has abandoned hope of the object being found by a Jew and restored to him; he will not transgress if he finds the object after the owner has abandoned hope of the object being restored to him. The result is the same if any of the other criteria is lacking; if so, the Torah obligations of the finder are not present.

7. However, there are circumstances under which one *may not* pick up the object (see Chapter 260); and there are circumstances under which he may or need not pick up the object, and if he does pick it up, he may keep it for himself (see Chapter 261).

8. And all of the criteria are present, so that the obligation to pick it up and to restore it are present.

turn aside" and "not to rob." If the finder, in a spirit of contrition,[9] decides to restore the object to the owner, he has still transgressed the negative commandment[10] of "not to turn aside."[11]

The Torah commandment "not to turn aside" and to restore the object to the owner is present whether the person who lost the object is known or not known to the finder, and whether the owner is close or far away from the finder. It does not matter whether the found object is animate or inanimate.

The commandment to restore the lost object

The person who finds the lost object must make every attempt to restore it to its owner, as described in these chapters.

Assume one picks up an object with the intent of restoring it to the owner. Afterward, the finder decides not to restore the object to the owner. The finder transgresses two commandments: the positive commandment of restoring the lost object and the negative commandment not to rob.

Assume the finder originally picked up the object with the intention to restore it to the owner. The finder delayed in restoring the object to the owner. The owner thereafter abandoned hope of recovering the object.[12] Then the finder decides to keep the object. He has nevertheless transgressed the commandment to restore the object, and the object still does not belong to him because he picked it up before the owner abandoned hope of the object being restored to him.

9. The finder must still perform such penance as will be dictated by a rabbi.

10. The other two transgressions, of restoring the object and not robbing, have been rectified. There is an opinion that when this finder restores the object after the owner has abandoned hope of ever recovering the lost object, the finder already has transgressed all three transgressions, and the restoring of the object is now a gift from the finder to the loser. Once there was the original intent not to restore the object, the three transgressions are violated and cannot be undone by the return of the object. If the finder returns the object before the loser abandons hope of its being restored, then the finder transgresses only the negative commandment not to turn aside.

11. The commandment not to turn aside can only be performed when the finder spies the object. His intent then, to keep the object for himself by not restoring it to the owner cannot be undone.

12. The abandonment of hope of recovering the object breaks the unity of all of the criteria being present, and there is no longer an obligation to restore the object to the owner.

Assume Shimon saw the object and did not pick it up. After Ruven, the owner, abandoned hope of the object being restored to him, Shimon went and picked up the object. He has transgressed the commandment not to turn aside from lost objects.

The law of restoring lost objects is not limited to objects that are literally lost, but applies to other situations as well. For example, if someone's animal is sick, a veterinarian must attempt to cure that animal. The veterinarian has the role of the finder and the owner of the animal has the role of the loser. Or if Shimon sees a river surging and threatening to overrun Ruven's real estate and/or Ruven's house and Shimon has the ability to place a barrier in the way of the river and save Ruven's property. Shimon is under the same obligation to help save Ruven's real estate as he is to restore Ruven's lost object. If one finds a cow grazing in vineyards or farms, he must remove the cow from the vineyard because of the damage that it can cause and must restore the cow to its owner. This holds true even if the cow is found in the vineyards or farm of a Gentile if the finder thinks that the Gentile may kill the cow for trespassing and causing damage to his fields. There is an opinion that if a person is wandering around aimlessly and as if lost, he must be taken to a place where he can be cared for. There is an opinion that the obligation of a doctor to heal the sick is part of restoring that which the owner has lost, his health in this case.

Criteria to activate the obligations

As stated above, it is not every object that the finder spies that he is obligated to pick up. There are certain criteria that have to be present and if any of them are missing, the finder is not under any obligation to pick up the object:

(1) The owner has not abandoned hope (or, under the circumstances, is not presumed to have abandoned hope) of the object being restored to him by a Jew who will find the object.

(2) The object must be identifiable.

(3) The object must be found in a place where the obligation exists to restore the found object.

(4) The object is a lost object.

(5) The object must be worth at least a *perutah.*[13]

(6) To restore the object must be consistent with the finder's dignity. (This criterion is discussed in Chapter 264.)

(7) The object must belong to someone to whom the finder owes a duty to pick up his lost object. (This criterion is discussed in Chapter 263.)

If all of the criteria are present, the finder must pick up the object so as to restore it to the owner. If any of these seven criteria are not present, the obligations under the Torah commandments to stop to pick up the object and to restore it to its owner are not applicable.

Criteria (1), the owner has not abandoned hope, and criteria (2), the object must be identifiable, are closely interlinked. If the object is identifiable, the owner will usually not abandon hope; if the object is not identifiable, the owner will usually abandon hope.

These criteria are now discussed.

(1) The owner has not abandoned hope

The obligation to pick up the object and to restore it to the owner is present if the owner has not (or is presumed not to have) abandoned hope of recovering the object from a person who will find it.[14]

The owner abandons hope if he states, "Woe is me that I've suffered a loss" or other words to that effect from which beth din can ascertain that the owner abandoned hope. This holds true even if the object has an identification mark.

If the finder picks it up *after* the abandonment, the object belongs to the finder.[15] **Caveat**: The abandonment of hope must precede the finder picking up the object. If the finder picks up the object and then the owner realizes that he lost the object and immediately abandons hope,[16] the item does not belong to the finder.[17] If there is some

13. See Glossary.

14. The other six criteria must also be present.

15. See Chapter 261.

16. Even if it is the type of object that one immediately gives up hope when he realizes that he lost the object, the abandonment must precede the finder picking up the object for the object to belong to the finder. Otherwise, the criteria of not abandoning hope is still not present.

17. This law centers around one of the most famous disputes in the Talmud (*Baba Metzia* 21b). For example, the owner lost the object at 6 A.M. The finder picked up the

doubt as to which came first, the finding or the abandoning of hope, the object must be restored to the owner.

There are times when the owner does not immediately realize that he lost the object. He cannot abandon hope until after he realizes that he lost the object. Under some circumstances there is usually no gap in time between the lost and the realization of the loss. For example, the object is valuable and the owner feels his pocket constantly to see if the object is still in his pocket. In such a situation the owner will almost immediately realize that he lost the object. Or it is heavy and the owner will almost immediately feel the loss because he realizes that the weight he was carrying is no longer there.

Absent a definite declaration from the owner, there is a presumption that if the object is identifiable, the owner did not abandon hope.[18]

An example[19] of the owner not abandoning hope is where the finder sees two men walking together and an object falls from one of them and the finder does not know from whom it fell. The object was picked up by the finder. Even if the object does not contain an identification mark, the owner has not abandoned hope.[20] If the finder picked up the item and the owner later did abandon hope, the item still does not belong to the finder. The result may be different if instead of two men there were three men and the object fell from one of them and the finder does not know from whom it fell.[21]

Related to the topic of abandoned objects are objects that are carried away by a raging river and other such acts of nature. As seen

---

object at 7 A.M. At 8 A.M., the owner realizes he lost the object and abandons hope of the object ever being recovered. The finder does not acquire ownership of the object.

18. Conversely, if the owner loses an object that is not identifiable, it is presumed that the owner abandons hope as soon as he realizes that he lost the object. See Chapter 261.

19. As stated above, many of these laws appear in this chapter as requiring the finder to pick up the object and restore it to the owner, as the same law with slight variations appears in Chapter 261, since with such variation in facts, all seven criteria are no longer present.

20. The owner has not abandoned hope since he thinks that the other person whom he was with took the object and will sooner or later admit that he took the object.

21. See Chapter 261.

in Chapter 261, if the finder, Shimon, rescues an object from a raging river or wild animals, the object belongs to Shimon.[22]

However if downstream there is an obstacle that will prevent the object from being washed out to sea, then there may be hope that the owner can reach such place and recover his lost object, and the laws of this paragraph apply. The result will depend upon whether the object has an identifying mark. (1) If it has an identifying mark, then the object belongs to the owner unless he has specifically abandoned hope of recovering the object.[23] It belongs to the owner even if he makes no effort to retrieve the object from the river as it is washing away his object. (2) If the object does not have an identifying mark, it will belong to the owner if (a) he immediately runs after the object to attempt to salvage the object before it is washed away; or (b) if the owner is not there when the river washes away his object, and, had he been there, he could have prevented the object from being washed away by the river. If either (1) or (2) is present then the object is presumed not to be abandoned and the finder must restore the object to the owner.

If the river is not a raging river but nevertheless carries objects away from the landowners along its banks, then the objects carried away by the river belong to the owner if (1) the owner immediately runs after the object and is not successful in rescuing his object; or (2) if the owner was not present when the river washed away his object, but when he became aware of it, he immediately made whatever effort could have been made.[24]

A river has a dam used by fishermen to catch fish. An object is

22. The reason is that if the actual intent of the owner is different from the standard of what a reasonable person does under the circumstances, that is, he abandons hope of ever recovering the object; the law presumes that this standard applies.

23. If the object has an identifying mark, then it is presumed that the owner did not abandon hope of recovering the object and the object must be picked up by the finder and restored to the owner. Thus either the owner will proceed downstream and recover his object, or else the people downstream, if they are Jewish, can be depended upon to salvage his object from the river and return it to the owner.

24. If by the time the owner heard of the river carrying off his object it was too late for him to do anything, then the object belongs to him, since the river is not a ravaging river and the people downstream will return the object to the owner if it has an identifying mark.

found behind the dam. The dam is set up by Jewish fishermen and is usually repaired by them. If an object is found there it has to be treated as an object that has not been abandoned. The result is otherwise when the dam is maintained by Gentiles.[25]

(2) The object must be identifiable

The finder is required to pick up an object that he spies on the ground only if it is identifiable. The identification may be a mark on the object, or the place where the object is found.

In the latter case it is identifiable if it appears that the object was deliberately left there with the intention of the owner to return there to retrieve his object.[26] Also, if the object is found in a place where the general public usually does not pass through, the object must be picked up to be restored to the owner, even if the object does not have its own identification mark.[27]

The identification mark need not be on the object itself, but may be the way the object is packaged, or how it is tied together, or the amount of the object,[28] or its weight, or a certain unique mark or thing about the object, or anything that makes the object identifiable by the owner when he comes to claim the object from the finder.

Even if an object does not have an identifying mark, if the item has

---

25. The role of Gentiles as finders of lost objects is discussed in Chapter 263. The Jewish owner of the lost object is presumed to assume that the object will be found by a Gentile and not be restored to him and thus he abandons hope of having the object restored. Therefore the object belongs to the finder. See Chapter 261.

26. This law differs slightly from the laws of Chapter 260, where the object was obviously placed where it is. There the finder is not permitted to pick it up to restore it to the owner. In this chapter the object is not that obviously placed where it is spied to alert the finder not to pick up the object. In the situations in Chapter 260, it is more obvious that the object was deliberately placed there and the owner will return to retrieve his object. For example, in these situations, the object is left in a more secluded spot.

27. Thus if the public place is used by many people, such as a loading platform on a pier, the place in and of itself is not an identification mark.

28. For example, fifty apples in a pile of apples, or three piles of apples, or some other identifiable number or height of the piles of apples.

been used by a scholar for some time and he states that he recognizes the object,[29] it is to be restored to the scholar.[30]

Each community has a beth din that can make rules for that community as to what objects are deemed to have identification marks, and those items that are not identifiable. If they are identifiable, then the second criterion is present regarding the obligation of the finder to pick up the object to restore it to the owner.[31]

(3) The place where the lost object is found

The next criterion that must be present for the finder to have the obligation to pick up and restore the object to its owner deals with the place where the object is found.

The Torah text quoted above refers to the lost object of one's brother, meaning a fellow Jew. If the object is found in a neighborhood where the majority of persons situated or passing through are Jews, then the laws of picking up and restoring found objects applies.[32] This is true even if the majority of the inhabitants of the entire town are Gentiles. The law presumes that the owner assumes that a Jew will find the object and return it to him and thus the owner does not abandon hope of the object being returned to him. Without the owner abandoning hope of the object being returned to him by the finder, the finder cannot acquire ownership of the object by picking it up.

(4) The object is a lost object

Only an object that was lost (and meets the other criteria) must be picked up and restored to its owner. If it was not lost, for example, if it was or appears to have been deliberately placed by the owner where it is now located, the finder must not pick it up. (See Chapter 260.)

If the object is not lost, but deliberately abandoned by its owner, the finder is not required to pick up the object. (See Chapter 261.)

---

29. There are some authorities who hold that the law of this paragraph applies only if the object is found in a place frequented by scholars.

30. The beth din of each community should establish guidelines regarding who is to be classified as a scholar for the purposes of this law.

31. In Chapter 261 there are examples of objects that do not have an identifiable mark and therefore may be retained by the finder.

32. Assuming that all of the other criteria are present.

(5) Value of the object

The requirement to pick up the found object is present only if the object is worth at least a *perutah*[33] (and the other criteria are also present). If it is worth less than a *perutah*, it need not be picked up.

The object must be worth at least a *perutah* at two time intervals: when it was lost and when it was found. If it was worth a *perutah* when lost, but worth less than a *perutah* when found, or worth a *perutah* when found and worth less than a *perutah* when lost, the obligation to pick up the object is not present. If it was worth a *perutah* when lost and also when found, the fact that it may have been worth less than a *perutah* in the interval between losing and finding does not affect the obligation of the finder to pick up the object. Similarly, if the object fell in value after it was found, this does not relieve the finder of the obligation to restore the object to the owner.

If an object belongs to more than one person, the share of each in the object must be at least worth a *perutah* to obligate the finder to pick up the lost object to restore to the owners.

(6) Consistent with the finder's dignity

The lost object must be one that the finder would have bothered to stop and pick up if it was his own. If he would not have picked it up for himself if he dropped it, he need not stoop down to pick it up for others. (This criterion is discussed in Chapter 264.)

(7) Must be a duty owed to the loser

The object must belong to someone to whom the finder owes a duty to pick up his lost object. (This criterion is discussed in Chapter 263.)

Examples of objects that must be restored

The community standards as decided upon by beth din will determine under which category a found object should be classified. This may change from community to community and from generation to generation.

---

33. See Glossary.

Objects that the *halachah* has traditionally from Talmudic times described as having identifiable marks are:[34]

a. bread or cake baked by a householder;[35]
b. dyed wool fleeces as delivered from a wool worker's shop;[36]
c. jugs of wine or oil bearing the mark of the producer, prior to the opening of the market season;[37]
d. large sheaves; a cake of figs with a piece of pottery in it;[38]
e. a loaf of bread with money in it;[39]
f. pieces of meat or fish cut in an unusual manner;[40]
g. any object that has an unusual feature about it so that the owner can identify it;
h. heaps of produce;[41]
i. produce in a vessel;[42]
j. needles or hooks or the like, found two or more at a time;[43]

34. The other criteria still have to be met, but usually if the object has an identifiable mark, the other criteria will be met.

35. Since every household baker bakes in a distinguishing manner, the bread is identifiable, as distinguished from bread or cake baked by professional bakers for sale in a bakery or supermarket where all the loaves of bread or cakes are standard.

36. See Chapter 261, page 39, that wool fleeces that come from the country before they have been worked on by a wool finisher may be kept by the finder.

37. Once the market season for these commodities has begun, the mark of the manufacturer is no longer relevant since it might have been purchased and lost by the buyer. By the same token, it would seem that the same holds true for most manufactured products that have not yet reached the market.

38. The uniqueness of the object is the identification mark, since a loaf of bread ordinarily does not have money in it.

39. In these last two cases, it is assumed that the pottery or money was deliberately placed there; thus it has an identification mark. It is unique to find a cake with a piece of pottery inside. This assumption holds true even if the possibility exists that the money or pottery accidentally fell into the object.

40. See Chapter 261, page 39, that if the pieces of meat or fish are not cut in an unusual manner, they belong to the finder.

41. If there are several heaps, the number may be its identification, and if only one heap, its location may be its identification. If it is scattered produce, see the section entitled "Scattered produce" in both Chapters 260 and 261.

42. If the produce is not in the vessel, see Chapter 261, page 40.

43. The number is deemed an identification mark. If found one at time, they belong to the finder. See Chapter 261, page 40.

k. a heap of money; three coins piled up in a certain manner;[44] or a specific amount of coins;[45]
l. money in a purse or a purse without money;[46]
m. a coin that has a unique marking such as a crack or split in the coin;[47]
n. bearer bonds or stocks that are identifiable only by a unique mark of the owner;[48]
o. money found in purchased produce;[49]
p. an object without an identification mark found in a vessel that has an identification mark;[50]
q. a mule without an identifying mark bearing a saddle that has an identifying mark.[51]
r. young birds with their wings tied together with an identifiable knot or in an identifiable place.[52]

---

44. If the three coins are one on top of the other in the shape of a turret, or two side by side and one on top of them, or part of one on top of them so that if a small stick was placed under them they could be picked up together, they must be restored to the owner.

45. The owner will identify the coins by the number of coins. There is an opinion that the number is of little probative value, since coins are very small and some of the coins may have been kicked away by the public going through the street.

46. However, if the money is scattered in front of the purse, the money belongs to the finder, unless it appears that both belong to the same owner. See Chapter 261, page 40.

47. This was stated when coins were the only type of money. Nowadays this can be used for coins of coin collectors.

48. Such as a smudge on a certain letter of the bond, and so forth.

49. This assumes that the money is tied up or placed there in such a manner that the owner can identify the money as his. If the produce comes from the original farmer, the money will belong to that farmer even if he cannot identify the money.

50. This topic is fully discussed in Chapter 261.

51. If the owner can identify the saddle, he will also have the mule restored to him. He must provide a valid reason why he cannot furnish an identifying mark for the mule, such as he just purchased the mule.

52. See Chapter 260, that the finder should not have taken the birds but should have left them where he found them. If the finder violated the law and took them, then if they have an identification mark, he must announce his find and restore them to the owner.

Chapter 260

SPYING AN OBJECT THAT WAS DELIBERATELY PLACED THERE

INTRODUCTION

In Chapter 259 there were set forth seven criteria that had to be met before the finder had the obligation to pick up the object that he spied on the ground and restore it to the owner. Criteria (4) states that "Only an object that was lost (and meets the other criteria) must be picked up and restored to its owner. If it was not lost, for example, if it was or appears to have been deliberately placed by the owner where it is now located, the finder must not pick it up."

If the object was deliberately placed there by the owner at the spot where it is found by the finder, it must not be picked up by the finder. Even if it has an identifying mark, it will put the owner to the expense and bother of having to locate the finder and to give the identifying marks and retrieve the object. Perhaps more importantly, if the object has no identifying marks, it will probably be lost to the owner forever. Thus the finder is admonished not to pick up such objects. This chapter deals with a few guidelines to the finder: (i) when he must not pick up the object because it was or appears to have been deliberately left there by the owner; (ii) when he must pick up the object with the intent to restore it to the owner; and (iii) when he may pick up the object to keep it for himself or leave it where it is. **Caveat:**

Whenever it is stated that the finder may keep the object for himself, it is assumed that the object was found in a place where found objects belong to the finder, or has no identifying characteristics to obligate the finder to announce his find so that the owner can reclaim the object, or is lacking one of the other criteria stated in Chapter 259.

Assume that the object was deliberately placed in a spot that is privately owned. According to (i) above, the finder must not pick up the object since the owner of the object will come back to that spot to take it. What if the object was deliberately left in this spot, but it was left such a long time ago that neither the current owner of the spot where the object was found nor any of his forebears left the object there? Does the object belong to the finder or the current owner of the spot where the object was found?

The first topic discussed by Rabbi Yosef Karo in this chapter deals with the object that is found in an ancient wall or pile of stones and other debris. Depending on the antiquity of the wall or pile of debris, there is a difference as to whom the object belongs. In this chapter I first deal with classifying deliberately placed objects, and then the topic of a nonancient wall is discussed, followed by a discussion of objects found in a rubbish dump.[1] The topic of an object found in an ancient wall, as well as many other topics discussed by Rabbi Karo in this chapter and Chapter 259, are also discussed by me in Chapter 261 since the found object very often belongs to the finder.

Assume that money is found in a store. The store as described in the Talmud and codes consists of an open area into which the customer enters the store and in which merchandise is available in front of the counter in the back of the store. The proprietor sits in front of that counter at the back wall of the store where he accepts the money in payment of the merchandise purchased by the customer. If money is found by a customer in the store, to whom does it belong, to the storekeeper or the finder? The rules can certainly be applied to any

---

1. The topic of finding something in a rubbish or garbage heap is found in the Talmud and has made its way into all of the codes. It was discussed at a time when people went to centrally located garbage dumps to dispose of their garbage and rubbish. On occasion people would hide their objects there for safekeeping. When Shimon finds the object is it to be considered an object that belongs to the finder because it was abandoned, or is it to be considered a deliberately placed object that may not be picked up by Shimon?

type of modern store, including supermarkets and shopping malls. There is also discussed in the codes the situation in which money is found on the floor of a money-changing business. This can certainly also apply to modern-day banks.

There are situations where the object consists of fruit found close to a privately owned orchard so as to indicate that the fruit was from the private orchard. Are there situations when the finder keeps the fruit?

There are times when the found object consists of grain found in the neighborhood of a threshing floor. The area alongside the threshing floor has some characteristics of being private, since the nearby threshing floor is privately owned, but it also has some of the characteristics of a public place since many farmers come to the threshing floor. When may the finder keep the grain?[2]

There are situations where the found object is a young bird; to whom does it belong?

The definitions of Chapter 259 are repeated here: The thing that was lost and then found is designated as "the object." The person who lost the object, the owner of the object, is designated herein as the "owner" or "Ruven"; the person who finds the object is designated herein as the "finder" or "Shimon." The term "restore" means to deliver the found object to its rightful owner.[3] The term "retain" means that the finder may acquire the object for himself by picking it up, and treat it as his own for all purposes. In this last situation the finder need not pick it up at all and may leave it where it is. The term "abandoned hope" means that the owner abandons hope of the object being restored to him by the finder of the object.

TEXT

Classes of deliberately placed objects

The *halachah* classifies objects that are deliberately placed or appear that they may have been deliberately placed where found into three

2. In the Talmud and codes this is the well-known case of finding "scattered fruit." See *Baba Metzia*, 21a.

3. I have not used the term "return" since it might be thought to mean that the person (the finder) who is delivering the object to its owner took it from him in the first place.

categories, with different results depending upon the amount of supervision in the area where the object is found: fully supervised, partially supervised, or unsupervised.

1. Assume that Shimon spies an object in a place that is fully supervised. For example, Shimon finds a garment or an ax next to a fence or next to a building, placed in a manner that men working in that building leave their belongs. Shimon must not pick up the object if he concludes that the owner deliberately placed the object there. This is true: (a) whether Shimon is certain of his conclusion or even if he has some doubts whether he is correct;[4] and (b) whether or not the object has an identifying mark. If Shimon does pick up the object, he may not leave the area where he picked it up unless he replaces the object from where he picked it up.[5] If Shimon picks up the object and takes it away he should take care of the object as he would of any found object. If it has an identifying mark, he should announce that he found the lost object. If it has no identifying mark, he should keep the object in his possession (but not use it) until it becomes known to him who the true owner is.

2. Assume that Shimon spies an object in a place that is only partially supervised, whether the finder is certain that the owner deliberately placed the object there or only thinks that the owner may deliberately have placed the object there. If the object has an identifying mark, the finder must pick up the object and must announce the find. If the object has no identifying mark, the finder must not pick up the object. If the finder does pick up the object, he must keep it (but not use it) until he ascertains who the owner is.

3. Assume that Shimon spies an object in a place that is not at all supervised. If the object has no identifying mark, it belongs to the finder, Shimon. This is true even if it appears that the owner deliberately placed the object down to later return to get it. If it has an identifying mark, the finder must pick it up and make the appropriate announcements.

---

4. The fact that it appears that the object was deliberately left there in a place that is fully supervised is sufficient reason for Shimon not to pick up the object. In this situation Shimon does not transgress the Torah commandment not to turn away from picking up lost objects because the object is not a lost object.

5. As was stated in note 4, since the object is not lost, there is no obligation on Shimon to take care of it and to restore it to the owner; he need only replace it where he found it.

Objects found in a rubbish heap

Shimon finds an object in a rubbish heap. If the rubbish heap is one that is not ordinarily cleared away, if the object seems to be concealed there, he must not pick up the object.[6] If the rubbish heap is ordinarily cleared away the presumption is that the object was abandoned by the owner and Shimon may keep the object. If the rubbish heap is ordinarily not cleared away, and the community decided to clear it away, Shimon should pick up the object and treat it as any other found object. If it has an identification mark, it should be announced. Even if it does not have an identification mark, the place where it was concealed may serve as the identification mark.[7]

Shimon, while passing a rubbish heap, finds an object consisting of a covered vessel. Shimon must not pick it up because the presumption is that it was deliberately placed there by the owner of the vessel. This holds true if the rubbish heap is not regularly cleared away. However, if this rubbish heap is regularly cleared away, Shimon may keep the object, since it is assumed that the owner realized that the object will be lost when the heap is cleared away and thus the object is abandoned.

Finding objects in a wall

Ruven finds an object in a new wall[8] on private property, that is, a wall that is known to have been built by the current owner of the property or his forebears who have continually owned the property. The result depends upon the side of the wall on which the object is found: in the side closer to the inside of the property or in the side facing the street.

If it is found on the side of the wall,[9] facing the outside, the street, and if the object has rust on it to show that it was left there some time

6. It is presumed that the owner left the object there for safekeeping.

7. For example, Ruven may come forward and state that he concealed a pistol without any identification mark at the southern end of the rubbish heap. The place, the southern end of the rubbish heap, together with the fact that Ruven knows that it was a pistol that he concealed there, will be controlling as an identification mark.

8. As distinguished from an ancient wall described in Chapter 261.

9. Even very deep in the ground at the base of the wall.

ago, the object belongs to the finder, even if the object has an identifying mark.[10]

However, if the object is found on the side of the wall facing inside toward the land owned by the owner of the property, the object belongs to the owner of the property. This holds true even if (1) the hole slopes toward that[11] side; and (2) the object has become rusty. The object will belong to the owner if he pleads that it is his. If the owner of the property inherited the property, beth din will, on behalf of the owner, raise the plea that he is the owner of the object.

If the hole in the wall from the inside edge to the outside edge, was filled with the object where it cannot be ascertained from which side in the wall the object was placed there,[12] the owner of the property and the finder divide the object. But if it appears that the object was placed there from the inside, the entire object will belong to the owner of the property; if it appears that the object was placed there from the outside, the entire object will belong to the finder.[13]

If the owner admits that the object is a found object, it belongs to the finder no matter where found.

Assume that a party wall belonging to the two adjoining landowners collapsed.[14] One of the landowners found an object. He may keep it if it has no identification mark.

Finding money in a store or in a bank

Ruven is the proprietor of a store. Shimon, who may or may not be a customer, enters into the store, spies money, and picks it up. If it is found on or behind the counter or in a place that is reserved solely for the proprietor of the store, it belongs to the proprietor, even if the majority of the customers are Gentiles, and even if the money has no

---

10. It is assumed that the object was left by a person other than the owner of the property and the person has forgotten about the object and has abandoned hope of finding it.

11. It is not assumed that the object rested in the other side of the wall and slid down to the side where it is now resting.

12. This holds true even if the object consists of one long piece.

13. For example, if the object was a knife, it is assumed that the knife was put into the hole with the handle outward, and if it was a purse, it is assumed that the purse was placed in the hole with the straps outward.

14. See Volume V, page 165.

identification mark.[15] If found in an area of the store not reserved for the proprietor or his employees, the money belongs to the finder.[16]

A person enters into a money changer's store or office or bank and finds money. If it is found in a place where only the moneychanger or his employees have access, the money belongs to the money changer or the bank, even if the majority of customers are Gentile. If it is found where the customer has access to proceed, it belongs to the finder.

Finding fruit alongside an orchard

Shimon finds fruit alongside an orchard on public property, such as a road. There are times when Shimon may keep the fruit and there are times when he must leave the fruit where he spied it. The latter situations are discussed below; the former situations are discussed in Chapter 261.

Ruven owns an orchard and some of the fruit from the orchard fell onto the public area.[17] Shimon spies the fruit. If the fruit tree is of the type that does not continually shed its fruit,[18] then the owner is not aware of the fruit falling. Therefore he has not abandoned hope of recovering this fruit and it belongs to Ruven. Even if Ruven later abandons hope of recovering the fruit, it still belongs to Ruven if Shimon picked it up before Ruven abandoned hope of recovery. If Shimon picked up the fruit after Ruven abandoned hope of recovery of the fruit, it belongs to Shimon.

Even if the fallen fruit is of a type that is usually abandoned by the owner of the orchard, there are times that the fruit is not abandoned. And if the ownership of the fruit is not abandoned, or cannot be abandoned, the fruit still belong to Ruven, the owner of the tree, and

15. The proprietor obviously lost it and did not abandon hope of recovering it.

16. It is not acquired for the shopkeeper by lying in the premises. One of the answers why not, is that the public must be excluded by the owner from entering onto the premises for the premises to acquire for the owner, and a store is a place where the proprietor wants customers to enter.

17. The tree from which the fruit fell may be entirely within the orchard owned by Ruven and the fruit, in falling, fell outside the orchard. Or the branches of the tree may have extended beyond the boundary of Ruven's orchard and the fruit fell off those branches.

18. The fruit of this type of tree has to be picked while yet on the tree, or falls onto the nets spread on the ground and the owner then shakes the tree to cause the fruit to fall onto the nets.

Shimon, the finder, must leave it without picking it up. The fruit that falls outside the orchard cannot be abandoned by the owner of the orchard if he is an orphaned minor. If the orchard is fenced in a manner that shows that the fruit that falls outside the orchard is not abandoned but rather still belongs to the owner, then it is forbidden for Shimon to pick it up.

Scattered produce

Shimon finds produce scattered about in the vicinity of a threshing floor. There are times that Shimon may keep the produce and there are times that he must not pick it up since the presumption is that the owner will return to recover his produce. The test is whether the owner of the produce would be willing to return to collect this amount of produce from the ground, spread over this amount of area. If it appears that the bother is too great for the amount of produce involved considering the size and the area covered, then the owner is deemed to have abandoned the produce, and it may be picked up and kept by the finder. If, considering the amount and the area, the bother is not too much for an owner, then it is presumed that the owner has not abandoned the produce; it still belongs to him and the finder must not pick it up.

Commencing with a standard stated in a Mishna the following rules regarding produce have become standard in all of Rabbinical literature:

1 kab[19] in 4 cubits[20] square, the produce belongs to the finder;
1 kab in less than 4 cubits square, the produce must not be picked up and must be left for the owner;
½ kab in 2 cubits square, the produce should[21] be left for the owner;

19. A kab contains about 160 cubic inches.

20. A cubit is about 21 inches and 4 cubits are thus about 7 feet. 4 cubits square is an area of about 49 square feet. See Glossary for definition of cubits.

21. I have used the term "should" instead of "must." The reason is that there are some authorities who hold that since the Talmud did not answer the question regarding these ratios between produce and area, the finder should not take the produce, and if he does he may keep it. But there are other authorities who hold that the produce belongs to the owner, since the Talmud did not answer the question to whom it belongs and laws that derive from a Torah source in which there is a doubt

2 kabs in 8 cubits square, the produce should[22] be left for the owner;

1 kab of two or three types of produce, such as dates, sesame, and pomegranates, the produce should[23] be left for the owner.

Finding young birds

Shimon while walking finds young birds[24] that cannot yet fly and can move from place to place by hopping. It is assumed that the young birds do not have any manner of identification so that the birds will belong either to the finder or to a person who has a dovecote close by. If it is within 50 cubits[25] of a dovecote, Shimon must not pick up the birds because they belong to the owner, and it is not assumed that the birds have been lost by a passerby.[26]

If there are two dovecotes, each not more than 50 cubits away from the found birds, the birds belong to the owners of both dovecotes if they are equidistant from where the birds were found. If the birds are found closer to one dovecote than the other, the birds belong to the owner of the closer dovecote. All of the foregoing in this paragraph applies only if both dovecotes contain the same number of birds. But if the birds in one dovecote are more numerous than in the second, the majority is decisive, even if that dovecote is more distant from where the young birds were found than the second dovecote.

If the young birds were found beyond 50 cubits from a dovecote, Shimon may pick them up and keep them.[27]

---

as to the answer must be decided in favor of the strict view. In this case the decision would be against the finder since the owner surely owned the produce.

22. See previous note.

23. See note 21.

24. If the birds are grown and can fly, if they seem to be ownerless, then the finder may keep them, no matter if there are dovecotes close by. If it is not known that they are ownerless, the finder cannot take them since he is robbing the owner of the birds.

25. See Glossary.

26. There is also authority that the laws of the text apply only if the young birds were not found on a road frequented by many passersby. If they were found on such a road they belong to the finder even if there is a dovecote within 50 cubits of the place where they were found.

27. The young birds belong to Shimon since young birds do not hop more than 50 cubits. If they were lost by a passerby, it is presumed that the owner abandoned hope of recovering the young birds.

If the young birds are found on a path in a woods or in gardens, vineyards, or orchards, they belong to the owner of the gardens even if they are found more than 50 cubits from the dovecote.

Young birds with their wings tied hopping behind a fence or behind a stone wall or on field paths belong to the owner.[28]

28. If the finder does take them, he must restore the birds to the owner if they have an identification mark, and if they do not have a mark they belong to the finder.

Chapter 261

OBJECTS THAT MAY BE KEPT BY THE FINDER

INTRODUCTION

What found objects may the finder keep for himself? Chapter 259 discusses objects that the finder must pick up, announce, and restore to the owner. Chapter 260 discusses objects that the finder must not pick up since they belong to the owners, who will undoubtedly return to retrieve them. All found items not covered by Chapter 259 or Chapter 260 are objects that the finder may keep for himself and are discussed in this chapter. Since the finder may keep the object if he so desires, he also has the option of leaving the object remain where it is, and another finder may then make the decision whether to pick it up to keep for himself or to leave it where it is.

As stated in Chapter 259, there are seven criteria that must be present before the finder has the Torah obligation to pick up and restore the object to the owner. If any of the criteria are absent, (and except as stated in Chapter 260) the finder may keep the object for himself or pass it by. The most common occurrence where the criteria will not be met is where there is an abandoning of hope by the owner that the object will be restored to him. This usually is based on the fact that the object does not contain an identifiable mark, or on the place where the object was lost. Many of the laws of this chapter are the reciprocals of the laws of Chapter 259.

Volume VI describes the various methods whereby ownership of an object of personal property is transferred from the owner to the purchaser or from the donor to a donee. There must be an act of acquisition that effects the transfer from the current owner to the new owner. Generally, the best method of acquisition is for the new owner to pick up the object into his own hands. That of course does not mean that anytime a person picks up an object, it belongs to him. If that were so, Shimon could go into Ruven's house, even by invitation, and commence picking up objects and plead that the objects now belong to Shimon. For an object to be acquired by picking it up there must be intent on the part of the current owner to part with ownership of the object to the new owner, and there must be intent of the new owner to acquire ownership of the object. If there is no intent on the part of the current owner to part with ownership to the new owner, the person who picks up the object to acquire it is a robber.

There are times, however, when the current owner abandons ownership of the object and then anyone can pick it up and acquire ownership of the object. Very often the loser of the object will abandon hope of finding the object or the hope that someone who finds it will restore the object to the owner.[1] It may be because the object has no means of identification to alert the finder who the owner is; or because the place where the object was lost is inhabited by Gentiles who are not bound by the Torah commandments and thus perhaps may not restore found objects to the loser. Or it may be that the circumstances are such that one quickly abandons hope of having the lost object restored, as when a flood carries off the object downstream. If the owner had abandoned hope of having the object found and restored, how is the abandonment manifested? Must there be a specific declaration of abandonment, or may the owner's conduct manifest such abandonment? Are there times when the *halachah* presumes that there has been an abandonment of hope by

1. It may be that the owner abandons hope of the object being restored to him, or the owner may, for any reason whatsoever, abandon the object, such as throwing his old sweater away in the street and telling his friends that he does not want the sweater any more.

the loser to ever finding the object or having it returned to him? What if the finder picks up the object prior to the owner abandoning it and then the owner abandons it? Can the finder perform another act to acquire the object? The objects that belong to the finder are discussed in this chapter.

The definitions of Chapter 259 are repeated here: The thing that was lost and then found is designated as the "object." The person who lost the object, the owner of the object, is designated herein as the "owner" or "Ruven," the person who finds the object is designated herein as the "finder" or "Shimon." The term "restore" means to deliver the found object to its rightful owner.[2] The term "retain" means that the finder may acquire the object for himself by picking it up, and treat it as his own for all purposes. In this last situation the finder need not pick up at all and may leave it where it is. The term "abandoned hope" means that the owner abandons hope of the object being restored to him by the finder of the object.

If the current owner of the object deliberately abandons the object, the finder of such an object can keep it for himself. This is the first topic discussed below.

Objects found in ancient walls are related to abandoned objects. In Chapter 260 there is discussed the finding of an object in a boundary wall on Shimon's property. That wall was not an ancient wall. The results of such finds are described in that chapter. Very often the object belongs to the owner of the wall but sometimes it belongs to the finder. The results may be different when the wall is an ancient wall, as described in this chapter. When the *halachah* on this topic was first being formulated, the Jews were about to cross the Jordan River under the leadership of Joshua. They would be taking over property owned by the nations who were on the land and thus the new inhabitants would not be familiar with the treasures or objects placed by the Amorites and other nations in their walls or piles of stones. Thus objects found in these ancient walls are deemed to be placed there by the ancient nations and do not belong to the new owners of the land. The text in this chapter has been reworded to reflect an object found in a wall that has been in existence for a very long time

2. As stated in Chapter 259, I have not used the term "return" since it might be thought to mean that the person (the finder) who is delivering the object to its owner took it from him in the first place.

so that the current owners cannot plead that it was placed there by their forebears.

Some of the other topics that follow are the topics of Chapter 259, but here they are the reciprocal of Chapter 259, such as "Abandoning of hope"; "Neighborhood where the object was lost"; "Objects lost to a raging river"; "Money found in a store or in a bank"; "Finding fruit alongside an orchard"; "Scattered produce";[3] and "Finding young birds."

There are situations where an owner leases his house or property to a tenant and an object is found there or an object such as a lame deer[4] enters upon the premises. To whom does it belong, the landlord or the tenant? This is discussed in the section entitled "Rights of a tenant to the found object."

There then follows a section of "other examples."

The final section of this chapter deals with a topic that should be the goal of all Jews, to act above the requirements of the law. This topic has been discussed in Volume I, Chapter 12; and Volume V, Chapter 175, Introduction.

TEXT

Abandoned objects

Assume the owner of an object abandons the object.[5] Whoever finds this object may pick it up or pass by the object.[6] Or the object is apparently abandoned, as where the owner leaves a jug of wine outside his house where insects and rodents can get to it. There is no Torah command to stop and pick up such an object. When the finder

3. This section is repeated from Chapter 260.

4. The lame deer can be acquired by the premises on behalf of the owner. If the deer is not lame it can be acquired only if the deer is caught.

5. The question of proof whether it was deliberately abandoned is for beth din to determine if the owner pleads that he did not abandon the object.

6. The object is technically not lost. But for the finder it has many of the attributes of a lost object. It is similar to an object whose owner has abandoned hope of having it restored to him.

picks it up, it belongs to him. The original owner can also pick it up and then it will re-belong to him.

Finding objects in an ancient wall

Ruven finds an object in an ancient wall or man-made pile of stones or debris, which wall or debris pile existed on the property long before the present owner (or his forebears[7]) acquired the property. The object *may*[8] be taken by the finder and retained by him.[9] This holds true if the following three conditions are all present: (1) there are no members of the community who recollect or were told by their forebears, who built the wall or made the debris hill where the object was found; (2) there is rust on the object or other indications that the object was placed in this location long before the current owner or his forebears acquired the property; and (3), the object is buried deep in the wall or deep[10] under the pile of debris, indicating it has been there since the ancient wall was built or the ancient pile of debris was first placed there.[11]

7. Even if his forebears have been on the property for several generations, if the object was obviously placed there long before his earliest forebears came into possession of the property, the finder may take and keep it.

8. Whenever the finder *may* pick up the object, he has the option to pick it up or to leave it where it is. In such situations, if the finder picks up the object it will belong to him and therefore he has the option not to pick it up. Where the finder *must* pick up the object, it will not belong to him, but rather he must try to locate the owner.

9. Volume VI, Chapter 200, discusses how a person's courtyard can acquire an object for him. If that is so, the question may be asked, why doesn't the courtyard containing the ancient wall acquire the object for the property owner rather than permit the finder to keep the object? One of the answers given by the commentators is that the law of acquisition by one's courtyard is effective only if the owner is aware of the object being placed or located in his domain. In the case in the text, the owner is not so aware. See also Chapter 260, note 18. The matter is discussed below in Chapter 262.

10. The theory is that the object was placed there in the wall when the wall was first built and that the wall sank so that the object was no longer visible, or that over the years the earth around the wall rose to cover up the object.

11. There are those commentators who hold that it is not necessary for both (2) and (3) to be present, and if either (2) or (3) is present together with condition (1), the object belongs to the finder.

Abandoning of hope

Caveat: The abandonment of hope must precede the finder's picking up the object. If the finder picks up the object and then the owner realizes that he lost the object and immediately abandons hope,[12] the object does not belong to the finder.[13] There are times when the owner does not immediately realize that he lost the object. He can not abandon hope until after he realizes that he lost the object. For example, the object is valuable and the owner feels his pocket constantly to see if the object is still in his pocket. In such a situation the owner will almost immediately realize that he lost the object. Or it is heavy and the owner will almost immediately feel the loss because he realizes that the weight he was carrying is no longer there. Even if there is some doubt as to which came first, the finding or the abandoning of hope, the object must be restored to the owner.

As stated in Chapter 259, the owner abandons hope if he states "Woe to me that I've suffered a loss" or other words to that effect from which beth din can ascertain that the owner abandoned hope. This holds true even if the object has an identification mark. If the finder picks it up after the abandonment, the object belongs to the finder.

The finder may keep the object that he finds if the owner has abandoned hope of recovering it.

The most common reason for the owner to abandon hope to recover his lost object is when the object is not identifiable by an identification mark or lacks a geographical identification such as the place where the object was lost.

Neighborhood where the object was lost

There may be another reason that the owner abandons hope of recovering the object. It was lost in a neighborhood where he has no hope of the finder restoring the object to him.

---

12. Even if it is the type of object that one immediately gives up hope when he realizes that he lost the object, the abandonment must precede the finder picking up the object for the object to belong to the finder. Otherwise, the criteria of abandoning hope is still present.

13. This law centers around one of the most famous disputes in the Talmud (*Baba Metziu* 21b). For example, the owner lost the object at 6 A.M. The finder picked up the object at 7 A.M. At 8 A.M., the owner realizes he lost the object and abandons hope of the object ever being recovered. The finder does not obtain ownership of the object.

If the majority of the neighborhood inhabitants or passersby where the object is found are Gentiles, the object is deemed to be abandoned and the Torah requirement to pick up the object and to restore it to the owner do not apply. The finder may pick up the object for himself or he may ignore the object and leave it where it is. This holds true even if the majority of the town is Jewish, the finder knows that the object was lost by a Jew, and the object has an identifying mark. Since the majority of persons situated or passing through this particular part of town are Gentiles, it is presumed that the owner abandoned hope of the object ever being returned to him, because he assumes that the object was found by a Gentile, who is not bound by Torah law to restore a lost object to the owner, and therefore will not return it to the owner. Under the foregoing circumstances, the finder may keep the object if it is the type that the loser will almost immediately realize that he lost it and immediately abandon hope of ever having the finder return it to him. Otherwise, when the finder finds it the owner may not yet have abandoned hope of finding it and the object, if picked up, still belongs to the owner. Once the object is picked up prior to the owner's abandonment, the finder cannot thereafter obtain ownership of the object even if the loser thereafter abandons hope of the finder returning the object to him.

There is an opinion that there is an exception to the laws of the last paragraph if the lost object was a Torah-related book,[14] since the owner thinks that the finder, even if a Gentile, will sell the book to a Jew who will then return the book to the owner. In such case the finder must pick up the book and restore it to the owner.

If a Jew finds a jug of wine in a place where the majority of the inhabitants or passersby of that neighborhood are Gentiles, the finder may keep the jug but the wine must be spilled out. He must spill out the wine since wine of Gentiles, even if not used in a Gentile religious ceremony,[15] is by Rabbinical enactment, entirely prohibited to Jews, but the prohibition does not extend to the vessels in which the wine was stored. If the owner turns out to be a Jew and gives the finder identifying marks to prove that the wine was lost by that Jewish owner,

14. Such as text of the Torah or other books of the Bible, or a tome of the Talmud and books that are uniquely used by Jews for their Torah study.

15. If some of the wine of that jug was used in a Gentile religious ceremony, the wind *and* its container are prohibited by Torah law for any use.

and the jug is still closed, the finder may drink the wine since the wine is not the wine of a Gentile.[16] Similarly, if a Jew finds an animal or fowl slaughtered according to Jewish ritual law[17] in a place where the majority of the slaughterers are Jewish, the finder may keep the animal or fowl only if the majority of the community are Gentiles. The finder may keep the animal because it is presumed that the loser abandoned hope of recovering the animal or fowl because the majority of the inhabitants of the community are Gentiles. Also, if a bird seizes a piece of meat that is recognizably kosher and drops it along its flight, the finder of the meat may keep it as a lost object, even if the majority of the town's inhabitants are Jewish, because it is presumed that the owner will have abandoned hope of recovering the object.

Objects lost to a raging river

As seen in Chapter 259, there are times when a river sweeps away an object from the banks of the river and it may still belong to the owner.

Very often it will belong to the finder. Shimon rescues an object from a raging river that has washed away the object, or from the ebb of the sea, or from a Gentile, or from a fire, or from a fierce animal such as a lion, bear, leopard, or panther. This is a situation in which the average person could not stop the river from washing away his object, or the fierce animal or the Gentile from taking the object.[18] The object belongs to Shimon, even if Ruven, the owner, runs after the object and/or shouts that he has not abandoned hope of recovering the object. Similarly, if the owner's fowl run far away and the owner cannot retrieve them, they are deemed abandoned and they belong to whoever finds them.

16. The wine belongs to the finder since it is presumed that the loser abandoned hope of the jug of wine ever being returned to him, because it was lost in a Gentile neighborhood. The wine is not prohibited since the jug was closed and none of the wine could have been used in a Gentile religious ceremony.

17. The method of slaughtering according to Jewish law and ritual are easily discernible and therefore it is certain that the owner of the meat was Jewish and the animal or fowl is kosher and may be eaten by a Jew.

18. The reason is that the intent of the owner is presumed to be that which a reasonable person would have under these circumstances, that is, he would abandon hope of ever recovering the object.

A river has a dam used by fishermen to catch fish. An object is found behind the dam. The dam is set up by Gentile fishermen and is usually repaired by them. If an object is found there it has to be treated as an object that has been abandoned.[19] The result is otherwise when the dam is maintained by Jews.[20]

Rights of a tenant to the found object

The owner of residential premises leases part of it to a tenant and the owner continues to also reside there. An object without an identification mark is found there by a third party not the landlord; it must be restored by the finder to the landlord or the landlord and the tenant as follows.[21] If the object appears to have been lost a long time ago,[22] prior to when the tenant moved into the premises, it belongs to the landlord. If it does not appear that the object was lost before the tenant moved in, the object belongs to both the landlord and the tenant. If the object has an identification mark, it must be picked up and restored by the finder to its owner.

The landlord, who does not reside on the premises, leases the premises to tenants and an object without an identification mark is found there by a party who is not a tenant. It belongs equally to all of the tenants currently residing there.[23] If the tenants moved in and moved out one after the other, the object belongs to the last tenant.[24] If the object has an identification mark, it must be picked up and restored to the owner.

If the landlord leases the property simultaneously to three Gentiles, or generally leases the property to Gentiles, he thereby converts the property into an inn and the object belongs to whoever finds it, even

19. The Jewish owner of the lost object will assume that the object will be found by a Gentile who would not be bound by Torah law to restore the object and therefore it would not be restored to him; thus he abandons hope of having the object recovered. The role of Gentiles as finders of lost objects is discussed in Chapter 263.

20. See Chapter 259, page 13.

21. It does not belong to the finder since it was found on private premises.

22. For example, it has rust on it.

23. For example, on January 1, the landlord leased the premises to Ruven, Shimon, Levi, and Yehudah. On February 1, Shimon moved out. An object is found by Dan, a nontenant, on March 1. The object belongs to Ruven, Levi, and Yehudah.

24. It is assumed as each tenant moved out he made a thorough search of the premises and the object was not there when he moved out.

if the object has an identification mark.[25] The foregoing holds true even if some of the tenants in the inn are Jews. If all of the tenants in the inn are Jewish and the object has an identification mark, it must be picked up and restored to the owner of the object.

Ruven, the landlord, lives together with Shimon, the tenant in one house with an adjoining courtyard. A lame deer or birds that cannot yet fly enter into the premises, or any other object is found on the premises that can be acquired by the premises. The deer or the birds or the other object belong to both Ruven and Shimon equally.[26]

Money found in a store or in a bank

It is stated in Chapter 260 that money found in a store or in a bank may in many instances belong to the proprietor of the store or to the bank. If the money is found in a part of the store or the bank to which the customers or general public has access, and not reserved for the employees of the store or the bank, the money belongs to the finder.[27]

Finding fruit alongside an orchard

Ruven owns a fig tree orchard. Some of the figs from the orchard fell onto a public area.[28] Shimon walking on a road alongside the orchard finds figs on the road. The figs belong to Shimon[29] since the

---

25. The landlord, by leasing the property to three heathens, has implicitly abandoned hope of retrieving the object.

26. For the purposes of acquiring the lost object, Ruven and Shimon are treated as partners. Chapter 262 discusses how a person's premises may acquire a lost object for the owner of the premises.

27. It is not acquired for the shopkeeper (or bank) by lying on his premises, since the public at large is invited onto the premises, and premises cannot acquire on behalf of the owner unless the premises are guarded so that the public cannot enter upon it.

28. The tree from which the figs fell may be entirely within the orchard owned by Ruven and the figs, in falling, fell outside the orchard. Or the branches of the tree may have extended beyond the boundary of Ruven's orchard and the figs fell off those branches.

29. They belong to Shimon, the finder, since Ruven, the owner, immediately abandons the falling figs outside his property because figs and similar fruits are spoiled by falling, or by worms and insects on the ground. Thus Shimon is not robbing Ruven's figs. What has been said about figs also applies to dates. However, the Rabbis

fig tree is of the type that continually sheds its fruit.[30] Therefore Ruven abandoned hope of recovering this fruit and it belongs to Shimon.[31] The figs will belong to Shimon even if they are dried figs found on the road alongside a field of figs that are drying.

As stated in Chapter 260, if the ownership of the figs is not abandoned, or cannot be abandoned, the figs still belong to Ruven, the owner of the tree, and Shimon, the finder, must leave them without picking them up. The figs that fall outside the orchard cannot be abandoned by the owner of the orchard if he is an orphaned minor. Or if the orchard of the owner is fenced in a manner that shows that the figs that fall outside the orchard are not abandoned but rather still belong to the owner, then it is forbidden for Shimon to pick up these figs.

Scattered produce

Shimon finds produce scattered about in the vicinity of a threshing floor. There are times that Shimon may keep the produce and there are times that he must not pick it up since the presumption is that the owner will return to recover his produce. The test is whether or not the owner of the produce would be willing to return and collect this amount from the ground spread over this amount of area. If the bother is too great for the amount of produce involved in relation to the large area covered, then the owner is deemed to have abandoned the produce, and it may be picked up and kept by the finder. If the bother is not too much for an owner, then the owner is not presumed to have abandoned the produce and, unless he expressly abandons the produce, it still belongs to him and the finder must not pick it up.

Commencing with a standard stated in a Mishna, the following rules have become standard in all of Rabbinical literature:

---

of the Talmud, by their observations in those days held that the same does not apply to olives or carobs. They belong to the owner of the tree.

30. As distinguished from fruit that has to be picked while yet on the tree, or falls onto the nets spread on the ground and the owner then shakes the tree to cause the fruit to fall onto the nets.

31. See Chapter 260, section entitled "Finding fruit alongside an orchard" where the fruit belongs to the owner.

1 kab[32] in 4 cubits[33] square, the produce belongs to the finder;

1 kab in less than 4 cubits square, the produce must not be picked up and must be left for the owner;

½ kab in 2 cubits square, the produce should[34] be left for the owner;

2 kabs in 8 cubits square, the produce should[35] be left for the owner;

1 kab of two or three types of produce, such as dates, sesame, and pomegranates, the produce should[36] be left for the owner.

Finding young birds

There are times when the finder of young birds may keep the birds for himself. This is discussed in Chapter 260 in the section entitled "Finding young birds."

Other examples

The community standards as decided upon by beth din will determine under which category a found object should be classified. This may change from community to community and from generation to generation. The following may generally be kept by the finder:

a. sheaves of grain;
b. cakes of pressed figs;
c. strings of fish or slices of meat not cut in any unique manner;
d. wool fleeces in the condition in which they arrive from the country;

32. A kab contains about 160 cubic inches.

33. A cubit is about 21 inches and 4 cubits are thus about 7 feet. 4 cubits square is an area of about 49 square feet. See Glossary for a definition of cubits.

34. I have used the term "should" instead of "must." The reason is that there are some authorities who hold that since the Talmud does not answer the question regarding these ratios between produce and area, the finder should not take the produce, but if he does he may keep it. But there are other authorities who hold that the produce belongs to the owner, since the Talmud does not answer the question to whom it belongs and laws which derive from a Torah source in which there is a doubt as to the answer, must be decided in favor of the strict view. In this case the decision would be against the finder since the owner surely owned the produce.

35. See previous note.

36. See note before previous note.

e. stalks of flax;
f. bread from a commercial bakery;[37]
g. opened jars of wine or opened jars of oil;[38]
h. produce in front of a vessel;[39]
i. a vicious animal such as a vicious dog or cat that kills children (such an animal may not be kept by the owner and whoever finds it may kill it and keep the carcass);
j. a single nail or a single needle;[40]
k. money scattered in front of a purse.[41]

To act beyond the requirements of the law

There are many instances where the lost object belongs to Shimon, the finder, although he knows that the object was lost by Ruven. The *halachah* recommends that Shimon restore the object to Ruven.[42] The *halachah* makes an exception where the finder is poor and the loser is wealthy, in which case the finder need not comply with this extra legal requirement. There is an opinion that if the finder is wealthy and the loser is a poor person, beth din will compel the wealthy finder to restore the found object to the owner.[43] There are also instances

37. See Chapter 259, page 16, regarding bread from a noncommercial baker.

38. Sealed jars of wine or oil must be restored to the owner. See Chapter 259, page 16.

39. The produce in front of the vessel belongs to the finder, but the vessel must be restored to the owner. This assumes that it appears to the finder and if the case arises to beth din, that the produce and the vessel belong to two different people. However, if it appears that the vessel and produce facing the front of the vessel belong to the same person, the finder must restore the produce as well as the vessel to the owner. However, if the vessel has a rim around the front and there is no produce left in the vessel, it is assumed that the produce was never in the vessel. If the back of the vessel faces the produce, the produce belongs to the finder.

40. If found two or more at one time, they must be restored to the owner. See Chapter 259, page 16.

41. The purse must be restored to the owner. If it appears that the money also belongs to the owner of the purse, the money too must be restored to the owner. See Chapter 259, page 17.

42. In *halachah* this is known as acting *lifnim mishurath hadin*. See Volume I, page 94, and also Glossary. See also author's article *Lifnim Mishurath Hadin*, Annual Volume of Young Israel Rabbis in Israel, Volume 2, Jerusalem (1988).

43. See Volume I, pages 94 and 95, where there is a discussion whether beth din may compel a person to act *lifnim mishurath hadin*. In the case under discussion in

where the law of the land requires that the object be returned to the loser although *halachah* would not enjoin the finder to do so. A Jew must abide by the law of the land and restore the object.[44] There is a reported case of the tenth century where a boat belonging to a Jew sank and was raised by a Gentile and sold to another Jew. The king decreed that whoever purchased the boat from the Gentile should restore it to the original owner of the boat. This case came before the beth din and it was held that the community must abide by the law of the land, that is, by the decree of the king; thus the Jewish purchaser had to restore the boat to the Jewish owner. The owner had to pay to the buyer the same price the buyer paid to the Gentile. There are communities where beth din requires a finder of a lost object to return the object to the loser although technically the object should belong to the finder, as where the object does not have an identifying mark or the majority of the inhabitants of the community where the object was found are Gentiles.

---

the text, the wealthy finder is not out of pocket since the object came to him without any payment.

44. See Glossary, *dina d'malchuta dina*; see Chapter 369.

Chapter 262

HOW A FOUND OBJECT IS ACQUIRED

INTRODUCTION

As seen in Volume VI, nothing can be acquired, not even an abandoned object, unless an act of acquisition has been performed. Until the act of acquisition is performed by the new owner, ownership of the object continues with its current owner; if the object is abandoned, it does not have any owner until someone acquires it by an act of acquisition.

The methods of acquisition of real property described in that volume are not relevant to this chapter dealing with the acquisition of found objects, since real property does not get lost. However, the methods of acquisition of personal property are relevant. Personal property can be acquired: by lifting or pulling the object, or having the object delivered to the person acquiring the object (Chapter 198); by the payment of money in unusual cases (Chapter 199); by the buyer's courtyard, or his 4 cubits, or his vessels (Chapter 200); by local law and local custom (Chapter 201); along with realty (Chapter 202); and by barter (Chapter 203). Obviously, some of these methods are not relevant regarding found objects. Rabbi Yosef Karo in *Shulhan Aruch Hoshen haMishpat*, chapter 268, deals with the acquisition of found objects; he also discusses there the acquisition by the finder's courtyard or by his 4 cubits. In his chapter 271 he discusses the acquisition of animals.[1] I have moved these topics from *Shulhan Aruch Hoshen haMishpat*, chapter 268, and *Shulhan Aruch Hoshen haMishpat*, chapter 271, to this chapter. See my rearrangement as stated in the introduction to Chapter 259.

TEXT

Acquisition of found objects

None of the objects that the finder may pick up and keep for himself belong to the finder until he performs an act of acquisition to obtain ownership of the object.

Ordinarily, picking up the object is the best method of acquisition of the object.[2] In certain situations, pulling the object is the best method of acquisition.[3]

The mere spying of an ownerless object is not an act of acquisition. Even if the finder falls upon the object in a public place, it does not belong to him, since lying down on an object is not a method of acquisition. Thus if Shimon spies the object and falls down upon it and then Yehudah puts his hand under Shimon and grabs the object, the object belongs to Yehudah, since he took the object into his hand, this being an act of acquisition. However, in those places where the 4 cubits square acquires on behalf of the finder, falling on the found object there will also act as an act of acquisition of the object.

Acquiring found objects by one's courtyard

In Chapter 200 it is stated, "The courtyard acquires on behalf of the buyer if it is guarded by either of two types of guarding: (1) there is a

1. Rabbi Karo, in chapter 271, also mentions that the laws dealing with found notes of indebtedness and receipts of payment are discussed in *Shulhan Aruch Hoshen haMishpat*, chapter 65, and the laws of found bills of divorce (*get*) are found in *Shulhan Aruch Eben haEzer*, chapters 132 and 153.

2. See Volume VI, page 147, that the object must be lifted up 3 *tefachim*, or about 10 inches. See Glossary for definition of *tefach*.

3. See Volume VI, page 145.

wall or fence around the premises, or (2) a person is guarding the premises."[4]

Assume an object falls into Shimon's courtyard, or an animal that cannot run fast or birds that cannot fly away are found in Shimon's courtyard. In all of these instances it must be presumed that the owner of the object has abandoned hope of having the object restored to him.[5]

Regarding found objects, the law is that Shimon's courtyard acquires a lost object on his behalf even if he is not present at the courtyard and even if he is not aware of the object in his courtyard. This holds true only if there is a wall or fence around the premises.

If the courtyard does not have a wall or fence around it, Shimon will acquire the object only if he is present there. There are several views as to whether Shimon, in addition to standing there, also has to expressly state that he desires that his courtyard should acquire the lost object on his behalf. One view holds that Shimon, in addition to being present, must also specifically state that he wants his courtyard to acquire the lost object on his behalf. If he is not present or does not make the statement, his courtyard does not acquire the object on his behalf, and anyone may take the lost object lying on his property. The other view holds that the mere presence of Shimon at his courtyard is sufficient to have the courtyard acquire the lost object on his behalf and no statement is necessary. There is another view that compromises the views. If the lost object is an animal that has a broken leg and cannot run fast or a bird that cannot fly, then the courtyard acquires on behalf of Shimon only if he makes the statement that he wants the courtyard to acquire on his behalf. All inanimate objects are acquired by the presence of Shimon without his having to make a statement.

Assume that the animals are running across Shimon's courtyard or birds are flying across his courtyard. They cannot be caught by Shimon and there are strangers running after these animals or birds. The courtyard has not acquired on behalf of Shimon and whoever catches them acquires them.[6]

---

4. See Volume VI, page 159.
5. See Chapter 259, page 10 (caveat).
6. See also end of Chapter 259; Chapter 260 section entitled "Finding young birds"; and Chapter 261 section entitled "Right of the tenant to the found object."

Acquisition by the finder's 4 cubits

It is stated in Volume VI, page 161, "As is seen in Chapter 268 the Rabbis have decreed that in the cases of acquiring found articles of personal property, if the found item is within the 4 cubits area of the finder, he acquires the found object even though he has not lifted it up. This decree is limited to objects found in a back street or in a *simtah* (an area that is part of the public street, yet is off to a side and is not frequently used), or in a field that does not belong to any person. The decree does not apply to the frequently used portion of a public street, since every person is entitled to walk in any area of the public street, and therefore there is no area of 4 cubits that the finder of the item can declare to be solely his. This decree also does not apply to realty belonging to a third party."[7]

The area of 4 cubits[8] is approximately 49 square feet.[9]

Two people, Shimon and Levi, both entered into the 4 cubit area where the found object rests. Or both of them are standing within the same four cubits and the object falls into these 4 cubits. Both of them acquire the object, although it may be closer to one of them. If one of them entered the 4 cubits before the other and the object was already there, then the one who entered first acquires the object.

There is an opinion that the four cubits acquire for the finder only if he is standing still in the 4 cubits. Others hold that the finder acquires the object whether he is standing still or walking through the 4 cubits.

Acquiring lost animals

Assume that an animal appears lost. For example, Shimon spies a cow or other domesticated animal grazing along a road in the daytime, even for several consecutive days. This law is that animal is not a lost animal and must not be taken.

However, if the animal is wandering along the road at the crack of

7. The reference to Chapter 268 should be changed to this chapter (262). See Introduction to this chapter, above.

8. See Glossary, cubits.

9. The object belongs to the person within the 4 cubits whether the person reached there first and then the object or the object was there first and then the person.

dawn and is still there at dusk for several consecutive days, the animal is presumed to be lost. If it is at night, in those communities where animal do not graze at night, the animal is considered a lost animal. Similarly, if one sees a horse whose saddle is not in place, or a mare that is running loose with its foal, these are considered lost animals.

If the animal is running along the road, if it is running toward town or toward a farmhouse, it is presumed not lost. If it is running away from town, it is deemed lost.

Community practices will be controlling as to whether an animal is deemed lost.

All animals that are lost must be restored to the owner, unless it is known that the owner has abandoned hope of having the animal restored to him.

Volume VI, page 149, discusses the acquisition of animals that are purchased. Generally, the same methods of acquiring animals that are purchased are used to acquire abandoned animals, that is, by pulling the animal or by riding the animal, in both cases so that it moves from the space where it was.

Chapter 263

LOST OBJECTS OF GENTILES OR OF SINNERS

INTRODUCTION

As is stated in Chapter 259, the laws dealing with the restoring of lost objects to the owner applies to lost objects of Jews. What about the objects lost by Gentiles? This chapter deals with such lost objects, as well as lost objects of Jews who are sinners.

TEXT

The lost object of Gentiles

The *halachah* distinguishes between the lost objects of Jews and the lost objects of Gentiles. The reason is that in many communities the Gentiles did not restore lost objects and were therefore not included in the laws dealing with the restoring of lost objects.

In those communities where the law is that all lost objects must be restored, the lost objects of Gentiles must be restored.

In situations where the restoration of a lost object will reflect well on the Jewish people, it must be restored.[1] Similarly, if the failure to return the lost object to a Gentile will reflect badly on the Jewish people, the object must be returned. Also, when the return of the object will enhance neighborliness between Jews and Gentiles, it must be done.

The lost objects of Jewish sinners

Whether Shimon, the finder of a lost object, has to restore the object to Ruven, a Jewish sinner who lost it, depends upon the type of sinner Ruven is. Unless Ruven is guilty of major religious sins, the object must be restored to him. But if Ruven spitefully[2] eats nonkosher food when he could just as easily eat kosher food, or publicly desecrates the Sabbath, he is treated as a sinner whose object need not to be restored to him.

1. For example, the Gentile who is not at all familiar with Jewish practices will praise the Jewish religion when the Jewish finder tells him that he is restoring the lost object.

2. A businessman who eats with fellow businessmen and is embarrassed to tell them that he would like to eat kosher food is not a spiteful sinner.

Chapter 264

THE DIGNITY OF THE FINDER

INTRODUCTION

The Torah, in setting forth the requirement to pick up the object lost by another person, states, "You shall not see the ox of your brother or his sheep or goat cast off and hide yourself from them; you shall surely return them to your brother."[1] The Talmud,[2] in discussing this verse, teaches us that it means that there are times when a person may indeed turn away from the object; that situation occurs when it would be inconsistent with the dignity of the finder to carry the object or to lead an animal home if the object or animal were his own. This chapter discusses those situations when the finder is not required to fulfill the commandment to pick up and restore the object that he finds. Is this exemption always present, or does it depend upon the place where the object is found, whether a rural area or an urban area? May the finder waive the exemption?

1. Deuteronomy 22:1.
2. *Baba Metzia* 30a.

TEXT

If a person spies a lost inanimate object that he would be embarrassed to carry if it was his own, he need not pick it up to restore to its owner.

It depends upon the person, whose dignity may be based on his position in the community or because he is a scholar who does not carry his own sacks or cartons in the street; in such a case he may pass the object without picking it up and he is not in violation of the commandment to restore the object to its owner. Every such person must examine his own conscience. If he would have taken these things for himself had they belonged to him, he must also restore them to the owner. But if he would consider picking them up or carrying them to be beneath his dignity had they belonged to him, he need not pick up the object.

If he did pick it up to restore and then thought that he does not want to be seen carrying this type of object, he is required to continue[3] his effort and must restore the object to its owner.[4]

The exemption of restoring live animals

If the finder spies a lost animal, such as a cow or sheep, he need not stop to take possession of the animal to restore it to its owner, if it is beneath his dignity to do so. However, if, with the original intent to restore the animal to its owner, he makes the animal move by, for example, hitting the animal with his hand or with a staff, then he must restore the animal to its owner in a safe place.

When the finder is obligated to restore the animal, he must take care of it according to the standards discussed in Chapter 266.

Location of the found object

If the scholar would restore certain objects in a rural area, but it would embarrass him to carry them in the city, he is not required to pick up

3. Once he has commenced the Torah commandment not to turn aside, he must also complete the Torah command to restore the found object to its rightful owner.

4. There is also an opinion that holds that in the case of found inanimate objects, even if a person picks it up and begins the process of restoring the object to its owner, he may change his mind and rely on his scholar's exemption.

such objects in the city. If the object is found in a suburban area, there is a difference of opinion as to whether the finder who is a scholar must restore the object in a suburban area. One opinion holds that since he would be exempt in a city, the exemption extends to the suburban area; the other opinion holds that the exemption applies where it specifically applies and not in other places.

There is another situation that exempts the finder from picking up and restoring the lost object. If the finder is a priest and the object is in a cemetery, the finder is exempt from picking up the object since a priest is forbidden to enter into a cemetery.

Not to rely on the exemption

The scholar is admonished not to rely on the exemption but rather to act the same as any other person in fulfilling the commandments to pick up and restore the lost object.[5]

There is another view that the scholar cannot waive his exemption, for to do so would be humiliating for other scholars. This view admits that all persons other than scholars should follow the view of the prior paragraph even if they could be part of the exemption because of their prominence in the community.

---

5. In *halachah* this is known as acting *lifnim mishurath hadin*. See Volume I, page 94, and also Glossary. See also author's article, *Lifnim Mishurath Hadin*, Annual Volume of Young Israel Rabbis in Israel, Volume 2, Jerusalem (1988).

Chapter 265

PRIORITY IN PICKING UP LOST OBJECTS

INTRODUCTION

The most likely scenario for the type of a situation described in this chapter would be where a river is sweeping away objects belonging to many people. Among them is an object belonging to Ruven, an object belonging to his father, and an object belonging to Ruven's teacher. Ruven is in a position to save only one object.[1] If only his father's object and his teacher's are involved, and Ruven can save only one object, whose object has priority?

The Torah states, "However, may there be no destitute among you."[2] The Talmud explains this to mean that the material object of the person in a position to save it takes precedence over the objects of all others.[3]

There are times when the finder has the option to save his own object or to save the object of another person other than his teacher

---

1. The teacher spoken of here is his pre-eminent Torah teacher from whom he learned most of his knowledge of the Torah and to whom he owes his total allegiance and total respect. See Maimonides, *Laws of Talmud Torah*, chapter 5.

2. Deuteronomy 15:4.

3. *Baba Metzia* 33a.

or his father. His own takes priority. What if the finder saves the object of the other person and thereby loses his own object? Is the finder entitled to compensation other than the possible compensation provided for in the next chapter? What if the finder stipulates with the other person as to compensation? Is it binding? What if the other person is not present and thus he cannot consent to the demands of the finder? What if the finder takes up the role of a helper for the loser of the object? Is he entitled to compensation?

A related question concerns Ruven, a person who undertakes to perform an act to benefit Shimon without Shimon's knowledge. Is Ruven entitled to compensation?[4] A specific example of benefiting another person occurred when Jews were often wrongfully imprisoned, to be held for ransom. Occasionally the duke or governor of a state or province would release certain Jews from whom he used to borrow money without any ransom payment, or upon a ransom payment would release other Jews in addition to the Jews who made the payment. What is the relationship between the Jews who interceded with the captors to release other Jews? A related topic is that of compensating the marriage broker or the business broker who is retained to obtain a result: in the case of a marriage broker, a suitable marriage for a woman or a man; in the case of the business broker, a sale or some other event for which he is retained. What is his measure of compensation if he seeks and is promised an exorbitant fee?

TEXT

To act beyond the requirements of the law

As is stated in many places in this work, a person should, and in certain circumstances, must act beyond the requirements of the law.[5] Thus Ruven in many of the examples given below should save his neighbor's object rather than his own if it will not cause a monetary

4. See Chapter 375.

5. In *halachah* this is known as acting *lifnim mishurath hadin*. See Volume I, page 94 and also Glossary. See also author's article *Lifnim Mishurath Hadin*, Annual Volume of Young Israel Rabbis in Israel, Volume 2, Jerusalem (1988).

loss to Ruven. Otherwise, in most situations regarding lost objects, the finder will find enough reasons why he is too busy with his own livelihood to take the time to restore a found object.

The Talmud states, "Jerusalem was destroyed because they [the judges] based their judgments [strictly] on Torah law, and did not go beyond the requirements of the law."[6]

The finder's lost object takes precedence

Ruven loses his own object and finds it and at the same time he finds the lost object of another person. If he can restore both of them, he must do so. However, if he can restore only one of the lost objects, his own object takes precedence over any other person's objects, even over the lost objects of his father or his teacher.

Ruven can insist on saving his own object instead of Shimon's, even if Shimon, who is unable to save his own object, offers to pay to Ruven the value of Ruven's object to save Shimon's object.[7]

Lost objects of his father and his teacher

Ruven finds the lost object of his father and of his teacher and can only restore one of them. If his father is a scholar of stature equal to that of his teacher, he must restore the object of his father.

If not, he must restore the object of his teacher.[8] However, the lost object of his teacher has priority only if his teacher was not paid for teaching him. But if he was paid by his father for teaching him, the father's lost object has priority. Similarly, if some other person other than Ruven's father paid the teacher, such other person's lost object and the father's lost object have priority over the teacher's object.

Ruven saves Shimon's object rather than his own

Two objects are being swept away by a river, Ruven's and Shimon's. Shimon can with great effort possibly save his own object. (If Shimon

6. *Baba Metzia* 30b.

7. Ruven can insist that he wants his object rather than the money value of his object.

8. Rabbi Yosef Karo writes in *Shulhan Aruch Hoshen haMishpat*, chapter 266, "If a father tells him [the son] not to restore a lost object, he should not listen to him."

cannot save his own object it is deemed abandoned, and if Ruven saves Shimon's object it belongs to Ruven.) Ruven can save only one object; he saves Shimon's object and loses his own object. He is paid by Shimon only that which he would have been paid (in those instances where payment is permitted as shown in Chapter 268) and is not compensated for the loss of his own object.[9]

The foregoing holds true only if Shimon is present to see that his object is being swept away and Ruven did not stipulate with Shimon that he expects to get reimbursed for the value of Ruven's object that will be lost. Ruven under such circumstances could have stipulated with Shimon that he will rescue Shimon's object if Shimon will pay to Ruven a certain compensation and also for the value of Ruven's object that is being swept away.[10] Ruven's failure to so stipulate evidences a waiving of any rights that Ruven may have to receive payment for his own lost object. However, if Shimon is not present to negotiate with Ruven, and Ruven saved Shimon's object, Shimon must pay to Ruven the value of Ruven's object together with the compensation, if Ruven would be entitled to any, as shown in the next chapter.

Similarly, Ruven in front of three people[11] states that he will rescue Shimon's object in order to be compensated for the value of his own object that will be lost, and for compensation for recovering Shimon's object; Ruven will be so compensated. One opinion states that this last law holds true only if Shimon is not present, and another view holds that this holds true even if Shimon is present.[12]

---

9. The example given in the Talmud and codes is as follows: The river is sweeping away Ruven's donkey worth $100 and Shimon's donkey worth $200. Ruven rescues Shimon's donkey and loses his own donkey to the river. Ruven receives the same compensation he might be entitled to as shown in Chapter 268, not the $100 for the donkey.

10. Ruven states to Shimon that he will rescue Shimon's object, and charge him a certain compensation and also for the value of Ruven's object, and Shimon remains silent. If Shimon sees Ruven perform the rescue, Shimon's silence will be deemed a sign of assent to the statement of Ruven.

11. Three men constitute a beth din.

12. Since Ruven could have so stipulated with Shimon, then why the necessity for the three men? It is answered that the stipulation that Ruven makes with Shimon is valid only if there are no other men present.

In those situations when Shimon must pay Ruven for Ruven's lost object, he will still have to make the payment even if Ruven later recovers his own lost object.[13]

In those instances in which payment is permitted under the laws of the next chapter, if Ruven is not successful in rescuing Shimon's object, Shimon need pay to Ruven only that which any person would have been paid for an attempted rescue that did not succeed. If the stipulation between Ruven and Shimon is that Ruven will be paid whether or not he succeeds in rescuing Shimon's object, Shimon must pay Ruven even if Ruven is not successful in rescuing Shimon's object. Conversely, if the stipulation is that Ruven will be paid only if he succeeded in rescuing Shimon's object, then Shimon does not have to pay Ruven if he is not successful. Beth din will have to determine the intent of the parties in each case. Also, beth din will have to determine if the rescue effort is successful, for example, if Ruven rescues the object and then it is swept away from the place where Ruven places it.

If there is no stipulation between the parties, and the efforts by Ruven to save the object are not successful, Shimon need not pay Ruven anything, not even for the time and effort expended.

Ruven saves Shimon's object by losing his own

Assume that Ruven is carrying his jug of wine and Shimon is carrying his jug of honey. Honey is worth much more than wine. Shimon's jug of honey developed a crack in it and the honey will pour out. Ruven seeing this spills out his wine and places his now empty jug beneath the honey and all of the honey is now caught into Ruven's jug. Ruven will be compensated for his efforts[14] in saving Shimon's honey but will not be paid for his lost wine. Since Shimon is there, if Ruven wants to be compensated for his efforts and also for the wine he is to spill

13. Shimon's obligation became effective when Ruven agreed to abandon his own object to recover Shimon's object. The fact that Ruven's object was later recovered by Ruven does not eliminate Shimon's obligation. Because Ruven's object was abandoned by him, anyone could have rescued Ruven's object and kept it for himself. Thus Ruven acquired the object that he had previously abandoned.

14. He will be paid according to the scale described in Chapter 268.

out, he should so stipulate to Shimon. If Ruven states he will save Shimon's honey by pouring out his own wine, and Shimon says nothing, then Shimon must pay for the wine as well as for Ruven's efforts.

Conversely, Shimon could have insisted that Ruven pour out his wine to save Shimon's honey and that Shimon pay Ruven for his efforts and for his wine. Ruven runs no risk since the honey is now in his jug and in his possession until he is paid.[15] There are those who dispute this holding and say that Ruven can refuse to spill out his wine to save that of Shimon if Ruven wants his wine.

Assume that Ruven leaves his jug of wine on the ground and Shimon is there with his jug of honey, which cracks. Shimon may take Ruven's jug of wine, spill it out, and let his honey flow into Ruven's now empty jug. Shimon owes Ruven the value of the wine.

The foregoing laws hold true only if Shimon could somehow have saved his honey in some manner or form. If it is obvious that he could not have saved his honey, then if Ruven puts his jug under that of Shimon's jug as the honey pours out, the honey belongs to Ruven as abandoned property.[16] In all events, there are laws of the land and rules of beth din that control many of these situations.

In all those situations in this chapter where Ruven stipulates with Shimon that Shimon will pay to Ruven more than the going rate for such efforts, the stipulation will be enforced only if Ruven will suffer some damages by his rescue effort. But if Ruven does not suffer any damages by his effort to save the objects of Shimon, Shimon need pay only the amount that a person receives for such efforts as stated in Chapter 268. Thus in the above example, if Ruven's jars were empty and Ruven before rescuing Shimon's honey insists that Shimon pay

---

15. Ruven can set a reasonable time limit for payment and need not have to sue for payment. If Shimon does not pay within such reasonable time, the honey belongs to Ruven.

16. The law is the same in similar situations. For example, there is a fire in the town and all of the residents are evacuating the town, which will surely burn down. Ruven runs into someone's home and takes something; it belongs to Ruven. The property is deemed to be abandoned property. However, if the owner of the property could have rescued his own objects with great effort, Ruven is to receive wages for the rescue, as determined by beth din, but the object belongs to the owner, and not to Ruven.

him an exorbitant sum[17] and Shimon agrees, Shimon need pay only such sum as beth din will fix for the amount of labor Ruven expended, as shown in Chapter 268.[18] Another example given in the codes is where Shimon is escaping from captors who have wrongly imprisoned him. He comes to a ferry and pleads for Ruven, the ferry operator, to take him across the river. Ruven demands an exorbitant fee, or Shimon himself offers an exorbitant fee. Once Shimon is taken across the river, he need pay only the normal fee. However, if the person with the boat is a fisherman who is fishing and Shimon offers to pay the fisherman an exorbitant fee for leaving his nets and for getting him across the river, and the fisherman leaves the nets and takes Shimon across the river, Shimon must pay to the fisherman that which he promised. In all of the situations where Shimon need not pay the exorbitant amount, this holds true if Shimon did not yet make the payment. However, if he made the payment to Ruven, then he may not receive anything back.

If Shimon deposited the exorbitant sum with an escrowee, the rules are as follows: If Shimon told the escrowee, release the sum to Ruven upon his rescuing the object, the escrowee must do so when Ruven rescues the object. However, if Ruven told the escrowee, the money that Shimon is giving to you is to be given to me when I rescue Shimon's object, and Shimon is silent, then the escrowee may not give the money to Ruven and Ruven will be paid for his efforts as stated in Chapter 268.

Exorbitant professional fees

What has been said about rescue efforts is also true of professional services. Ruven is a doctor and Shimon comes to him for a cure. Ruven asks for an exorbitant fee, and Shimon agrees to pay it if Ruven heals him. Ruven heals Shimon; Shimon must pay the agreed-upon fee. However, if they discussed a medicine and Shimon agreed

17. The term "exorbitant" as used in this chapter refers to any fee that is in excess of the normal fees for the service rendered.

18. Shimon's promise to pay the exorbitant amount is deemed to be a promise made without any intent, more in the nature of a jest.

to pay an exorbitant amount, Shimon need pay only the normal price.[19]

A person retains a marriage broker or a business broker and promises the broker a fee that is in excess of the ordinary fee. When the matter is completed, the broker is entitled only to the normal fee, not to the agreed-upon higher fee. There is an opinion that the agreed-upon fee must be paid. A third opinion holds that where there is a community-fee, then that fee is controlling, and if the community does not have a set fee, then the agreed-upon fee must be paid.

However, according to all opinions the agreed-upon fee must be paid if the agreement was concluded and made binding by a *kinyan*,[20] or by a handshake in those communities where a handshake is the equivalent of a binding *kinyan*, or by oath to make the payment. Also if the broker was retained for an extraordinary task that is not usual, then the agreed-upon fee must be paid according to all opinions.

Ruven, a broker, undertook to represent Shimon without a fee. Just before the entire performance of Ruven was completed, Ruven demands a fee for his work; Shimon has expended moneys in reliance of the completion of Ruven's performance. Shimon agrees to pay to Ruven the fee that he demands and makes the payment. Somehow Shimon holds moneys belonging to Ruven and wants to offset the money he is holding against the fees that he paid to Ruven. Shimon pleads that Ruven originally undertook to represent Shimon without a fee and made his demand for a fee after Shimon had expended money that he stood to lose if Ruven did not complete his task. Thus the money paid to Ruven was in the nature of robbery and can be recovered by Shimon. It was held that the fee belongs to Ruven and Shimon must return the money to Ruven. The reason is that even if Ruven undertook to work without a fee, he is not obligated to complete his undertaking. However, if Ruven's services were no longer needed by Shimon and Shimon could have completed the project himself if Ruven removed himself from the project, and now Ruven demands money not to interfere and ruin the project unless he is

19. The medicine is not part of the professional fees that Ruven may charge and that Shimon agreed to pay.

20. See Glossary; see Volume VI, Chapter 195.

paid, Shimon may recover any money that he paid to Ruven under such circumstances.

Benefiting another without his authorization

Anytime that Ruven, without any request from Shimon, performs any service for Shimon's benefit, for which Ruven expects to be paid, Shimon need not make any payment unless there is some actual benefit conferred upon Shimon. If some benefit is received by Shimon, he must make some compensation to Ruven, as determined by beth din, considering the effort and time expended by Ruven and the actual benefit received and retained by Shimon.[21]

Intercession by Ruven on Shimon's behalf

Ruven and Shimon are imprisoned. Without any agreement between Ruven and Shimon, Ruven intercedes with the authorities by expending money to free himself. He was freed together with Shimon. If beth din determines that Shimon would have in all events been released without the intercession of Ruven, Shimon does not owe any money to Ruven, since Ruven and Shimon did not stipulate that Ruven would make a payment to the captors and obtain the release of Shimon, for which Shimon would pay an agreed-upon sum to Ruven.

Had Ruven and Shimon stipulated that Shimon would pay an agreed sum of money to Ruven if Ruven would intercede on Shimon's behalf by making a payment to the captors, then Shimon must pay to Ruven the agreed-upon sum. If Shimon pleads that he would have been freed without Ruven's intercession, and beth din so determines, beth din will fix a sum that it determines is the value of the benefit conferred upon Shimon as if Ruven had been the cause of Shimon being freed. If beth bin finds that the entire expenditure was for Ruven freeing himself and no extra expenditure was made for the freeing of Shimon, Shimon does not owe anything to Ruven, even if Shimon agreed to pay Ruven for his expenditures and efforts. This is true even if Shimon would not have been freed if Ruven did not make the expenditure to free himself. But if beth din determines that the

21. See Chapter 375.

expenditure freed both Ruven and Shimon, Shimon owes to Ruven half of the expenditure.[22]

If Shimon is kidnapped and Ruven expends money to free him, Shimon must reimburse Ruven for the money he paid for the rescue.

22. As an outgrowth of these laws, the following laws evolved. The libraries of Ruven and Shimon are about to be seized by the authorities. Ruven saves his books and the books of Shimon by making an expenditure to the authorities. Assume that Ruven went to the authorities with the intent of saving only his books. If Ruven did not have to make any extra expenditure to save the books of Shimon, then Shimon need not pay to Ruven any part of his expenditure. However, if Ruven went to the authorities with the intent to save both his books and Shimon's books, then beth din must determine a sum that Shimon will have to pay to Ruven for the books of Shimon being saved.

Chapter 266

THE CARE TO BE GIVEN TO A FOUND OBJECT

INTRODUCTION

Ruven finds an object that he is required to pick up and to restore to its owner according to the Torah commandments.[1] Because the object must be restored to its owner, it cannot be acquired by Ruven. Ruven must anticipate that the owner will imminently come to claim his object.

What is Ruven to do with the object until he restores it to its owner? What if he never finds the owner? What is the degree of care that Ruven must take to preserve the object? Most of the examples given in the codes follow the discussion in the Talmud and thus the objects discussed may not seem to be all that relevant today. I therefore recommend that the degree of care be left to beth din, which should set community standards and make rules to protect the interests of both the loser and the finder. In those communities that have laws relating to lost and found objects, these laws may often be controlling.

1. It meets all of the requirements as described in Chapter 259.

TEXT

The responsibility of the finder to the owner

The finder of an object must take care of the object that he found until it can be restored to its owner. In taking care of the object, the finder has the responsibility of a paid bailee[2] regarding the object,[3] that is, he is responsible if anything happens to the object while under his control.[4] He is responsible to make restitution to the owner if the object is again lost or stolen or destroyed or if he is negligent in his care of the object. He is not responsible if the object was lost or destroyed by an act of God or *force majeure*. If no owner appears after the finder has advertised that he found the object as described in Chapter 267, he is obligated to take care of the object until the coming of the prophet Elijah.[5]

Examples of care to be given to the object

The finder must take care of the object with the same degree of care as do people in the community with their own objects. The finder must constantly examine the object to see that its condition is not deteriorating. The finder must examine the object to see that it is not spoiling or wasting away.[6] Some of the examples of the care to be taken of found objects as found in the Talmud and codes follow: (When it is stated that some things may not be done it is because it was found that such conduct may cause damage to the object.)

The type of garment or cloth will determine the care to be taken.

---

2. He has the responsibility of a paid bailee because he benefits from the role as a guardian of the object. While he is occupied with taking care of the object which is a Torah commandment, he may be exempt from fulfilling some other Torah commandments.

3. There is an opinion that the finder has the same laws as an unpaid bailee.

4. See Chapter 303.

5. See Volume II, page 174–77. It states, "There is a concept in *halachah* known as 'setting the matter aside until the prophet Elijah appears.' The prophet Elijah is the harbinger of the coming of the Messiah. When there are matters that the beth din cannot decide because they cannot ascertain the facts, such matters are held in abeyance, with neither party to the dispute obtaining judgment."

6. The examples that follow below also apply to a person who is a bailee of an object whose owner has gone abroad for an extended stay.

There are constantly new types of materials manufactured and the manufacturer's instructions must be followed.

A garment or cloth made of wool must be shaken out once in 30 days. It must be shaken out by one person and not by two people, nor may it be beaten with a stick.

A garment or cloth made out of linen must not be shaken out.

All types of cloth may be spread on a couch if it is to air out the cloth, but not if it also benefits the finder so as to cover a piece of furniture.

Wooden utensils should occasionally be used to prevent them from rotting.

Copper utensils may be used with hot or cold water, but not over a fire.

Silver utensils may be used with cold water, but not with hot water.

Gold and glass vessels may not be used.

Garden instruments may be used on ground that is soft, but not if the ground is hard.

A scroll[7] must be read once in 30 days, and if the finder cannot read, he should unroll it and roll it up every 30 days. The finder may not: study the scroll if this is the first time that he studies this particular subject matter; read a section from the scroll and then reread the section; read a section and then translate it; open it to more than three columns at one time; permit two persons to read in it two different sections; permit three persons to read it at one time. Appropriate modifications of these rules would apply to bound books.

If Shimon finds *tefilin*[8] he may have their value assessed and keep the *tefilin*, or sell them, since they are readily available and the owner can purchase a new pair with the money. Based on this law, there is an opinion that the same applies to all objects that can be easily purchased. The other opinion holds that the loser wants his own object to be restored to him rather than money to buy another object.

Live animals have special rules:

a. the animal must be fed and cared for.
b. a sheep must be sheared of its wool.

---

7. The old codes speak of scrolls since they were written prior to the invention of movable type, which made possible mass production of bound books.

8. See Glossary.

c. If it works and eats, such as a mule, the finder should hire it out, take the rental, and feed the animal. If the rental is more than is needed to feed the animal, the surplus belongs to the owner. This must be done for 12 months. After the 12 months, beth din[9] assesses the animal's value.

d. If the animal produces milk, or a hen lays eggs, the finder sells the milk or the eggs and feed the animals with the proceeds. This must be done for 12 months. After the 12 months, beth din assesses the animal's value.

e. Calves or foals must be taken care of for 3 months if they can be grazed and for 30 days if they must be fed.

f. Large geese or hens must be taken care of for 30 days. Small ones that cost more to feed than they can earn must be kept for 3 days. The finder may then sell them with permission of beth din.

g. In all events, if the expense of feeding the animal exceeds its income, the seller may, after 3 days, sell it and keep the money for the owner. The statement of the finder as to how much he spent on feeding the animal is sufficient and he need not take an oath to sustain his plea. Similarly, if he hired them out and made income and had expenses, his statement is sufficient and he need not take an oath.

h. Fruit that has begun to spoil or anything similar may be sold with the permission of beth din.

In all of the situations where there is money substituted for the found object, it may used by the finder who holds it for the owner, as borrowed money. Therefore he is responsible if the money is lost or stolen or even if lost by *force majeure*.[10] This holds true even if he has not used the money.

If one finds money, he may not make use of it; therefore if it is lost by *force majeure*, he is not responsible.[11]

9. There is an opinion that holds that the finder may make his own appraisal.

10. See Chapter 340.

11. He has the status of a paid bailee, as stated in the text, or as an unpaid bailee, as stated in note 3 above.

Chapter 267

THE ANNOUNCEMENT AND THE RESTORING OF THE FOUND OBJECT

INTRODUCTION

The finder now has in his possession an object that he must restore to its owner, as described in Chapter 259. How does he go about restoring it? What if he cannot tell who the owner is, although the object has an identifying mark by which the owner can identify the object as the object that he lost. How does the finder make it known that he found an object? How does the owner identify the object to the satisfaction of the finder? What if two persons claim the found object? What if the owner claims that the object as restored to him is incomplete and that the finder took some of the object for himself?

TEXT

Where the owner of the lost object is known

Assume the owner of the lost object is known to the finder. It may be unique and everyone knows that it belongs to Shimon, the owner.

Ruven, the finder, will restore the object to Shimon. Or it has an identification mark on it that contains the name of the owner.[1]

The finder should contact the owner by the best method available: telephone, fax, letter, e-mail, or whatever method that will best inform the owner that the finder has the lost object and wants to restore it to the owner. After contact has been made, the owner should come to the finder to retrieve his lost object.

Assuming that the finder cannot contact the owner, the finder may leave the found object at the home of the owner with a person of suitable age with instructions to give the object to the owner.

Or the finder may leave the object in a courtyard or other place belonging to the owner that is guarded so that it will not be stolen from that place.[2] This may be done although the owner is not aware that the object is left at his guarded premises. If the object was left in a place that is not guarded, then the finder is responsible if the object gets lost or stolen.

If the restored lost object is again lost and the finder again finds it he must restore it again and again. For example, the lost object is a goat. The finder, without the knowledge of the owner, restores the goat to an enclosed pen that the owner keeps for the goats. As the finder leaves, he sees that the goat has again escaped from the pen. The finder must again take the goat and return it to the pen.

In the final analysis, beth din will have to decide if the finder exercised appropriate care in restoring the object to the owner.

Where the owner of the lost object is not known

Ruven finds an object that has an identification mark, but the mark does not show to whom the object belongs.[3]Ruven must announce

1. For example, a name tape on a garment, or an identification card in a wallet or pocketbook, or a letter with a name on it, or any other thing that will help the finder identify who the owner is.

2. Such as in a mailbox or the owner's courtyard that has a high fence around it, or any other place or premises belonging to the owner where it is reasonably expected that the owner will spy the object as soon as he passes by his premises and retrieve it.

3. For example, Ruven finds a sweater that was obviously knitted at home as distinguished from a store-bought sweater, the knitting being loose and sloppy. Also, the colors are very unique, such as the fist knitted line being purple, the next line pink,

the fact that he found something.[4] The announcement must be made in such manner and places as will make it likely that the owner who lost the object will come forward to try to identify the object and reclaim it. The codes speak of making the announcement in the synagogue on those days when most frequent the services, and at such interval in the services as to make it likely that the announcement will reach the owner. Where to best make the announcements depends upon the community or place in which the object is found and beth din may have to issue directives. It may be that the most effective way is to advertise in a newspaper or in the community or synagogue bulletins, or to place notices on lamp poles, or on trees, or on school bulletin boards, all according to the directives of beth din.

In those societies where it is dangerous to announce that an object has been found, then the finder must initiate a word-of-mouth announcement to reach the owner.

There was a decree made by a synod of Rabbis in the eleventh century that the owner who lost something should also make an announcement so that the one who finds it will know where to restore it to the owner and also so others will be able to tell the person who found it where to find the owner. The decree also provided that persons other than the finder and the owner could not refuse to cooperate to bring together the owner and the finder on the grounds that these other persons were sworn to secrecy not to disclose to the owner who the finder was.

The wording of the announcement

The wording of the announcement has to be in such language that it is not too obvious what was found so as to reduce the likelihood that a dishonest person can come forward to claim the object, nor must it be so obscure that the owner will not know that it is his object that has been found.

One of the purposes of the announcement is to enable anyone who may own such an object to go home or to look in his pockets or other places to see if he has lost such an object. The announcement

---

the next line orange, the next line aqua, the next line red, and so forth and the pattern repeats itself at certain intervals.

4. The terms of the advertising is stated in the next section.

will tell him that it may be his object that the finder found. The owner will go to the finder and describe the object that he lost. Or the owner knows that he lost the object and does not know who found it.

The identification by the owner

There are three categories of identification of lost objects by the alleged owner.

1. The alleged owner states that he lost a blue coat (the announcement having said that a coat was found). This type of identification does not carry any weight; it may be a fortuitous guess. Identification such as "the coat that I lost is blue and has black buttons" likewise does not rise to the level of good identification.

2. There is a higher level of identification. For example, the coat is blue with black buttons and is a size 44. Or it was lost in Cohen's restaurant, the same place where Ruven found the coat.

3. There is the highest level of identification. For example, the owner states that the coat has a tiny hole on the inside lining about 4 inches from the zipper of the lining on the right side. Only the true owner could be so specific.

Beth din should establish criteria for the identification of lost objects depending upon the type of object that was found; they should set up the categories in each community.

If an alleged owner makes an identification under category 1, he should not get the object from the finder.

If a person is a known liar, he too should not be given the object that he allegedly lost even if he identifies the object by category 2. He is to be given the object if he produces two witnesses that he lost that object or if he identifies the object by a category 3 identification.[5]

If the alleged owner employs category 2 identification, he must be known to be an honest man or have witnesses testify that he is honest, in order to get the object from the finder.

Assume that Shimon and Levi each comes forward and each correctly identifies the object using the same level of identification, for example, both identify using category 3 identification. The object

5. There is an opinion that a known liar will not be given the object even by a category 3 identification; he will only be given it if he produces two witnesses that say the object is his.

is given to neither Shimon nor Levi.[6] It may be suggested to them that one should, without conceding that the object is not his, waive his rights to the object. Or else they should compromise in some way. If one can produce two witnesses[7] that the object is his, he will get the object.

If one produces even category 3 identification and the second produces witnesses, the object is given to the one who produces witnesses. The witnesses need not testify that they saw the second one lose the object; they need only testify that they know that the object belonged to the second one.

If Shimon and Levi each produce witnesses that the object belongs to him, even if one identifies the object by category 3 identification, it still leaves two witnesses against two witnesses, and the object is given to neither Shimon nor Levi.

The traditional codes give some rules in determining who has established the identification in a manner more satisfactory than the other claimant.[8]

Beth din has to establish rules and has to judge each case anew, because very rarely are there two situations exactly alike.

The finder need not take an oath

Ruven finds a wallet and restores it to Shimon. Shimon pleads that the wallet as restored by Ruven contains only $100, while when he lost the wallet it contained $200. Shimon pleads that Ruven should take an oath that when he found the wallet it contained just $100. Ruven need not take an oath that the wallet was restored in the same condition in which he found it.[9]

---

6. It has been suggested that if one employs category 3 identification and the other category 2 identification, the object should be given to the one who employs category 3 identification.

7. Producing one witness does not alter the situation in favor of the person producing the one witness to bolster his identification.

8. If the found object is a cloak, and Shimon produces witnesses that he wove the cloak and Levi produces witnesses that the cloak fell from him, the cloak is given to Levi. If Shimon identifies the length and Levi identifies the width, the cloak is given to Levi.

9. If the finder would always be required to take an oath, people would be loath to pick up lost objects.

Chapter 268

NOT TO TAKE COMPENSATION FOR RESTORING A LOST OBJECT

INTRODUCTION

Ruven finds Shimon's object. As stated in Chapter 259, there are Torah commandments that compel Ruven to pick up the object and restore it to Shimon. In addition to fulfilling the Torah commandment, which is reward enough, can Ruven demand and receive compensation for restoring the object to Shimon? In Chapter 265, in the section entitled "Ruven saves Shimon's object rather than his own," it is shown that there are times when Ruven, the rescuer (or finder) of Shimon's object is entitled to be compensated, in addition to the Heavenly reward of complying with the Torah commandments.

TEXT

Compensation to be paid to the finder

As stated in the Introduction above, the Heavenly reward for fulfilling the Torah commandments to pick up and restore a lost object should be sufficient.

However, the *halachah* does not require a person to lose money in performing these commandments. There are several suggested compensation scales suggested by the authorities, based on the reading of the relevant Talmudic passage.[1]

Assume that Ruven the finder earns $10 an hour at his work and the object is worth $50.

Ruven, on his way home from work, finds Shimon's object, which contains Shimon's address, and without going out of his way, Ruven restores the object to Shimon. Ruven should not receive any compensation.

Ruven, on his way home from work, finds Shimon's object and must take a taxi to deliver the object to Shimon. Ruven is entitled to receive the taxi fare from Shimon.

Ruven can only deliver the object to Shimon during the time that he works. The restoring of the object takes 2 hours. Ruven will lose $20 from his wages and should receive such compensation.

If Ruven were unemployed, he would accept any type of menial job and receive $2 an hour. If he had obtained a job as a deliverer of objects, he would be paid $4 an hour. Although there are several views as to how much Ruven may charge for restoring the object, I set forth the two most popular views. One view holds that he may charge $4, which is the compensation of an unemployed worker ($2 an hour X 2 hours). Another view holds that Ruven may receive $8, the compensation of a person who is employed specifically to deliver the lost object ($4 an hour X 2 hours).

In no event may Ruven be paid more than the value of the object.

Ruven makes a prior demand to be compensated in full

The compensation set forth above applies only if no other arrangements have been made for the compensation to be paid Ruven.

Assume that Shimon is present when Ruven agrees to restore to Shimon the object that Shimon lost. Shimon is too weak to climb up a tree where his pet cat has climbed. Ruven, on his way to work, comes by and volunteers to climb the tree and restore the cat to Shimon if Shimon will pay him the amount of time that Ruven will lose because of coming to work late, and Shimon agrees. It took Ruven 1 and 1/2

1. See *Baba Metzia* 30b and 31b.

hours to get his ladder and to climb the tree and to return the ladder to his house. Shimon must pay to Ruven $15 (1 and 1/2 hours X $10 an hour).

Assume that Shimon is not present and Ruven sees Shimon's cat up the tree, and Ruven will have to take 1 and 1/2 hours off from work to restore the object to Shimon. Ruven may convene a beth din or any three persons and stipulate in their presence that he will restore the object to Shimon and will seek compensation from Shimon according to the amount of time that he loses from his work. Ruven will be entitled to $15 from Shimon, the same as in the prior paragraph.

Although there are many formulas, Ruven should whenever possible rely on the Heavenly reward rather than on money for restoring the lost object.

Chapter 269

PICKING UP A LOST OBJECT FOR OR WITH ANOTHER PERSON

INTRODUCTION

Shimon loses an object that has no identification marks or in some other way does not comply with the criteria stated in Chapter 259 for restoring lost objects, and the finder may keep the object. Or else Shimon specifically declares that he abandons the object. Ruven and Levi see the object. Ruven may pick it up to acquire the object for himself or he may pick it up so that Levi acquires the object. Does Levi become the owner of the object? May Ruven change his mind and keep the object for himself? What if both Ruven and Levi pick it up?

For the purpose of this chapter and under the law, an object that is lost and does not meet the criteria for restoring lost objects is designated as an abandoned object.

TEXT

Ruven picks up an abandoned object on behalf of Levi

Assume that Shimon's lost object is now deemed abandoned by Shimon. Ruven sees the object. Levi may also be present and asks

Ruven to acquire the object for him, Levi. Or else Ruven desires to acquire the object on behalf of Levi even if Levi is not present.[1] The object belongs to Levi as soon as Ruven lifts the object 3 *tefachim*.[2]

The intent of Ruven to acquire the object on behalf of Levi may be orally expressed by him, or may be only in his mind. We will know his prior state of mind if he later states that he picked the object up with the intent to acquire it on behalf of Levi.

Once Ruven acquires the object on behalf of Levi, Ruven cannot later state that he changes his mind and will not deliver the object to Levi.

However, if Ruven, not at the request of Levi, picks up the object without any specific intent in mind and later states that he intended it to be picked up on behalf of Levi and then states that he was jesting when he said that, and he really intended the object to be acquired for himself, the object belongs to Ruven.[3] But if Levi had asked Ruven to pick up the object for Levi, and Ruven picked up the object without any comments, it is assumed that he intended the object to be acquired on behalf of Levi. For example, Levi is in his automobile and sees the object on the ground and asks Ruven, a passerby, to acquire the object for Levi, and Ruven, knowing that the object is abandoned, does so; it belongs to Levi. The object will belong to Ruven if, as he picks up the object, he states that he is picking up the object for himself, even if he was requested to do so by Levi.

A case analogous to the case of picking up an object for someone else who so requests is the case of Ruven asking Levi to purchase merchandise on behalf of both of them so that they can be partners regarding the sale of the merchandise. Levi purchases the merchandise and later first declares that he purchased it for his own account only. There is an opinion that the merchandise belongs to both of

1. A person may acquire something for a second party without the knowledge of the second party. This is under the theory that one can confer a benefit on a person, such as acquiring an object for another, without his knowledge if it is beneficial for him. See Volume VII, Chapter 243.

2. About 10 inches. See Volume VI, page 147. Also see Glossary for definition of *tefach*.

3. Ruven is believed since at the time that he picked up the object he said nothing and also Levi did not request that he pick up the object for Levi.

them.[4] This is modified by another opinion that this holds true only if Ruven had the money to purchase his half of the merchandise when Levi went to purchase it.

Two persons acquiring together

There is an object on the ground abandoned by Shimon.[5] Both Ruven and Levi pick up the object.[6] It belongs to both of them. As stated above, the object must be picked up 3 *tefachim* for the finder to acquire the object. As Ruven picks up one end of the object the other end is still on the ground and does not belong to him. Simultaneously,[7] Levi picks up the other end and acquires that end. Neither has acquired the entire object and thus the object is theoretically still ownerless. In order to give effect to the aspirations of both Ruven and Levi, the *halachah* presumes that Ruven picks up his half and intends that the other half shall belong to Levi, and Levi picks up his half and intends that the other half shall belong to Ruven. Thus between the two of them the entire object is acquired by both of them as equal owners, and no third party can pick up the middle and claim that the middle is acquired by him.

This assumes that there is no impediment to Levi in acquiring the object. However, if there is some impediment (as stated in the next chapter) as where Levi is a minor, a deaf-mute, or a mentally deficient person, then Ruven acquires only that portion of the object that he actually raises 3 *tefachim* off the ground, the minor acquires only that portion that he lifts up from the ground, and a third party can acquire the balance of the object.[8] There is an opinion that if the second

4. This opinion holds that it is similar to the situation where Levi asks Ruven to pick up the object and Ruven does so without comment.

5. It may be actually abandoned by Shimon or lost by him and it has no identification mark or is lacking any of the other criteria to obligate the finder to restore the object to him.

6. This case is not the same famous Talmudic case described in Volume IV, Chapter 138. There each pleads that he is the only person who picked up the entire object and it was acquired solely by him and that the other person has not acquired any part of the object. In this chapter each admits that the other picked up his part of the object.

7. Or at any time prior to Ruven having picked up the entire object.

8. The rest of the object is still ownerless and does not belong to Ruven since the

person who picks up part of the object is a Gentile, then the entire object will belong to Ruven and the Gentile.

If both Ruven and Levi are minors, deaf-mutes, or mentally deficient, then the object will belong to both of them, since it is a decree of the Rabbis as stated in the next chapter that they can acquire found objects.

---

minor cannot acquire any part of the object for Ruven. The presumption that one acquires for himself and for the second person is not present.

Chapter 270

OBJECTS FOUND BY A DEAF-MUTE, A MENTALLY DEFICIENT, OR A MINOR

INTRODUCTION

Rabbi Yosef Karo in *Shulhan Aruch Hoshen haMishpat* includes in chapter 270 the laws of the acquisition of found objects by deaf-mutes, mentally deficient persons, minors, one's wife, his children, or his employee. I have divided the topics into two chapters: Chapter 270 deals with the acquisition of found objects by the deaf-mute, the mentally deficient, or the minor; Chapter 271 deals with the acquisition of found objects by one's wife, his children, or his employees. That which Rabbi Karo discusses in chapter 271, the finding of animals, has been included in other chapters.

Throughout this work, reference is made to the fact that the law recognizes that there are certain persons with legal impediments: the deaf-mute, the mentally deficient, and the minor.

In Volume I, at page 51, the term "minor" is defined and his eligibility to act as a judge is discussed; at page 117 the ability of a minor, a deaf-mute, and a mentally deficient to sue in beth din is discussed; at pages 254 and 256 the capacity of these three classes to act as witnesses is discussed.

Volume II, Chapter 46, discusses the role of a minor to authenticate instruments;

Volume III, Chapter 96, discusses "Oaths imposed by disqualified persons";

Volume IV, Chapter 110 discusses "A levy is not made on the property of minors";

Volume V, Chapter 149 discusses "Those who cannot obtain a presumption"; at page 228, "Minors in partition or demand situations"; at page 254, "Sale to a minor" as it affects the right of first refusal;

Volume VI, Chapter 188 discusses, "Ineligible agents";

Volume VII, Chapter 227 discusses, "Acts of agents," and Chapter 243, "Gifts acquired by the donee's agent" and the acts of a guardian of persons under a disability; Chapter 235, "Persons who are ineligible to participate in a sale"; Chapter 247, "Division of Gifts."

TEXT

A person with a legal disability finds an object

If a deaf-mute, a mentally deficient person, or a minor finds a lost object, the object would not legally belong to them under Torah law. They do not have the capacity to acquire a thing unless the seller, employer, or donor gives it to them, or some qualified person enables them to acquire it.[1] But in the case of found objects which have been abandoned by the owner, there is no one to aid them to acquire the object.

Thus, if someone were to take the objects that they found, the taker would not be robbing them since legally it does not belong to them.

However, the rabbis of the Talmud decreed that the objects found by any of these three classes of persons belongs to the finder.[2] If someone did take the object from them, the person with the legal disability cannot sue in beth din to obtain the object from the taker. The taker will have to give an accounting to Heaven.[3]

---

1. Thus the wages paid to them, or an object sold to them, or a gift given to them belongs to them and anyone who takes it from them is a thief.

2. The Rabbis of the Talmud, in order to protect the peace of society, decreed that objects found by these three classes of person should not be taken away from them and that they may keep that which they found.

3. A person is not forgiven in Heaven unless he also makes payment on earth to the injured party.

Chapter 271

OBJECTS FOUND BY CLOSE RELATIVES OR BY AN EMPLOYEE

INTRODUCTION

This is the last chapter dealing with lost and found objects.

There are certain classes of persons whose belongings are sometimes deemed to belong to others because of their relationships. This chapter deals with some of these relationships. Regarding one's children, the results may depend upon whether the father is supporting the children or whether they are independent. Regarding one's wife, the reasons for the laws as set forth in the text below depend upon ancient decrees enacted for the tranquility of the family. Regarding one's employee, it depends upon the type of work the employee was doing at the time.

TEXT

Objects found by one's children

Objects found by children who are supported by their father belong to the father.[1]

---

1. This is by a decree enacted by the Rabbis of the Talmud. The reason is that the father does not have the responsibility to support his children after the age of 6. The

Objects found by male children who are not supported by the father belong to the children.

Objects found by female children under the age of 12 years, 6 months, and 1 day belong to the father.[2] The foregoing holds true only as long as the father is alive. When the father dies, although the daughters are still supported out of his estate, the objects found by the minor daughters need not be given by them to their brothers who inherit their father's estate.[3]

Objects found by someone supported by Ruven who is not Ruven's child do not belong to Ruven, whether or not such person is male or female, and whether or not a minor has reached majority.

Objects found by one's wife

In consideration of decrees made by the Rabbis of the Talmud in favor of the wife, they also decreed that the objects that a wife finds belong to her husband.[4]

Objects found by an employee

Ruven hires Shimon to work for him and the work does not entail looking for objects. Shimon finds an object; it belongs to Shimon. If the work entails looking for objects and Shimon finds an object, even of a completely different kind than the kind he was hired to look for, the object belongs to Ruven.[5]

Rabbis enacted that the father must support his children until they attain their majority. In return for this support, the objects found by the children so supported belong to the father.

2. The reason is that the father has the right to betroth a daughter until she attains the age of 12 years, 6 months, and 1 day. The findings of the daughter belong to the father so that there should not be any enmity between them.

3. Gifts given to a child who has reached his majority belong to the child, whether or not the child is supported by his or her father. If the child is a minor and is supported by the father, the gift belongs to the father.

4. See Volume II, page 164, note 2, where the decrees of the Rabbis regarding the obligations of the wife and the husband are set forth.

5. For example, the river has been dammed and Ruven hires Shimon to find fish that the river carried from upstream, and Shimon finds a wallet with money. The money belongs to Ruven.

Chapter 272

HELPING TO LOAD, UNLOAD, AND RELOAD ANIMALS: RIGHT OF WAY OF PASSAGE

INTRODUCTION

The laws of the first part of this chapter are included mostly for their background to teach how a Jew must act towards his fellow Jew and the regard that a Jew must have for the welfare of animals. There is thus included a section on the contemporary applications of the laws of this chapter dealing with loading, unloading, and reloading of animals. The second subject matter of this chapter dealing with priorities of passage may also have contemporary application.

Rabbi Yosef Karo, in *Shulhan Aruch*, calls this chapter "Laws of Animals Or Boats That Meet." I have changed the title to reflect the actual contents of the chapter; the second half of the title has been retained in deference to the *Shulhan Aruch*. The priority of passage of animals or boats takes up only a few of the eighteen paragraphs in this chapter of *Shulhan Aruch*.

A few definitions: The owner of the animal to be loaded, or unloaded, or reloaded is designated as "Shimon." Ruven is the passerby who sees Shimon's animal about to be loaded, or staggering[1]

1. This is called "crouching" or "falling" in the Torah verses.

under its burden, or about to be reloaded. "Burden" is the objects that are placed on, or taken off from, or about to be replaced on Shimon's animal. "Load" as used here is a verb and refers to placing the burden on an animal in the first instance, that is, where this burden has not yet been on the animal. "Unload" as used here refers to taking off the burden from an animal that was previously loaded. "Reload" as used here refers to replacing on the animal the burden that has been unloaded from the animal because it was staggering under the burden.

Shimon's animal is about to be loaded by him in the first instance. Ruven happens to pass by. What, if any, are Ruven's obligations to Shimon to help him load the burden on the animal?

Shimon's animal is staggering under its burden. Assume that Ruven did not help load the burden on the animal. What, if any, are Ruven's obligations to help unload the burden from the animal?

Shimon's animal has been unloaded from the staggering burden that Ruven may or may not have helped to unload. What, if any, are Ruven's obligations to help reload the burden on Shimon's animal?

In Chapter 259 in the section entitled "The commandment not to turn aside from a lost object," there is set forth the Torah commandment as it appears in Deuteronomy 22:1–3. The commandments regarding the restoring of found objects also appear in Exodus 23:4. Each of these Torah sections dealing with found objects is immediately followed by a concomitant commandment dealing with a parallel theme; namely, to help one's neighbor to unload his animal if it is overloaded, and to help reload (or load in the first instance) his neighbor's animal.

> Exodus 23:4–5
>
> 4. If you meet your enemy's ox or his donkey going astray, you shall surely bring it back to him again. 5. If you see the donkey of someone you hate crouching under its burden, would you refrain from helping him?-You shall help him repeatedly.

> Deuteronomy 22:1–4
>
> 1. You shall not see the ox of your brother or his sheep or goat cast off, and hide yourself from them; you shall surely return them to your brother. 2. If your brother is not near you and you do not know him, then gather it inside your house, and it shall remain with you until your brother inquires after it, and you return it to him. 3. So shall you do for

his donkey, so shall you do for his garment, and so shall you do for any lost article of your brother that may become lost from him and you find it; you shall not hide yourself. 4. You shall not see the donkey of your brother or his ox falling on the road and hide yourself from them; you shall surely stand them up with him.

The fact that in both Exodus and Deuteronomy the verses are parallel and also appear one after the other shows the Divine intent that the laws of one will be similar to the laws of the other. As is seen in the text below, the laws of found objects and of loading, unloading, and reloading animals are parallel to each other: the three commandments, two positive and one negative; the violations of the commandments by "turning aside"; the exemptions afforded to certain classes of people; the compensation or lack of compensation to be paid; and to act beyond the requirements of the law.[2]

Also, a section dealing with caravans discusses whether all of the members of the caravan are responsible for each other if an animal of one of them is disabled, which is similar to a person requiring help with loading, unloading, or reloading his animal.

Rabbi Yosef Karo treats all of the laws of loading and unloading, and right of way of passage in one long chapter, while the laws of found objects are spread over many chapters; however, many of the laws in the first category are similar to or the same as those in the latter category.

There is another underlying theme in this chapter, namely the pre-

2. Maimonides in *Laws Concerning Murder and The Preservation of Life* writes: The person referred to in the verse as the enemy does not mean an enemy from the heathen nations, but rather a Jewish enemy. How can a Jew have a Jewish enemy? The Torah states 'You shall not hate your brother in your heart.' [Leviticus 19:17] The Sages stated that if one all alone sees another commit a transgression and warns him and he does not desist, one is obligated to hate him until he repents and departs from his evil ways. Yet even if he has not yet repented and he finds himself alarmed with the bundles [on his animal] one is obligated to help him load and unload, and not to leave him to possibly die because he may delay leaving the place because of his belongings and find himself in danger. The Torah is very solicitous for the lives of Jews, whether they are wicked or righteous, since they [are presumed] to acknowledge God, and believe in the essentials of the religion. As it is written "As I live saith the Lord God, I have no pleasure in the death of the wicked but that the wicked turn from his way and live." [Ezekiel 33:11]

vention of cruelty to animals. There is a dispute in the Talmud whether the concept of treating an animal kindly is of Torah or Rabbinical origin. The prevailing view is that the concept is of Torah origin.

In addition to the laws dealing with loading, unloading, and reloading another's animal, this chapter also deals with the right of way to be given to one of two or more animals or boats traveling along a river or path when there is only room for one of them to pass through at a time.

TEXT

The Torah commandments to load, unload, and reload an animal

The Torah verses as above stated teach two positive commandments and one negative commandment regarding the loading, unloading, and reloading of an animal, in this case someone else's animal.

There is the positive commandment that if Ruven sees Shimon's animal staggering under the weight of its burden, Ruven must help unload the burden. There is also the positive commandment for Ruven to help Shimon raise the animal after the burden has been removed and to help reload the animal. If Ruven leaves Shimon helpless and neither unloads or reloads the animal, he transgresses the fulfillment of the two positive commandments as well as the negative commandment not to see his brother's animal and hide himself from helping to unload the animal. If he unloads and does not reload, he transgresses only one positive commandment, that to help reload. If the animal is not overloaded, but a bundle fell off the animal, and if Ruven does not help load this bundle back onto the animal, he transgresses the negative commandment not to hide himself and the positive commandment of reloading.[3]

The commandment of "reloading" may follow and be combined with the commandment to "unload"; or "loading" may be performed independently. For example, if one helps his neighbor unload his animal, he then helps him reload it. Or he may see a bundle fall off the

3. He does not violate the commandment to help unload.

animal along a road and he helps his neighbor reload this particular bundle on the animal.

The performance of the unloading and loading commandments

Ruven sees Shimon's animal staggering under the burden that is on its back. Ruven must perform the commandments of unloading if the animal is within about 466 feet[4] from Ruven.[5] It does not matter if the burden is its normal load or if it is overloaded; the obligation to help unload the bundles from the animal applies.[6] The obligation is always there because of the suffering of the animal; the fact that Shimon overloaded the animal is no reason for Ruven to permit the animal to suffer.[7]

If this particular animal is always overloaded and its natural gait is to walk bent over, the obligation to unload the animal is not present. However, while not being under an obligation to unload the animal because of the Torah commandment to unload, Ruven has the obligation to unload some of the bundles because the Torah enjoins him to prevent any animal from suffering.

Once Ruven has performed the first commandment of unloading the animal, he now has to perform the second commandment of helping to reload the animal.

If Ruven sees a bundle that has fallen from the animal, Ruven must assist Shimon in loading that bundle onto the animal.

In loading or reloading the animal, Ruven must take care to see that the animal is not overloaded. If Shimon wishes to overload the animal, Ruven must not assist him and should protest to Shimon that Shimon should bring another animal to carry the overload.

---

4. The Talmud and the codes speak of a distance not exceeding 266 and 2/3 *amoth* (plural of *amah*). I have defined an *amah* as being the approximate equivalent of 21 inches (see Glossary, *tefach*). Thus 266 2/3 *amoth* would be approximately 5,600 inches or 466.67 feet.

5. While the obligation to perform the commandments is not present if the animal is at a further distance as stated, there is still an obligation to help unload a suffering animal.

6. Ruven cannot plead that since Shimon overloaded the animal, Ruven does not have to help unload it. Shimon may have inadvertently overloaded the animal, and in any event the animal should not be permitted to continue suffering.

7. The Torah prohibits a Jew from permitting animals to suffer.

Assume that Ruven helped unload and then helped to reload and a bundle fell off the animal, or the animal is once again staggering under the burden, Ruven must once again assist Shimon in unloading and reloading the animal. Not only must Ruven assist Shimon as many times as is necessary to unload and reload, or load the animal; Shimon is required to accompany Shimon with his animal for a distance[8] to see that all is now well with the animal carrying its burden. Shimon may waive the requirement[9] for Ruven to accompany him and the animal for that distance.[10]

Compensation of the assister

Ruven assists Shimon in loading, or in unloading and reloading, Shimon's animal and accompanies Shimon and the animal for the required distance. Ruven may not ask for any compensation for the unloading of Shimon's animal. But Ruven can demand compensation for loading or reloading Shimon's animal, and also for accompanying Shimon and the animal. The amount of compensation is the same as the compensation for one who finds a lost object, when there is a requirement for the ɪinder to be compensated, that is, an amount that will compensate Ruven for the resulting loss of earnings. See Chapter 268.

The animal owner's presence

Above it is written that the Torah states, "If you see the donkey of someone you hate crouching under its burden, would you refrain from helping him? You shall help him repeatedly." The Torah also states, "You shall not see the donkey of your brother or his ox falling and hide yourself from them; you shall surely stand them up with him."

These two verses seem to imply that the obligation for Ruven to

8. The distance mentioned in the Talmud (*Baba Metzia* 33a) and the codes is that of a *parsah* (or sometimes called a *parsang*). A *parsang* is the equivalent of 4 *mils* and each *mil* is the equivalent of 200 *amoth* (plural of *amah*). I have defined an *amah* to be 21 inches (see Glossary, *tefach*). Thus a *mil* is 42,000 inches and a *parsah* is 168,000 inches or 14,000 feet or 2.65 American miles.

9. Shimon by waiving the requirement for Ruven to accompany him is relieved of compensating Ruven for walking with him.

10. There is an opinion that Ruven need accompany Shimon and his animal for a distance of one *mil*, or about 2/3 of an American mile.

load, unload, and reload Shimon's animal is binding only when the owner Shimon is also present. This is true only if Shimon is present and does not participate in loading, unloading, and reloading the animal. However, if Shimon is not present, Ruven must perform the commandments of unloading and reloading. There are times when even if the owner is present and does not participate in the loading, unloading, and reloading Ruven must load, unload and reload. For example, if Shimon is too old or too weak to participate, the original loading having been done for him by someone else.

Exemptions from the commandments

There are times when Ruven is exempt from the obligation to perform the commandments of loading, unloading, and/or reloading. Some examples are:

If Ruven is a *kohen*[11] and the animal is in a cemetery, the *kohen* must not go to the cemetery to help unload or load the animal. The reason is that a *kohen* is not permitted to go into a cemetery.[12] If Ruven is a scholar, or an old sage, or wealthy, or highly respected, and does not ordinarily perform such tasks as loading or unloading animals, he need not help to load, unload, and reload the animal. Regarding the persons listed in this paragraph, the test is would such a person load, unload, and reload his own animal? If he would not do it for himself, he is not obligated to do it for Shimon. However, if Ruven is truly pious, he will help to load, unload, and reload even if he would not have done so for himself.[13] In case of suffering of the animal, all persons should help if they are physically able to do so.[14]

If the animal belongs to Shimon and is being driven by a heathen,

---

11. God commanded Moses to set aside Aaron and his sons to serve as priests in the Holy Tabernacle and later in the Holy Temple. (See Exodus, chapter 28.) All the descendants of Aaron are priests. The Hebrew word for priest is *kohen* (or *cohen*). A *kohen* may not enter into a [Jewish] cemetery. (See Leviticus 21:1.) See next note.

12. There are authorities that the laws prohibiting a *kohen* (a priest) apply only if the cemetery is a Jewish cemetery.

13. In *halachah* this is known as acting *lifnim mishurath hadin*. See Volume I, page 94, and also Glossary. See also author's article *Lifnim Mishurath Hadin*, Annual Volume of Young Israel Rabbis in Israel, Volume 2, Jerusalem (1988).

14. None of the laws regarding acting beyond the requirements of the law apply to a *kohen* when the animal is in a cemetery. The prohibition against the *kohen* not entering the cemetery overrides the obligation to help unload and reload and load.

Ruven need not assist in unloading and reloading, or loading the animal, even if the bundles on the animal belong to a Jew. If the heathen is not present then Ruven must perform the commandment if the bundles belong to a Jew. Also, if the animal belongs to a Jew, Ruven must perform the commandment even if the bundles on the animal belong to a heathen. However, if the animal and the bundles belong to a heathen, then Ruven must assist him only if it will lead to better relations between Jews and heathens. Nevertheless, in all those instances where Ruven is not obligated to assist, he should nevertheless do so to prevent suffering by the animal.

Priorities in performing the unloading, reloading, or loading

Ruven encounters two animals belonging to two different people, Shimon and Levi, both of whom are friends of his or both of whom are his enemies. Shimon's animal is staggering under its burden and requires to be unloaded; Levi's animal is not yet loaded because Levi cannot find anyone to help him load the animal. Ruven is obligated to first help to unload Shimon's animal. The reason is to relieve the suffering of Shimon's animal.

However, if Levi is Ruven's enemy, and Shimon is Ruven's friend, then Ruven is obligated to first load Levi's animal and then to unload Shimon's animal. This is done to subdue Ruven's evil impulse.

A caravan traveling together

In all that is said in this section, if there is a custom as to how to proceed, or if there are rules, such customs and rules must be adhered to. What follows are instances where there are no customs, rules, or laws to follow.

A caravan of mules is traveling together, either all of them loaded with bundles or all of them unloaded. The leg of one of the mules became injured so that it cannot proceed as quickly as the other mules. The remaining animal owners cannot proceed quickly but must proceed at the pace of the injured animal. If the injured animal will be able to proceed after a short wait, the other owners must wait for that period. However, if the injured animal cannot proceed at all the other owners are not required to wait for that owner.

The caravan is parked for the night and is attacked by pirates[15] or thieves, or by an army that is battling another army. The thieves were paid off and left the caravan. Each member of the caravan has to give his share of the ransom paid in proportion to the value of the goods he is carrying.

Members of a caravan hire a guide to get them to where they are going, through a dangerous place, and they pay the guide in proportion to the value of the goods being carried and also according to the amount of people in each vehicle.

The members of the caravan may make any type of stipulations regarding losses and expenses.

A vessel carrying goods for several merchants is about to sink and the merchants are told that the vessels will not sink if a certain weight of goods were thrown overboard. All of the merchants must pay their proportion of the value of the goods jettisoned according to the value of the goods, and not according to the weight.

Contemporary applications

Instead of mules or other beasts of burden, the owner is proceeding in a vehicle, a car or a truck that breaks down or has a flat tire, or is stuck in a sand drift or a snow drift. A driver who passes by must try to help the driver of the broken-down vehicle who has a flat tire or who is stuck, if providing such help will not endanger the passerby. This includes helping to unload the truck or other vehicle and helping to reload it. Or if a truck is proceeding and a carton falls off the truck, and the driver needs help in reloading the carton, other drivers must help him.

Once the broken-down vehicle is in a position to proceed, the helping driver should accompany him to see if the vehicle is indeed now able to travel.

In most instances, police or other safety vehicles will help the driver of the broken-down vehicle. However, many drivers have had experience where a car was stuck on a lonely, dark road and there was no

15. See *USA Today*, October 10, 1996. Piracy on the high seas throughout the world dipped slightly to 125 cases from January to September, with Indonesia still recording the most cases.

way to communicate with the police. A helping hand at that moment would be a Godsend.

Priority in proceeding

A vehicle driven by Ruven and a vehicle driven by Shimon both appear at a bridge going over a small river. The bridge can hold only one vehicle or the lane on the bridge is so narrow that only one vehicle can cross the bridge. Or as sometimes happens, there is only room for one more vehicle on a ferry. Most communities have laws, rules, and regulations governing such situations and these are controlling. Assume, however, that the community does not have traffic laws to govern which vehicle may proceed first. If one of them is a commercial vehicle carrying cargo and the other is a passenger vehicle, the commercial vehicle has priority. If they are both commercial vehicles and one is loaded and the other unloaded, the loaded vehicle has priority. If one is a passenger vehicle and the other an unloaded commercial vehicle, the passenger vehicle has priority.

If both are commercial vehicles, whether both unloaded or both loaded, or both passenger vehicles, then they can arrive at some adjustment between themselves or else cast lots as to who proceeds first. If there is a financial gain by going first, then there may be a money adjustment made by the parties.

That which has been said regarding vehicles holds true for ships.

Chapter 273

OWNERLESS PROPERTY

INTRODUCTION

Rabbi Yosef Karo calls this chapter "Laws Of Acquiring Ownerless Property, And How Something Becomes Ownerless."

It is accepted in Jewish law that a man can abandon things that belong to him, and they become ownerless. The main topics of this chapter are to define the three classes of ownerless property; how one declares his own property to be ownerless; and how one acquires ownerless property.

There are three classes of ownerless property, as seen in the section entitled "Classes of ownerless property." One class is where the object has never been owned; the various situations under that class are discussed. Another class is where the owner declares, or is presumed to decide, that an object that he owns is ownerless, that is, he abandons ownership of the object; most of the chapter deals with this type of abandoning ownership of the object. The abandoned object may be real property and/or personal property. Must there be anyone present when he abandons the ownership of the project? When does the abandonment take effect? Can the owner rescind the declaration of abandoning ownership of the object?

Can the declaration limit the class of people for whom it is abandoned? For example, Ruven instead of making a specific unequivocal and unambiguous declaration of abandonment of ownership of the object, makes a declaration that the abandonment of the object should be limited to a class of people, or should exclude a certain person or class of people, such as this object is abandoned to only poor people, or not to people who are born in China. Can the declaration limit the time that it is effective, or specify that the time it is effective commences in the future?

The owner is hereinafter designated as "the owner" or "Ruven"; the person who acquires the ownerless object is "the acquirer" or "Shimon."[1] The object can be acquired by Shimon only if he performs an appropriate act of acquisition as stated in Volume VI. The laws of acquiring ownerless real estate are discussed by Rabbi Karo in chapter 275, which deals with the property of a proselyte who dies without heirs. His property is ownerless and his real estate can be acquired by anyone. How much of his real estate is acquired and the methods of *hazakah* are discussed there. It may be that Rabbi Karo discusses these subjects in chapter 275 because there are laws that apply only to the ownerless real estate of a proselyte as well as laws that apply to all ownerless real estate.

TEXT

Classes of ownerless property

A person can only abandon ownership of an object that is in his possession and/or control. He cannot abandon ownership of an object that is not under his possession or control, such as an object of personal property that was stolen from him. Ruven can abandon an object that Levi is holding for him.

There are three classes of ownerless property, whether the property is real property or personal property: (1) property that has always

1. Whenever it is stated that Ruven declares that he abandons ownership of an object and that Shimon performs an act of acquisition to acquire the object, one of the acquirers can be Ruven himself.

been ownerless; (2) property that the law deems to be ownerless; and (3) property declared by the owner to be ownerless.

(1) Examples of property that has always been ownerless are deserts, rivers, and streams on public lands and all that is found in them.[2] The governments may have laws affecting the ownership of such places, such as retaining ownership of them or permitting subdivisions of the government to own them. Absent such laws, these areas and all that is found therein, such as trees, minerals, growth, fruits, fish, fowl, birds, animals, and the like, are ownerless.[3] Regarding fish in the seas and birds or beasts, the laws of ownership are as follows: (a) If Shimon catches fish in the seas or oceans or in rivers, or if he catches birds or any species of beasts, Shimon acquires ownership to them since they are ownerless. While Shimon should not catch these objects in property belonging to Levi, if he did catch them there, they belong to Shimon. (b) If the fish are in fisheries owned by Levi, or birds or animals are enclosed in enclosures (no matter how large) owned by Levi, they belong to Levi, and should Shimon catch them, he is a robber. (c) If Shimon takes fish from Levi's net while it is in the water, or if Shimon takes an animal from Levi's trap while it is yet in the forest, the object belongs to Shimon, although he has transgressed a decree of the Rabbis in the Talmud.[4] However, if the net or trap has a hollow shape like a vessel, the objects caught therein belong to Levi, and if Shimon takes them he is a robber.[5] (d) Shimon sets a trap in Levi's field and the trap catches a wild bird or animal. It belongs to Shimon,[6] although he does not have the right to place his trap there. However, if Levi stands within his field and declares that all animals or birds are acquired for Levi by his field,[7]

2. There is authority that these areas are not ownerless in the Land of Israel when the tribes are on their allotted lands, but rather that these areas belong to the tribe where they are located.

3. The reason is, that they have been ownerless since the creation of the world.

4. While Levi cannot sue Shimon, because the decree of the Rabbis is to preserve peace, it is left for the judgments of Heaven to punish Shimon. Generally speaking, while beth din cannot enforce any payment, the person still is not free of his obligations to Heaven until he makes the appropriate payment.

5. And Levi can sue Shimon in beth din to recover his loss.

6. The reason that the object does not belong to Levi is that he could not have gotten control of the object and also that his property was not guarded.

7. Or Levi is able to catch them.

then the animals or birds belong to Levi, and Shimon does not acquire the animals or birds in the trap.[8] (e) If fish jump into Shimon's boat, he acquires ownership of the fish.[9] (f) Levi, a poor person, lops olives off the top of an olive tree and they fall to the ground.[10] Shimon, who is also a poor person, picks them up from the ground. Shimon is deemed a robber by Rabbinic enactment, although technically the olives are ownerless and do not belong to Levi since he did not take them into his hands to acquire them. However, had Levi taken the olives into his hands before he dropped them to the ground, Shimon, if he then took the olives, would be a robber.[11]

(2) If a proselyte dies without any heirs, all of his property is deemed ownerless.[12] Other examples of personal property that are deemed lost and ownerless are objects that are carried off by a raging river or tides into the ocean.[13] The Talmud and the codes include the following case of an object being deemed ownerless. If Shimon picks fresh cress growing in Levi's flax field, it is not deemed robbery because the cress spoils the flax in the field and Levi is perfectly happy to have Shimon pick the cress. But if the cress is already dried then taking it is robbery, since whatever harm the cress will do to the flax is already done. If the cress in on the edge of the field, it is forbidden for Shimon to take it even if it is fresh.[14]

(3)A Jew or Gentile who is the owner of real property and/or personal property can declare his property to be ownerless if he complies with the procedures stated below.

---

8. The caught animal or bird belongs to Levi even if he is not standing within the field if the field is protected by a wall.

9. The reason is that the boat is like a field that is guarded.

10. The olives were left by the owner of the tree to fulfill the Torah command to leave gleanings for the poor. Both Levi and Shimon are poor.

11. The difference between a robber under Torah law and a robber by Rabbinic enactment is that the former can be sued in beth din to recover the loss, while the latter cannot be sued in beth din to recover the loss.

12. A person who converts to Judaism is deemed to be a newborn person without any legal personal relationship to any of his former relatives. Thus if the proselyte does not have a child with a Jewess conceived after he converts and starts a family, he has no heirs.

13. This is true even if the owner specifically states that he does not abandon the swept-away property. See Chapter 261.

14. The same laws apply to all situations where Shimon does Levi a favor by getting rid of unwanted growth.

The declaration of abandoning ownership

The owner's intent to make the object ownerless cannot be done by the owner solely in his mind. The declaration of abandoning the ownership of an object must be made by the owner (and not by an agent) in the presence of at least three people;[15] it cannot be made by the owner without anyone present.[16]

The declaration must be unequivocal and unambiguous.

A declaration of abandonment of ownership made in error or under duress is not effective.

Limited abandonment of ownership

Ruven cannot limit the class of Jews who may acquire the abandoned ownerless object. He may not limit it to animals and not to humans; or to Gentiles and not to Jews; or to Jews and not to Gentiles; or to poor and not to rich; or to rich and not to poor.[17]

Ruven may limit the time during which the abandonment of ownership is effective, and if Shimon performs an act of acquisition during such period, the object belongs to Shimon. Otherwise, ownership remains with Ruven. For example, Ruven, on January 1, declares in front of witnesses that ownership of the object is abandoned between January 1 and February 1. Shimon performs an act of acquisition on January 15. Ownership of the object is with Shimon and does not cease and revert to Ruven on February 1. If Shimon performs an act of acquisition on February 2, the object does not belong to him and remains with Ruven.

Ruven may declare his object of personal property to be ownerless

15. Two persons to be witness that the declaration was made, and the third person to be able to acquire the object.

16. According to Torah law, the declaration could be made in the presence of only one witness, but the Rabbis of the Talmud, to publicize the event, decreed that the declaration of abandonment of ownership must be in the presence of three persons. In certain limited cases, where the purpose of the declaration is to prevent the owner from transgressing a Torah law, it is permitted to declare one's personal property abandoned without anyone else being present.

17. For example, if Ruven declared an object to be abandoned for the poor and not for the rich, even if a poor person performed an act of acquisition on the object, it does not belong to the poor person.

as of a future date.[18] If the object of personal property is located on that future date in a place not belonging to Ruven, it is ownerless.[19] Until that future date Ruven may rescind the declaration.[20]

There is a difference of opinion as to whether a declaration of abandonment of ownership of an object made on the Sabbath is effective.

When the owner's abandonment takes effect

Ruven declares his object to be ownerless. There are two views in the Talmud[21] and the codes as to when the declaration takes effect and the object becomes ownerless. The first view holds that the object immediately becomes ownerless and that anyone, such as Shimon (and even Ruven himself[22]) can now acquire the ownerless object.[23] The second view holds that the object continues to be owned by Ruven until Shimon acquires the object by performing an act of acquisition.[24]

There are opinions that according to both views, Ruven can rescind

18. For example, Ruven declares on January 1 that an object of personal property belonging to him shall be ownerless on February 1. If the object is located in a place not belonging to Ruven, it is ownerless on February 1. Ruven may at any time through January 31 rescind the declaration and the object belongs to him as if the declaration had not been made.

19. If the place where the object of personal property is located belongs to Ruven, then Ruven's property acquires the object for him.

20. Ruven may rescind the declaration even beyond the three-day period mentioned below.

21. Actually, there are two opinions as to what are the two views. I have set forth only one of those opinions as to what the two views are. See *Nedarim* 43a.

22. Since the object is now ownerless, Ruven is now a former owner, and he has the same rights to acquire the object as does anyone else.

23. The object can be acquired by Shimon (or even by Ruven himself) only by employing one of the methods of acquisition stated in Volume VI.

24. This view holds that the abandoning of ownership of an object is similar to giving Shimon a gift of the object. There is a necessity for the owner to confer ownership on the recipient when the recipient of the gift performs an act of acquisition on the object that is the gift. Similarly, in the case of Shimon acquiring the ownerless object, the owner must confer his intent for Shimon to acquire the object. Even according to the first view, there may be the consent of Ruven for Shimon to acquire the object by Ruven's consent being given when he abandons ownership of the object.

the declaration within three days of making it. If Ruven does rescind his declaration of abandonment within the three days, the declaration is rescinded and of no effect even if Shimon performed an act of acquisition during the three-day period.[25] There is also a difference of opinion whether the law of this paragraph applies to both real estate and personal property or only to real estate.

According to the second view stated in the first paragraph of this section, Ruven should be able, even after three days, to rescind his abandonment until Shimon performs an act of acquisition on the object, whether real estate or personal property. However, Ruven must not do so because declaring an object to be ownerless is similar to making a vow,[26] and a person should never fail to live up to his vow.[27]

Acquisition of ownerless objects

Whoever is the first person[28] to perform an act of acquisition to acquire the object becomes the new owner of the object.

There must be intent on Shimon's part to acquire the ownerless object. For example, if he does not know that something is ownerless and picks it up so that he can restore it to its owner, Shimon has not acquired the ownerless object.

Shimon (or Ruven himself) can acquire the ownerless objects by performing any of the methods of acquisition for purchasing an object described in Volume VI, such as *hazakah*[29] for real estate; and lifting, pulling, delivery, by one's courtyard, or by Shimon's 4 cubits,[30]

25. There is a dissent that holds that once Shimon performs an act of acquisition of the object, Ruven can no longer rescind the declaration.

26. If the owner Ruven dies after he has declared the object to be ownerless, then according to the second view in the text, the heirs of Ruven can rescind the declaration if Shimon has not as yet performed an act of acquisition, since it was still owned by Ruven when he died and the heirs are the inheritors but are not bound by the vow of their father.

27. Only if Ruven has not yet performed an act of acquisition on the object, Ruven can seek absolution from the declaration as he can from any vow, by consulting a rabbi who will tell him the procedure.

28. This includes Ruven himself.

29. See Volume VI, Chapter 192; see Glossary; see Chapter 275 as to how to acquire ownerless real estate.

30. See Volume VI, page 161.

for personal property.[31] Other methods of purchasing objects such as money or a deed for real estate or money for personal property or *kinyan*[32] for both types of objects, are not applicable since the former owner does not transfer the object to the person performing the act of acquisition of the ownerless object. There is a difference of opinion if Shimon can acquire the ownerless personal property "along with" (*agov*)[33] the acquisition of ownerless real property if he performs an act of acquisition to acquire the real property.

If Shimon stands guard over abandoned objects to prevent anyone else from acquiring the object, the object does not belong to Shimon. Gazing at or guarding an object is not an act of acquisition.

---

31. See Volume VI, Chapters 197–203.
32. See Volume VI, Chapter 195; see Glossary.
33. See Volume VI, Chapter 202; see Glossary, *agov*.

Chapter 274

THE TEN DECREES OF JOSHUA

INTRODUCTION

Rabbi Yosef Karo calls this chapter "There Are Other Things That Belong To Other People That I Am Permitted To Use Although They Are Not Ownerless." He has one paragraph that refers the reader back to chapter 194. I have discussed these laws in Volume VI, Chapter 194, page 122.

Rabbi Moses Isserles in his emendations discusses the ten decrees promulgated by Joshua after he led the Jews across the Jordan River into the Land of Israel.[1] They are included in this chapter since they resemble the situation where one's land is treated as ownerless for some purposes.[2] He also adds another law discussed below in the section entitled "Swarm of bees."

Ruven is the owner of the property and Shimon is the person acquiring the right to use Ruven's property.

---

1. Rabbi Isserles remarks that he does not know why Rabbi Karo omitted these laws from *Shulhan Aruch.* He adds that perhaps they were omitted since they may not be relevant nowadays because they deal with Jews owning fields and vineyards, and this is not usual in the Diaspora.

2. See *Baba Kamma* 80b; Maimonides, *Laws of Damage by Chattels*, chapter 5, paragraph 3.

TEXT

The ten decrees promulgated by Joshua

When Joshua apportioned the Land of Israel among the tribes of Israel, he and his court promulgated ten decrees:[3]

1. Shimon may pasture small cattle, such as sheep and goats, in woods consisting of large trees belonging to Ruven. However, large cattle, such as cows and bulls, may not be pastured by Shimon there. Neither small nor large cattle may be pastured in Ruven's woods consisting of small trees, except with Ruven's consent.

2. Shimon may gather wood from Ruven's field, provided that it is taken from trees of little value equal in value to thorns, for example, prickly shrubs and thistles, and further provided that the wood is still attached to the ground and fresh, and that Shimon does not tear out the roots. Other woods are forbidden.

3. Shimon may collect plants no matter where they grow wild, except in a field sown with fenugreek for fodder.

4. Shimon may take a cutting from any tree, including trees owned by Ruven, other than the stumps of olive trees. The amounts of the cuttings are limited as follows: from the olive tree, up to the bulk of an egg; from reeds and vines, above the joint; from other trees, only from the side branches and not from the middle stem. The cuttings may be taken only from newly grown twigs that have not yet produced fruit, and only from that side of the tree that does not face the sun.

5. When a new spring emerges from the ground, the inhabitants of that city only may use it as a water supply, although its source is not on their property but on Ruven's property. No others can supply themselves with water from this new spring.

6. Anyone may catch fish in the Sea of Galilee if he uses a fish hook but not with a net, nor may he use a boat. If he is a member of a tribe in whose territory the lake is located, he may spread a net or keep a boat there.[4]

7. Shimon, who must relieve himself, may leave the road, go behind

3. Although these decrees were promulgated by Joshua when he entered into the Land of Israel, they are applicable everywhere, even outside the Land of Israel.

4. Presumably, the same applies to all of the waterways in the Land of Israel.

the nearest fence, and relieve himself there, even if the place belongs to Ruven.

8. If Shimon is lost among vineyards belonging to Ruven or similar cultivated real estate, he may cut his way through and go in any direction until he finds his way out.[5]

9. Whenever the road becomes too muddy or waterlogged to walk thereon, Shimon may go to the sides of the road and walk there or even on paths owned by Ruven.

10. An unclaimed dead body acquires ownership of the spot of land on which it lies and must be buried there. This does not apply if it is lying across a boundary of a city or within the border strip of a city. If it is found on a boundary or within such a border, the body must be taken to a cemetery.[6]

King Solomon decreed that travelers during the summer may walk on privately owned field paths until the falling of the second rains.[7]

Swarm of bees

Shimon has a swarm of bees that left his premises and settled on a branch of a tree belonging to Ruven. According to one opinion, Shimon may cut the branch off the tree and compensate Ruven for the branch: according to another opinion, Shimon may not do so.

5. Shimon must pay Ruven for the damage that he caused.

6. This law applies outside the Land of Israel only if it is permitted by the law of the land.

7. This is provided that the fields are not sown.

Chapter 275

PROPERTY OF A PROSELYTE WHO DIES WITHOUT HEIRS

INTRODUCTION

This is the last chapter dealing with acquiring property, whether real estate or personal property other than by purchase, or by gift, or by inheritance. After Rabbi Yosef Karo in *Shulhan Aruch* states the laws of found property, that a finder may sometimes keep the objects that he finds for himself, he sets forth the laws of ownerless property and the property of a proselyte who died without heirs, so that his property is now also ownerless. The laws of this chapter are rather unlikely to be practiced. Even if there should be a proselyte who dies without heirs according to *halachah*, the laws of the land will usually hold that he has heirs according to the status that he had prior to his conversion to Judaism.

A non-Jew converts to Judaism.[1] When the proselyte becomes a Jew, he is no longer related to former relatives according to *halachah*. Thus all of his relatives, his wife, his parents, his children, brothers, and sisters are not recognized in *halachah* as his relatives.

1. This assumes that all of the laws of conversion have been scrupulously followed.

Thus, if he does not have children conceived after he converts,[2] he has no heirs according to *halachah* and his property, whether real estate or personal property is ownerless. In Chapter 273 it is stated, "The laws of acquiring ownerless real estate are discussed by Rabbi Karo in chapter 275, which deals with the property of a proselyte who dies without heirs. His property is ownerless and his real estate can be acquired by anyone. How much of his real estate is acquired and the methods of *hazakah* are discussed there. It may be that Rabbi Karo discusses these subjects in chapter 275 because there are laws there that apply only to the ownerless real estate of a proselyte who died as well as laws that apply to all ownerless real estate."

What was stated in Chapter 273 is the basis of the subject matter of Chapter 275. I have divided the acquisition of the assets owned when a proselyte died heirless into two parts, personal property or real estate.

Some of the methods of *hazakah* are also discussed here, and they are not necessarily the same methods of *hazakah* that are performed to acquire real estate by purchase as discussed in Volume VI, Chapter 192.

Unless otherwise noted, the proselyte spoken of in this chapter is a proselyte who dies without leaving any heirs. The person who attempts to acquire the ownerless property of the deceased proselyte is designated as "Shimon." Whenever a marriage is spoken of (unless otherwise noted) it means a marriage according to *halachah*.

TEXT

The property of a proselyte who dies without heirs

A person is born Jewish only if his mother at the time of his birth is Jewish, whether the mother was born Jewish or converted to Judaism prior to the child's birth. The religion of the father does *not* determine the religion of the child. Thus when a Jewish woman gives birth to a

2. Or if he had children after he converted, but they were conceived before his conversion, although born after his conversion, they are not his heirs in *halachah* for the purposes of heirship.

child, the child is Jewish regardless of the religion of the father. And if the mother is not Jewish at the time she gives birth, the child is not Jewish regardless whether the father is Jewish. Should the non-Jewish mother convert to Judaism after she gives birth to the child, the child must undergo its own conversion to be Jewish.[3]

When a Gentile converts from any other religion to Judaism, he is considered to be a newborn person. All former relatives are no longer his legal relatives. His prior marriage is not considered a marriage and his wife is not his wife according to *halachah*.

After his conversion, the proselyte, whether or not he was married before he converted: (a) might not ever marry;[4] (b) may marry his former wife, if she is Jewish when they now get married, either because she was born Jewish or converted to Judaism prior to this new marriage; or (c) may marry any other Jewish woman.[5] When he now marries a Jewish woman she is his wife in *halachah* and children born to them are his recognized children[6] according to *halachah*. Thus if the proselyte does marry and raise a family after he converts, the children conceived after his conversion are his heirs, the same as the family of any other Jew. If the child was conceived prior to his conversion,[7] the child is not considered heir to his property.

If the proselyte dies without having any children conceived after he converted,[8] and if he left no will disposing of his assets, his objects, both real estate and personal property, are ownerless.

It is rumored about that a proselyte died without heirs. Jews seized his assets. It is then rumored that he did not die, or that if he did die

3. Therefore: (i) if the proselyte, before he converted fathered children by a non-Jewish mother, the children are not Jewish. (ii) If after his conversion he fathers a child by a non-Jewish mother, the child is not Jewish. (iii) If before his conversion the proselyte fathered children by a Jewish mother, his children are Jewish. (iv) If after his conversion he fathers children by a Jewish mother, his children are Jewish.

4. There is a Torah commandment to beget children, and he may, under certain circumstances, be violating such commandment if he does not marry after he converted and beget children.

5. The proselyte has to comply with the laws of the land against bigamy if he marries a woman who was not his wife before his conversion and he did not divorce her according to the laws of the land.

6. They are his children but not his heirs if conceived prior to his conversion.

7. Even if the mother was Jewish prior to conception of the child.

8. According to *halachah*, children conceived before he converted are not considered heirs in case of his dying intestate.

he has surviving him a child conceived after he converted or a widow who is pregnant by him after his conversion. The Jews must return the assets that they seized.[9] If it turns out that the rumors were true, that he died without heirs or that his child died before the proselyte died, or that his wife had miscarried, then it belongs to whoever thereafter seizes the objects, and not to the first Jews who had seized and then returned his assets.

Acquiring the ownerless objects of the deceased proselyte

As is the situation with all ownerless objects, whoever performs an act of acquisition on the object, *with the intent to acquire the object*, acquires the object.[10] The act of acquisition may be done by an agent on behalf of Shimon.[11]

If Shimon digs (or performs some other act of *hazakah*), thinking that he is digging on his own field, Shimon does not acquire the field of the proselyte since he lacks the requisite intent to acquire the field of the proselyte. However, if Shimon digs in a field that belonged to proselyte 2 (who died heirless), thinking that it belonged to proselyte 1 (who died heirless), hoping to acquire the real estate of proselyte 1, the real estate of proselyte 2 in which he dug belongs to Shimon, since he intended to acquire ownerless real estate.

The person acquiring the objects of the deceased proselyte is not obligated[12] to pay for his funeral expenses.[13]

---

9. In the case of the pregnant wife, if she gives birth to a child who was conceived after the proselyte converted, the assets will belong to the child.

10. See Chapter 273, "Acquisition of ownerless objects."

11. The act of the agent is the act of the principal, even if the agent did not realize that the real estate belonged to the proselyte and that by his act he is acquiring the real estate for the principal. See Volume VI, Chapter 182.

12. The reason given is that as soon as the proselyte dies, his objects are immediately ownerless. There is no lien on his possessions for his funeral expenses that have not yet been incurred. The same holds true if a creditor seizes the property of a deceased debtor to the extent necessary to repay his debt; he is not obligated to pay for the debtor's funeral out of the property that he seizes.

13. There is also a dissent that holds that it is not equitable to have a person acquire the dead proselyte's assets and not use some of it to pay his burial expenses. This may lead to quarrels between the people who will bury the proselyte and those who have seized his assets.

When a proselyte dies heirless, all of the debts due to him are canceled.

A proselyte loaned money to Yehudah and received collateral security. The proselyte died in possession of the collateral. Naftali seized the collateral from the house of the proselyte. Naftali must return the collateral to Yehudah.[14] The same holds true if the proselyte held a mortgage on the field of Yehudah, as soon as the proselyte died, the mortgage lien terminated and Yehudah owns the real estate free of the lien.[15]

Conversely, perhaps Yehudah had loaned money to the proselyte and received collateral security from the proselyte. The proselyte then died heirless and Naftali seized the collateral from Yehudah. Naftali must pay to Yehudah the amount of the debt and the collateral belongs to Naftali. Naftali acquires the overage only if the collateral was not resting in the possession of Yehudah or his fenced-in courtyard; if it was so resting in Yehudah's possession or his fenced-in courtyard,[16] the entire collateral belongs to Yehudah. The laws of this paragraph apply not only to collateral held by Yehudah, but equally to objects of personal property that the proselyte had deposited with Yehudah for safekeeping or that Yehudah had rented or borrowed from the proselyte.

The proselyte owed money to Jews and he died heirless. Other Jews seized the assets of the proselyte. They must restore the assets to the creditors[17] of the proselyte in inverse order of the seizings.[18]

14. At the instant when the proselyte died, the lien on the collateral terminated and reverted to Yehudah.

15. If Naftali had performed an act of acquisition to acquire the real estate that the proselyte held as security for the debt owed by Yehudah, Naftali will have to give the real estate back to Yehudah.

16. Yehudah's fenced-in courtyard acquires for him even if he was not aware that it was there. See Chapter 262, section entitled "Acquiring found objects by one's courtyard."

17. The creditors, in addition to having to prove their claim, must take an oath that the debt is unpaid.

18. For example, on January 1, the date of death of the proselyte, he had debts of $100 and assets of $130. On January 2, Dan seized $20 worth of assets from the possession of the estate of the proselyte. On January 3, Gad seized $30 of assets from the possession of the estate of the proselyte. On January 4, Ephraim seized $30 of assets from the possession of the estate of the proselyte. On January 5, Menashe seized $50 of assets from the possession of the estate of proselyte. The creditors will first

The proselyte died heirless owing money to Yehudah[19] and Naftali seized the assets of the proselyte. Naftali stands in a position similar to that of an heir of a decedent who must pay the debts of the decedent to the extent that he inherited assets; Naftali must pay the debt owed to Yehudah out of the seized assets,[20] and the balance, if any, belongs to Naftali.

The act of *hazakah* to acquire the real estate of the deceased proselyte

Real estate: (1) of a deceased proselyte that is now ownerless; or, (2) that is otherwise ownerless; or, (3) that can be acquired although paid for when a Jew purchases the real estate from a Gentile and becomes temporarily ownerless[21] can all be acquired by the acquirer performing an act of *hazakah* that is the same in all three situations.[22]

All the acts of *hazakah* to acquire real estate when there is a

---

retake the $50 from Menashe, leaving a balance of $50. They will then retake $30 from Ephraim, leaving a balance of $20. They will then retake $20 from Gad, leaving him with $10; and Dan will keep the $20 he seized.

19. The debt is evidenced by a note of indebtedness or by witnesses or by a promissory note executed by the proselyte, or by any other evidence that Yehudah can use to enforce the payment of the debt in beth din.

20. Yehudah will have to take an oath that the debt is still unpaid.

21. See Volume VI, page 122. It is there stated, "The Talmud relates the following dictum: A Gentile sells land to a Jew (hereinafter referred to as the 'Jewish buyer'). According to the view taken by the Gentiles in that community as soon he paid the money for the realty he ceases to be the owner. [As far as the Gentile was concerned he ceased to be the owner.] According to *halachah* the Jew does not become the owner until he receives the deed from the Gentile. [This may be based on the fear the Jew has that the Gentile will later deny receiving the money and selling the realty to the Jew.] There is thus an interval in time when the realty is considered by *halachah* to be ownerless, from the time the Jewish buyer gives the money to the Gentile until the time that the Gentile gives the deed to the Jewish buyer. If a second Jew comes along during that interval and makes a *hazakah* on the realty, the second Jew becomes the owner."

22. There are four ways in which a purchaser can acquire real estate: (a) by the purchaser making a money payment; (b) by the seller giving the purchaser a deed; (c) by the purchaser performing an act of *hazakah* on the real estate; and (d) by a *kinyan*. See Volume VI, Chapters 190, 191, 192, and 195, respectively. In acquiring ownerless real estate, the only method of acquisition is by *hazakah*, the other three methods are not appropriate since there is no seller to accept the money, or to give a deed, or to perform a *kinyan*.

purchase are also effective when acquiring real estate that is ownerless, with one notable exception: If Shimon eats of the produce of the real estate that is ownerless, he does not acquire that real estate, which under certain conditions may be an act of acquisition in the case of a purchase of the real estate from a seller. He does not acquire the real estate even if he eats of the fruit of the trees for many years. Shimon must perform some other act of *hazakah* on the land or do some work on the trees.[23] Therefore, if Shimon finds the field of the deceased proselyte already plowed and Shimon sows it with seed and later eats of the produce, he does not acquire the field.[24] If he covers the seed he acquires ownership of the field.

Conversely, there are acts of *hazakah* that acquire in the case of ownerless real estate but do not acquire in the case of purchase of real estate from a seller. Here are a few examples, in all of which situations Shimon (or Levi) acquires ownership of the real estate:

a. Shimon comes to a large palace built on the real estate of the proselyte or on other ownerless real estate and he puts on a coat of paint or whitewash or he paints a mural or decoration on the wall opposite the door, and the mural or decoration is at least 1 *amah*[25] square;

b. Shimon draws a picture on the real estate of a deceased proselyte;

c. Shimon spreads out mattresses or sleeping bags on the real estate of a proselyte;

d. Shimon plows the field of the deceased proselyte;

e. Shimon trims the twigs of vines or the branches of trees or the leaves of trees on the real estate of the deceased proselyte and he intends[26] to improve the trees;[27]

23. The Talmud, *Baba Bathra* 54a, tells of an incident where a woman ate the fruit of a palm tree for 13 years and then some man came along and performed an act of acquisition by doing some work on the tree. The man had acquired ownership of the tree.

24. When Shimon sows the seeds into the soil, he does not effect an improvement to the field. When the produce grows, it does so by itself.

25. See Glossary.

26. If he prunes the trees on both sides, it is deemed that his intention is to improve the trees; but if Shimon prunes the trees on one side, then it is deemed that his intention was to acquire the trimmings rather than to improve the tree.

27. However, if Shimon's intent is to use the trimmings to feed his cattle or for

f. Shimon gathers twigs, grass, or stones in the field of the deceased proselyte and he intends[28] the improvement of the field;[29]

g. Shimon levels the field of the deceased proselyte with the intent[30] to improve the field;[31]

h. Shimon opens a water channel onto the land of the deceased proselyte intending[32] to improve the land;

i. Shimon builds a structure on the real estate of the deceased proselyte without completing the entire structure to a point that it is usable, such as not yet having installed the doors to the structure.[33] Levi puts on the doors.[34] Levi acquires ownership of the real estate, because only now can the structure be used[35] and thus the real estate

---

some purpose other than helping the trees, he does not acquire ownership to the real estate.

28. If Shimon picks up both the large and the small stones and twigs it is deemed that he does so for the improvement of the field. If he picks up the larger ones and leaves the smaller ones, it is deemed that he does it for some other purpose.

29. However, if Shimon gathers these things because he needs them, such as the stones for building or the twigs for fuel, he does not acquire ownership of the field.

30. If Shimon takes earth from the hilly places and places it into the depressions in the earth, it is deemed that he does so for the improvement of the ground. If he throws the earth around in a haphazard manner, then it is deemed that he needs a particular level place for some other purposes. In all of these situations where his actions are deemed to be not for the improvement of the real estate, his declaration to the contrary is of no effect. His actions speak louder than his words.

31. If Shimon levels the field for some other purpose, such as to use it as a storage area, he does not obtain ownership of the field.

32. If the channel has only an opening onto the land, it is deemed to be for the benefit of the land. If there is an opening as the water enters upon the land, and he makes another channel so that the water may run off from the land, then it is deemed that the channel was not made for the improvement of the land but for some other purpose, such as to catch fish. However, if it is beneficial for the land to have two openings, then this will be an act of *hazakah*.

33. Shimon's acts are the equivalent of piling stones on a field, which in and of itself does nothing to improve the field. The structure cannot ordinarily be used without doors to protect the occupant. It may be that an interior door is sufficient, depending upon the type of structure.

34. There is an opinion that even if Shimon installed the doors but did not install a lock, and Levi locked the door, the real estate belongs to Levi, since the structure cannot be used if the doors cannot be locked. Where the structure belongs to Levi, he will have to reimburse Shimon for the materials.

35. If the structure is secure without the doors and can be used without the doors, the real estate belongs to Shimon.

acts as the foundation of the structure.[36] If Shimon built a structure that can be used for the purpose that it was built without doors, then the structure is complete without doors and the real estate belongs to Shimon. If Shimon digs a foundation for the structure, there is a difference of opinion if the digging of the foundation is equivalent to improving the real estate.

The part of the deceased proselyte's real estate that is acquired

Shimon performs an act of *hazakah* to acquire the real estate of the proselyte. If the real estate is one contiguous tract, delineated by boundaries, Shimon acquires ownership of the entire tract the moment he performs an act of acquisition, such as turning a shovel-ful of earth. If it is not delineated by boundaries, Shimon acquires ownership to the tract by plowing the tract[37] from one end to the other and then plowing another furrow back again.[38]

If the tract of land owned by the deceased proselyte before he died

36. There is an opinion that the structure belongs to Levi only if Shimon used materials that did not belong to him, that is he used materials that belonged to the proselyte and Shimon did not intend to acquire them when he used them, or else built the structure with workers (who probably did not intend to acquire the materials for Shimon; they were busy building and not thinking whose materials they were using). In these instances both the structure and the real estate belong to Levi when he installs the doors. However, if Shimon used his own materials or intended to acquire the materials from the predeceased proselyte when Shimon picked them up, the structure belongs to Shimon. Levi, by placing the doors on the structure, acquires nothing since the structure belongs to Shimon, and the underlying real estate is still ownerless, and whoever performs an act of acquisition to the real estate will acquire the real estate. There is an opinion that goes even further and holds that even if Shimon used his own materials, if Levi puts on the doors, the real estate and the structure belong to Levi. (The real estate, since Shimon did not acquire it by not putting on the doors, and the structure, since Shimon intended the materials to be part of the real estate that he had hoped (mistakenly) to acquire.) Since he did not acquire the real estate, the materials are deemed ownerless in this situation.

37. Although the *halachah* speaks of his plowing with a team of animals, the law will be the same if he plows with a tractor.

38. There are several views as to what exactly Shimon must do to acquire the entire tract. One view holds that Shimon plows the field from end to end, either from north to south or from east to west, and then back again. Another view is that he plows along the southern and northern boundaries, or along the eastern and southern boundaries. Local custom or the rules of the beth din will prevail. As stated in the

without heirs contained interior boundaries, then if Shimon performs an act of acquisition on one side of the boundary, he does not acquire the area on the other side of the interior boundary. The items that form interior boundaries are generally those listed in the Talmud and subsequent codes, but would include such other boundaries as are now in effect to divide areas within tracts of land. The listed dividers are: a designated boundary, the *chatzav* hedge, a river, a rivulet, a ravine, a water-filled ditch, a road (whether public or private),[39] paths (whether public or private)[40] used both in rainy seasons and dry seasons, different types of grasses, and anything that is the custom of a community.

When there is a large tract of land belonging to the deceased proselyte without any interior boundaries or any of the other dividers, then Shimon acquires much of the area that is considered as one unit as is associated with the name of the proselyte.[41]

The proselyte dies owning two tracts of land adjacent to each other, tract 1 and tract 2, divided by a boundary line or other divider. Shimon performs an act of acquisition on tract 1 to acquire tract 1; he acquires that tract. Shimon performs an act of acquisition on tract 1 to acquire both tracts 1 and 2; he acquires only tract 1. He performs an act of acquisition on tract 1 to acquire tract 2; he acquires neither tract.[42] Shimon performs an act of acquisition on tract 1 to acquire

---

introduction, the laws of this chapter are rather rare. Even if a proselyte will die without heirs according to *halachah*, he will probably have heirs according to the secular laws of the land where he was domiciled.

39. The difference between a public road and a private road is that the former is at least 16 *amoth* wide and the latter is at least 4 *amoth* wide. (See Glossary for definition of *amah*, the singular of *amoth*). Both are used for travel by both pedestrians and vehicular traffic. If either of these roads divides a tract, it separates the tract into two parts, and an act of acquisition performed in one part does not give Shimon ownership of the other part.

40. Paths are distinguished from roads in that paths are used solely for pedestrian traffic. These paths act as dividers between various parts of the tract of land only if they are used in all seasons, even when there are crops on the land.

41. There is an opinion that this law applies only to fields that are irrigated by springs throughout the year. But if they are rain-irrigated fields, where the rainy season is limited to certain seasons, then Shimon acquires only that area in which he performed an act of acquisition.

42. He does not acquire tract 2, since he did not perform an act of acquisition in tract 2. He does not acquire tract 1, since he had no intent to acquire tract 1.

tract 1, tract 2, and the divider between the two tracts, or he performs an act of acquisition on the divider to acquire both tracts. The law is that if another person, Levi, thereafter performed an act of acquisition on tract 1 and/or tract 2, before Shimon performed an act of acquisition on the tracts themselves, the tracts on which Levi performed an act of acquisition belong to Levi.

The proselyte died owning two houses, house 1 in the front facing the street and house 2 behind house 1. Shimon performs an act of acquisition on house 1; he has acquired house 1. If he performs an act of acquisition on house 1 to acquire both houses 1 and 2, Shimon acquires only house 1. If he performs an act of acquisition on house 1 to acquire house 2, he acquires neither house.[43] There is an opinion that if Shimon performs an act of acquisition on house 2 with the intent to acquire both houses, he acquires both houses.[44]

Assume that when the proselyte acquired the real estate he received a deed, whether it was a deed of purchase or a deed of gift. After the death of the proselyte, Shimon takes possession of the deed. He has not acquired ownership of the real estate described in the deed. He does own the deed.[45]

---

43. See previous note.

44. The reasoning in this case is that since when he acquires the back house 2 he also acquires an easement through house 1 to reach house 2, he thus also acquires house 1, which he also intended to acquire. According to this opinion, what has been said in the previous paragraph when Shimon performs an act of acquisition on tract 1 to acquire both tracts 1 and 2 that he acquires only tract 1 would hold true only if the tracts were alongside each other. However, if tract 1 was an interior tract that can be reached only by going over tract 2, Shimon would also acquire tract 2.

45. He may use the deed to hang on his wall as a decoration or some other similar thing.

Part II

LAWS OF INHERITANCE

Chapter 276

LAWS OF INTESTACY

INTRODUCTION

This chapter is the first of a series of chapters devoted to the laws of inheritance of a person who dies intestate, that is, he dies without a will disposing of his assets, neither did he make a gift *causa mortis* before he died disposing of his assets.[1] The person who dies intestate (the "decedent") will be designated as "Ruven." Ordinarily, the assets of a decedent who dies intestate are disposed of as set forth by the secular civil intestate statutes of the jurisdiction where the decedent dies.

However, the surviving members of the decedent can agree to divide the assets of the decedent according to the laws of intestacy as stated in *halachah*. In many orthodox circles, such agreements are not infrequent; most importantly, many orthodox people write their wills to conform to the laws of these chapters as if they died intestate under the *halachah* system, or at least try to approximate these laws

1. The subjects of gifts *causa mortis* and wills are discussed in the end of Volume VII, commencing with Chapter 250.

in their wills.[2] The laws of distribution of assets of the decedent upon his death are based on the Torah command found in Numbers 27:6–11 dealing with the laws of intestate inheritance and Deuteronomy 21:15–17 dealing with the laws of primogeniture.

> Numbers 27:6–11
> 6. God said to Moses, saying. 7. The daughters of Zelophehad speak properly. You shall give them a possession of inheritance among the brothers of their father, and you shall cause the inheritance of their father to pass over to them. 8. And to the Children of Israel you shall speak, saying: If a man will die and he has no son, you shall cause his inheritance to pass over to his daughter. 9. If he has no daughter, you shall give his inheritance to his brothers. 10. If he has no brothers, you shall give the inheritance to the brothers of his father. 11. If there are no brothers of his father, you shall give the inheritance to the relative who is closest to him of his family, and he shall inherit it. This shall be for the Children of Israel as a decree of justice, as God commanded Moses.

> Deuteronomy 21:15–17
> 15. If a man will have two wives, one beloved and one hated, and they bear him sons, the beloved one and the hated one, and the firstborn son is the hated one's; 16. Then it shall be that on the day that he causes his sons to inherit whatever will be his, he cannot give the right of the firstborn to the son of the beloved ahead of the son of the hated one, the firstborn. 17. Rather, he must recognize the firstborn, the son of the hated one, to give him the double portion in all that is found with him; for he is in his initial vigor, to him is the right of the firstborn.

As is seen in the text below, if there are female and male heirs on the same level of kinship, the males inherit and the females are not included in inheriting the estate; lacking males or their descendants to the end of the line, the distribution is made to females on the same level of kinship.[3] The effects of this principle are certainly ameliorated by the decrees of the Rabbis in the Talmud regarding the obligations

2. See Volume VII, Chapter 257.

3. There are many cogent reasons for keeping the family assets within the tribe, especially the family real estate allotted to the families and tribes by Joshua.

of the estate and the male heirs toward the widow and the daughters of the decedent. The first section in the text deals with the status of the widow and daughters of the decedent. Thereafter follows the section dealing with the order of inheritance in cases of intestacy; this section contains a chart setting forth the distributees in the case of intestacy followed by a list of those who inherit in the case of intestacy, correlated to the chart. The numbers above the persons named in the chart is their order of inheritance as set forth in the list. The notes accompanying the list expand on the concise list. I have only shown five generations: the generation of the decedent, the two prior generations, and two subsequent generations. In almost all cases, such a span of generations should be sufficient. In the remote possibility that it is not sufficient, the list can be extrapolated either forward or backward.

The descent is by the method called *per stirpes* and not *per capita.* These terms are explained in the section called "*Per stirpes* distribution."

I have also set out a section regarding the heirs of a woman who was married when she died or was a widow when she died. In many respects the chain of heirship is similar to that when a man dies; however, there are a few significant dissimilarities.

Rabbi Moshe Isserles, in his emendations at the end of the chapter in *Shulhan Aruch*, writes that it is not possible for the heirs to inherit things that are not physical[4] nor to transmit such items to one's heirs. There was a time that these things did not have independent value that could be stated; also there was a time that these were not transferred by *kinyan*. Now that the *kinyan* has replaced other methods of acquiring and transferring items, it also includes things that are not physical. I have therefore omitted the laws, declaring it impossible to transmit such items from this Restatement.

4. See Volume VI, Chapter 212 which discusses transferring nonphysical items, such as air rights, the right to live in an apartment, the right to eat fruit from a tree, and so forth.

TEXT

Obligations of the heirs to the widow and daughters of the decedent

The widow is entitled to be maintained by the heirs of her deceased husband out of the property that they inherited from her husband. She is entitled to food, clothing, and shelter. She may continue to reside in the family residence occupied by her late husband and has the services of all household employees such as maids and chauffeurs that she had before he died. All of these things are to be provided in keeping with her station or her husband's station, whichever is higher. If the widow becomes ill, she can obtain unlimited medical treatment from the estate; if she requires limited medical treatment, she must pay for it by herself from her *kethubah*.[5] If she dies, the husband's heirs must provide for her burial. All income from the property that she brought into the marriage belongs to her.[6] All of these are provided to her until the earliest of three happenings: (1) her death; (2) her remarriage; (3) her claim to her *kethubah*.

Upon the death of a father, a fund is taken from his estate to provide his daughters with a livelihood, according to his station in the community. If there is no way for beth din to know how much he would have given, each daughter receives 10 percent of the estate.[7] The estate is also responsible for the maintenance of the daughters until they reach their legal majority at the age of 12 years, 6 months, and 1 day, or become betrothed, whichever is sooner. The maintenance includes food, clothing, and shelter.

Beth din always has the right to see that the widow and daughters are adequately provided for out of the estate. If there are not sufficient assets in the estate to provide for both the widow and the daughters, the rights of the widow have priority.

5. See Volume VII, Chapter 257, note 53, and accompanying text; also see Glossary.

6. See Glossary, *nichsai melog*.

7. In practice, the first daughter to get married gets 10 percent of the estate, the next daughter gets 10 percent of the remainder of the estate, and so on. Otherwise, if there were ten daughters, there would be nothing left for the sons; and if there were eleven daughters, the last daughter to get married would get nothing.

The order of inheritance in cases of intestacy

The *halachah* assumes that every Jew[8] has relatives surviving him.[9]

Assume Ruven dies without a will and not having made gifts disposing of all of his assets. His heir or heirs are determined as of the moment of his death in accordance with the priorities set forth below.

Priority is given to the descendants of the decedent and failing to leave surviving descendants, the chain of inheritors goes up first one generation to the father of the decedent and then to the descendants of the father; failing that the chain goes to the grandfather of the decedent and then to his descendants. This continues until there are heirs of the decedent.

All descent is through the father and not through the mother of the decedent. Ruven's widow is *not* an heir of Ruven. The mother is not an heir of her children, nor does she confer heir status on persons who are only related through her. Thus brothers by the same mother do not inherit each other. Brothers by the same father inherit each other whether or not they have the same mother.[10] Thus, if a child is born and his father is not known and therefore there are no relatives from his father's side, the members of his mother's family are not his heirs. If he leaves no descendants, then his property is ownerless, the same as that of a proselyte who dies without heirs.[11]

Whenever there is an heir, his pedigree does not affect his heirship, even if the heir is a bastard.

In the distribution chart, Ruven, the decedent, is in the third generation.

---

8. That is, except for a proselyte who dies without leaving surviving children or the descendants of his children. They are his heirs only if the children were conceived after his conversion into Judaism. See Chapter 275.

9. There are problems relating to survivors of the Holocaust where entire Jewish families perished without a trace of any other survivors. Very often the birth records of the community in which they were born were also destroyed. A competent *halachik* scholar should be consulted in such an event. This may be remote since many survivors started new families, or else have wills so that the laws of intestacy do not apply.

10. There is no difference between a brother by the same father and mother or a brother by the same father only.

11. See Chapter 275.

Distribution chart

generation number

I.

- **(14) Isaac**

II.

- **(7) Yaakov** son of Isaac
- **(22) Devorah** daughter of Isaac
- **(15) Pinchas** son of Isaac

III.

- **RUVEN *THE DECEDENT*** son of Yaakov
- **(8) Levi** son of Yaakov
- **(11) Dinah** daughter of Yaakov
- **(23) Shimon** son of Devorah
- **(26) Rivka** daughter of Devorah
- **(16) Mosh** son of Pinchas
- **(19) Merl** daughter of Pinchas

IV.

- **(1) Samuel** son of Ruven
- **(4) Sara** daughter of Ruven
- **(9) Peretz** son of Levi
- **(10) Yael** daughter of Levi
- **(12) Shlomo** son of Dinah
- **(13) Michal** daughter of Dinah
- **(24) David** son of Shimon
- **(25) Jane** daughter of Shimon
- **(27) Saul** son of Rivka
- **(28) Rona** daughter of Rivka
- **(17) Bob** son of Mosh
- **(18) Ann** daughter of Mosh
- **(20) Ezra** son of Merl
- **(21) Else** daughter of Merl

V.

- **(2) Seth** son of Samuel
- **(3) Penina** daughter of Samuel
- **(5) Amnon** son of Sara
- **(6) Naomi** daughter of Sara

List of distributees

The heirs of the decedent Ruven inherit in the order set forth in the following list, always recognizing that the next category comes into effect only if there is no one to inherit under the category before it.

1. The sons of Ruven, regardless of whether Ruven also had daughters or the daughter's descendants survivors surviving him[12] (in the chart: Samuel).
2. The male descendants of Ruven's sons to the end of the line[13] (in the chart: first Seth and then to his descendants if Seth did not survive Samuel).
3. The female descendants of Ruven's sons to the end of the line[14] (in the chart: first Penina and then to her descendants to the end of time, if Penina did not survive Samuel).
4. The daughters of Ruven[15] (in the chart: Sara).
5. The male descendants of Ruven's daughters to the end of the line[16] (in the chart: Amnon).
6. The female descendants of Ruven's daughters to the end of the line[17] (in the chart: Naomi).

---

12. Ruven dies and leaves three surviving sons, Samuel, Charles, and Arthur; and three daughters, Sara, Shirley, and Shulamith. Samuel, Charles, and Arthur inherit the entire estate of Ruven to the exclusion of the three daughters, Sara, Shirley, and Shulamith.

13. Ruven dies leaving no sons surviving him, but leaving grandsons, Seth, Ralph, and Harold; the sons of Ruven's predeceased sons, Samuel, Charles, and Arthur. Seth, Ralph, and Harold inherit the estate of Ruven.

14. If Samuel, Charles, and Arthur die before Ruven and none of them has sons surviving them, but Samuel has a daughter, Penina; Charles has a daughter, Shoshana; and Arthur has a daughter, Tamar; then Penina, Shoshana, and Tamar will divide Ruven's estate.

15. Ruven dies leaving no sons or descendants of sons; he does leave surviving him three daughters, Sara, Shirley, and Shulamith. They inherit the entire estate of Ruven.

16. Ruven dies leaving no sons or descendants from sons; he leaves no daughters surviving him, but his daughters, Sarah, Shirley, and Shulamith each left a son, Amnon, Sidney, and Chaim, respectively. Amnon, Sidney, and Chaim inherit the entire state of Ruven, although they also have sisters.

17. Sara, Shirley, and Shulamith predeceased Ruven and left no sons, only daughters, Naomi, Shoshana, and Blanche, respectively. Naomi, Shoshana, and Blanche inherit the entire estate.

7. The father of Ruven[18] (in the chart: Yaakov).
8. The brothers of the decedent[19] (in the chart: Levi).
9. The male descendants of Ruven's brothers to the end of the line[20] (in the chart: Peretz).
10. The female descendants of Ruven's brothers to the end of the line[21] (in the chart: Yael).
11. The sisters of the decedent[22] (in the chart: Dinah).
12. The male descendants of Ruven's sisters to the end of the line[23] (in the chart: Shlomo).
13. The female descendants of Ruven's sisters to the end of the line[24] (in the chart: Michal).
14. The grandfather of Ruven[25] (in the chart: Isaac).
15. The decedent's uncles[26] (in the chart: Pinchas).

---

18. Until now the heirs are descendants of the decedent, going from generation III on the chart to generations IV and V. Now the distribution goes up one generation to II.

19. The brothers born to the decedent's father, Levi, Odet, and Adrian, irrespective of whether these brothers have the same mother as the decedent; that is, whether half brothers or full brothers. As it were, the brothers do not inherit directly from the decedent but take the share that their father, Yaakov, would have inherited from Ruven.

20. Levi, Odet, and Adrian predecease Ruven. They leave sons Peretz, Bernard, and Hillel, respectively, who survive Ruven. Peretz, Bernard, and Hillel inherit the entire estate although they also have sisters.

21. Levi, Odet, and Adrian left no sons nor descendants of sons surviving Ruven. Levi, Odet, and Adrian left daughters surviving Ruven, Yael, Sheila, and Adele, respectively. Yael, Sheila, and Adele inherit the entire estate.

22. The sisters born to the decedent's father, Dinah, Ruth, and Renee, irrespective of whether these sisters have the same mother as the decedent; that is, whether half sisters or full sisters. As it were, the sisters do not inherit directly from the decedent but take the share that their father, Yaakov, would have inherited from Ruven.

23. Dinah, Ruth, and Renee did not survive Ruven. However, their sons, Shlomo, Julius, and Shamai, respectively, did survive Ruven. Shlomo, Julius, and Shamai inherit the entire estate of Ruven, whether or not they have sisters.

24. Dinah, Ruth, and Renee left no sons nor descendants of sons surviving Ruven. Dinah, Ruth, and Renee left daughters surviving Ruven: Michal, Eva, and Jeanne, respectively. Michal, Eva, and Jeanne inherit the entire estate.

25. The grandfather referred to is the father's father only. The heir is now from generation I, two generations prior to the decedent.

26. The uncles, Pinchas, Boris, and Denis, are only those who are the sons of the decedent's grandfather.

16. The male descendants of the uncles[27] (in the chart: Mosh).
17. The male descendants of the male descendants of the uncle to the end of the line[28] (in the chart: Bob).
18. The female descendants of the male descendants of the uncle to the end of the line[29] (in the chart: Ann).
19. The female descendants of the uncles (in the chart: Merl).
20. The male descendants of the female descendants of the uncle to the end of the line (in the chart: Ezra).
21. The female descendants of the female descendants of the uncle to the end the line (in the chart: Else).
22. The decedant's aunt[30] (in the chart: Devorah).
23. The male descendants of the aunt (in the chart: Shimon).
24. The male descendants of the male descendants of the aunt to the end of the line (in the chart: David).
25. The female descendants of the male descendants of the aunt to the end of the line (in the chart: Jane).
26. The female descendants of the aunt (in the chart: Rivka).
27. The male descendants of the female descendants of the aunt to the end of the line (in the chart: Saul).
28. The female descendants of the female descendants of the aunt to the end of the line (in the chart: Rona).

Heirs of a woman who was married

Sarah dies. Either she was married at the time of her death or was a widow (or a divorcee) at the time of her death. If Sarah and her

---

27. The uncles, Pinchas, Boris, and Denis, all predeceased Ruven. They left three sons, Mosh, Yosef, and Ben, respectively, who survive Ruven. Mosh, Yosef, and Ben inherit the entire estate of Ruven, whether or not they have sisters. They happen to have sisters, Merl, Zippy, and Zahava.

28. Thus if Mosh has two sons, Bob and Steven, and two daughters, Ann and Sally, Bob and Steven would inherit the entire estate of Ruven. This category could have been included in category (16) by adding the words "to the end of the line." I have set up a separate category to once again illustrate how males have priority over females on the same level of kinship.

29. Ann and Sally, mentioned in the prior note, would inherit the entire estate of Ruven. This category too could have been included in category (16) by adding the words "to the end of the line." See prior note.

30. The aunts, Devorah, Faige, and Madeline, are only those who are the daughters of the decedent's grandfather, Isaac.

husband were divorced, for the purposes of this section it is the same as if she was a widow.

A husband is the heir of his wife,[31] and if he is not alive, then her estate is inherited by her sons and their descendants. If she left no sons or descendants of sons surviving her, her estate is inherited by her daughters and their descendants if her daughters predeceased her. If she left no daughters or descendants of daughters, her estate is inherited by her father. If she is not survived by her father, then her father's sons inherit her.[32] If there are no sons of her father or their descendants surviving Sarah, then her father's daughters are Sarah's heirs, and if she had no such sisters or sister's descendants surviving her, the estate goes to her father's father, her grandfather. If he did not survive her, the estate goes to the grandfather's sons and descendants or then to the grandfather's daughters and their descendants.

A son who predeceased his mother is not her heir so as to transmit his inheritance to his brothers by his father only. Ruven, the sole son of Sarah died and then his mother, Sarah, a widow, died. Ruven's sons inherit Sarah, since Sarah does not have a husband surviving her. If Ruven left no descendants and his next of kin is his brother, Levi, from the same father but not from Sarah, Levi does not inherit Sarah. However, if Ruven had survived Sarah[33] and inherited her, then his heirs are the same as listed above; if his brother Levi is his heir, then Levi will inherit that which Ruven inherited from Sarah, although Levi is not related to Sarah.[34]

Per stirpes distribution

Per stirpes and *per capita* can best be defined by giving an example. Ruven, the decedent had three sons during his lifetime, Samuel, Charles, and Arthur. Only Samuel survives Ruven, Charles and Arthur having died before Ruven died. Samuel has two sons, Seth and Alex,

31. See Rabbi Yisroel Lau, *Yachel Yisroel*, Volume 2, page 369, Jerusalem, 1992.

32. These are her brothers who have the same father that she has. They may be full brothers or half-brothers, having the same father and a different mother. Her brothers who have the same mother but a different father do not inherit her.

33. No matter what his age, even 1 day old, and no matter how long he survived, even moments, he is the heir.

34. Once Ruven inherits Sarah that which he inherited is the same as any of his other assets.

alive when Ruven dies; Charles left two sons who are alive when Ruven dies, Ralph and Jeff; and Arthur left three daughters who are alive when Ruven dies, Selma, Thelma, and Arlene.

RUVEN, the decedent

sons:	Samuel*		Charles			Arthur	
grandchildren:	Seth*	Alex*	Ralph*	Jeff*	Selma*	Thelma*	Arlene*

*Survived Ruven

If the estate is divided *per stirpes*, it means that the estate of Ruven is divided into the number of sons that he had in his lifetime. Thus the estate is divided into three shares. Samuel receives one-third share of the estate. Ralph and Jeff each receive one-sixth share of the estate (one-half each of their father's (Charles') one-third share). Selma, Thelma, and Arlene receive one-ninth each (one third each of their father's (Arthur's) one-third share).

If the estate is divided *per capita*, then the estate would be divided into six shares according to the number of persons entitled to share in the estate. Samuel, Ralph, Jeff, Selma, Thelma, and Arlene each would receive one-sixth of the estate.

In *halachah*, the heirs of the same degree divide the estate equally. If there is more than one level of kinship, then the lower level receives that which their ancestor who is in the same level as the person in the earliest generation who shares in the estate.

Inheriting things that are not physical

There is an opinion that Ruven cannot transmit to his heirs things that are not physical, such as a leasehold or airspace, or the right to eat fruit.[35]

35. See note 4 above and accompanying text.

Chapter 277

LAWS OF PRIMOGENITURE

INTRODUCTION

The Torah states:

> 15. If a man will have two wives, one beloved and one hated, and they bear him sons the beloved one and the hated one, and the firstborn son is the hated one's; 16. then it shall be that on the day that he causes his sons to inherit whatever will be his, he cannot give the right of the firstborn to the son of the beloved one ahead of the son of the hated one, the firstborn. 17. Rather, he must recognize the firstborn, the son of the hated one, to give him the double portion in all that is found with him; for he is his initial vigor, to him is the right of the firstborn.[1]

It is seen from this that the firstborn has a special portion of the estate of his father, that of primogeniture.

This chapter and the next chapter describe this special portion. I have divided this chapter into three parts, (1) Who is a firstborn? (2) How does he prove he is a firstborn? (3) What portion of the father's estate does the firstborn receive? This last topic is continued in the next chapter that deals with those items to which the laws of

1. Deuteronomy 21:15–17.

primogeniture do apply and to which items the laws of primogeniture do not apply.

The firstborn is designated as "Ruven"; the father is designated as "Yaakov."

TEXT

Definition of a firstborn

Primogeniture is the *halachah* provision whereby a firstborn, if a male, receives a special portion of the estate of his father. For the purposes of primogeniture, the firstborn is the firstborn to the father,[2] whether or not he is also the firstborn to his mother.[3] The firstborn receives a primogeniture share only if he is the firstborn to the father and only from the father's estate. He does not receive a primogeniture share of his mother's estate even if he is her firstborn and also the firstborn of his father. He receives a portion of his mother's estate equal to that of her other sons.

In order to be the one whom the *halachah* recognizes as the firstborn, he must be born while the father is still alive.[4] For the purpose of these laws the word "born" means that his forehead emerged from

2. For example, his mother was married to her first husband and had children with her first husband. The first husband divorced her or he died. She then married Yaakov, who had no previous children, and has a child, Ruven, by Yaakov. Such child, Yaakov's first, is Yaakov's firstborn for the purposes of primogeniture, although he is not the firstborn of his mother.

3. The Torah commands that a firstborn son must be redeemed by paying five silver coins to the *kohen* (priest) (Exodus 34:19). For this purpose the firstborn is the one who is firstborn to the mother, although the son is not necessarily the firstborn to his father. See Maimonidies, *Laws of First Fruits*, chapter 11.

4. For example, the father died while his wife was pregnant. After the father died, his widow gave birth to twin sons, one of whom was born first. The rules of primogeniture do not apply to him. Or, when it was possible for a man to have two wives, the husband had two wives. When the husband died, both wives were pregnant, and one of them gave birth to a son and then the other gave birth to a son. The rules of primogeniture do not apply to the son who was born first.

the womb while the father was still alive.[5] There is an opinion that if the father was in a coma when Ruven was born, and died without recovering, Ruven is not considered the firstborn for the purposes of this chapter.[6]

If the first baby born to the father is a *toomtoom*,[7] he is not considered the firstborn male for the purposes of inheritance. This holds true even if there is a subsequent operation performed on him and it is then revealed that he was a male.

Ruven was the first child born to Yaakov after a prematurely born child to the same father, Yaakov, died within 30 days of birth.[8] Ruven is the firstborn of Yaakov for primogeniture purposes. Or, if a child was born to Yaakov in the ninth month of pregnancy, but was dead when its head emerged, and Ruven is the next child born to Yaakov, Ruven is the firstborn for the purposes of primogeniture.[9]

The firstborn to Yaakov, Shimon was born by a sectional birth, and thereafter Ruven was born through a normal birth. Neither Shimon nor Ruven have the status of a firstborn in accordance with the laws of primogeniture.

Avraham is a proselyte, who before he converted had children with a non-Jewish woman; his firstborn with a Jewish woman after he converts does not have the status of a firstborn regarding primogeniture.[10]

---

5. Yaakov had two wives, Leah and Rachel. Leah conceived first but Rachel gave birth first to a boy, Ruven. Ruven is the firstborn.

6. The verse says that the father "must recognize the firstborn" and if he is in a coma he cannot recognize him.

7. A *toomtoom* is a person whose genitals are not visible. Although his gender cannot be determined, he is in reality either a male or a female, not a third gender. (There is an opinion in the Talmud that the *toomtoom* should be considered a third gender.) Since his maleness is not recognizable at the time that he is born, he does not become a firstborn for the purposes of primogeniture.

8. The *halachah* recognizes a premature child to be one born in other than the seventh or ninth month of pregnancy and who does not survive 30 days.

9. If the first child was born in its ninth month and was alive when its head emerged, then Ruven, who is the next born to Yaakov, is not considered his firstborn for the purpose of primogeniture.

10. The prior children follow the father's status and are his relatives as being non-Jewish because his wife was not Jewish. Since he had children who had the same status as he had, his firstborn child after he converts and has a child with a Jewish mother is not his firstborn child.

A non-Jewish man has a child with a Jewish woman and after he converts has another child, a son (whether or not with the same Jewish woman). This latter son is considered his firstborn for the purposes of primogeniture.[11]

A Jew, Yehudah, fathered a child with a non-Jewish woman; such son is not considered his son. Yehudah thereafter has a son by a Jewish woman. Such latter son is considered a firstborn for primogeniture purposes.

If the firstborn, Ruven, is a bastard,[12] he is considered a firstborn for the purposes of primogeniture. Similarly, if the father Yaakov is a *kohen*[13] and fathers a son, Ruven, with a woman who is a divorcee; Ruven is considered a firstborn for the purposes of primogeniture.

Proof that one is a firstborn

The question may arise as to whether Ruven is actually the firstborn. The testimony of witnesses is the highest form of proof as to whether or not Ruven is the firstborn of his father. There may be documentary evidence such as letters of the father, birth records, or writings in a family Bible. The statements of the father made to people may be introduced as evidence if beth din deems it proper. If Ruven died and the eulogy referred to him as the firstborn, it may be adequate to so establish him as the firstborn. Beth din has to decide each case on the facts peculiar to that case.

Absent cogent proof, the following rules are usually followed by beth din.

The doctor (or the midwife) who delivered Ruven is believed to state that Ruven is the firstborn of twin boys. He is believed if his statement is made contemporaneously with the birth, that is, until he

11. The son that the non-Jew has with a Jewish woman is not considered his son according to *halachah*. The son is considered Jewish because the mother is Jewish, and the father, who was not Jewish at the time the son was born, is not considered related to his son. Thus his first son after he converted born to a Jewish woman is deemed to be his first son for the purposes of primogeniture.

12. The term bastard is defined in Volume I, page 49.

13. A *kohen* is a person who traces his ancestry back to Aaron, the first priest in Israel. A *kohen* is not permitted to marry a woman who had previously been divorced. If he fathers a child with such a woman, the child is called a *chalal*, a profaned person.

leaves the delivery room. The mother is believed to state that Ruven is the firstborn of twin boys during the first 7 days after his birth.[14]

The father is always believed if he states that Ruven is his firstborn. He is believed even if he names a person who was not known to be his son that he is his firstborn. Once the father states that Ruven is his firstborn, he may not later state that he is not his firstborn. Conversely, the father may state that Ruven is not his firstborn, although everyone thinks that he is. If the father was a mute, then statements made by him when he was alive using sign language, or writings, or even nodding with his head when asked if Ruven was his firstborn is adequate proof.

In situations where it is not established that Ruven is the firstborn, there must be proof produced that he is the firstborn. For example, one of the sons of the father demands that Ruven prove that he is the firstborn of their father. Perhaps there was a child born before Ruven?

There can be a situation where the firstborn was confused with another son to the point where it cannot be positively decided that Ruven is the firstborn; neither takes the extra portion of a firstborn.[15] In such a situation there is a difference in result depending upon the facts of the case. If it was ever known who the firstborn was but because of circumstances it is not now known, then the two sons, Ruven and Shimon, either of whom may be the firstborn, write a power of attorney to each other and take their primogeniture share when inheriting the estate with the other brothers, and then they divide this extra share.[16] If it was never known who is the firstborn, they may not follow the procedure of the prior sentence, and no one receives the primogeniture extra portion of the father's estate.

Assume a situation where a woman has just given birth to a child.

---

14. On the eighth day is the circumcision ceremony and the father takes the son from the mother.

15. There may be a situation where the surviving sons know that Ruven is the oldest son, but it is not known whether there was another child born to the father, Yaakov, prior to the birth of Ruven. If there was, then Ruven is not the firstborn for the purposes of primogeniture.

16. One does not have to go back to antiquity to find such situations. The Holocaust that occurred just a half century ago left too many people who did not know anything about when they were born, nor who was the oldest or the next oldest within a family.

She married her current husband, Yaakov, when she was divorced[17] only two months from her prior husband, David.[18] Seven months after her marriage to her current husband, Yaakov, she gave birth to Ruven. Ruven can be the child of the first husband and born after nine months of gestation, or the son of the current husband after a seven-month gestation period. If her current husband Yaakov is the father then the new baby is the firstborn of the father. Neither Ruven nor a child born to the father after Ruven is deemed a firstborn[19] for the purposes of primogeniture.[20]

The portion received by the firstborn

Assume that the father, Yaakov, died and there was a firstborn, Ruven. In most situations Ruven receives a double portion of the estate of the father. The estate of the father is divided into as many parts as their are sons plus one more, (n+1) and the firstborn receives one portion and then all of the brothers including the firstborn receive one of the remaining portions. Assume that there are three sons, one of whom is Ruven the firstborn. The estate is divided into four parts (3+1) and the firstborn receives one part (one-quarter) and then he and the other two sons equally share the remaining three-quarters. The firstborn thus receives one-half of the estate and the other two sons receive one-quarter each.[21] Assume ten sons, including Ruven, the firstborn. The estate is divided into 11 portions (10+1); one-eleventh is given to

17. Or her prior husband died two months before she married her current husband.

18. The law is that a widow or divorcee cannot marry another man prior to the ninety-first day after the death of the prior husband or the divorce.

19. The other sons can insist that Ruven and the other son prove the facts that they are the firstborn children.

20. Such a child may end up not inheriting the first husband nor the second husband. The heirs of the first husband plead that he is an heir of the other husband, and the heirs of the second husband plead that he is an heir of the other husband.

21. It has been said that the firstborn receives two portions and then the remaining sons divide the balance of the estate. In most instances this is correct. Thus when there are three sons the estate is divided into 4 parts and the firstborn receives 2 parts and the other sons 1 part each. In this situation the result is the same. However, as will be seen in the text below, there are times when this is not accurate. I have thus set the *halachah* to be that the firstborn receives one portion and then he and the remaining sons divide the remaining portions equally.

Ruven. Then the remaining ten-elevenths is divided among the ten sons including Ruven. Ruven thus receives two-elevenths and the other nine sons receive one-eleventh each.

In determining how many sons are to be included in the calculation for the primogeniture portion, only those sons who were born prior to the death of the father are included; sons born during the father's lifetime but who predeceased their father are included.[22] Yaakov had two sons, Ruven, the firstborn, and Shimon, both having predeceased Yaakov. Ruven left a daughter, Sarah, and Shimon left a son, David. Sarah inherits two-thirds of Yaakov's estate and David inherits one-third.[23] Any sons born after the father's death are not included in this calculation regarding the primogeniture portion, but such afterborn sons are included in the calculation in dividing the balance of the estate.

It was stated in the prior paragraph that the relationship of primogeniture applies even if the firstborn and/or the other sons do not survive their father, and apply *per stirpes*, not *per capita*. For example, Yaakov had three sons, Ruven (the firstborn), Shimon, and Levi. All three died before Yaakov. Ruven left two surviving daughters, Leah and Rachel; Shimon left two surviving sons, Moshe and Aaron; Levi left three surviving sons, Issacher, Dan, and Naftali, and a daughter, Sarah. All of these grandchildren were alive when Yaakov died. Since there were three sons, the estate is divided into four equal portions (n+1). Leah and Rachel, the daughters of Ruven, inherit one-half of the estate or one-quarter to Leah and one-quarter to Rachel. Moshe and Aaron, the sons of Shimon each inherit one-eighth of Yaakov's estate. Issacher, Dan, and Naftali each inherit one-twelfth of the estate.

Assume that Ruven is the firstborn. He has two brothers, Shimon and Levi, and also a *toomtoom* in the family. The *toomtoom* undergoes

---

22. Yaakov had three sons, Ruven (the firstborn), Shimon, and Levi. Levi predeceased Yaakov, leaving no children. When Yaakov dies his estate is divided into four parts (3+1), and Ruven the firstborn receives one part (one-quarter) as his primogeniture portion. The remaining three-quarters is divided between Ruven and Shimon, each receiving 37.5 percent of the estate. Ruven thus receives 62.5 percent of the estate.

23. Yaakov's estate is divided into three parts (2+1). Two portions are given to Ruven, and since he is not alive, his share goes to his heir Sarah. The remaining one-third goes to Shimon, and since he is not alive it goes to his heir, David.

an operation and it is determined that he is a boy.[24] Since it was not known at his birth that he was a boy, the *toomtoom* is not included in determining the primogeniture portion of the estate. Thus only the two sons, Shimon and Levi, and the firstborn, Ruven, are counted so that there are four portions to be divided (3+1). Ruven receives one-quarter of the estate leaving the balance of three-quarters of the estate to be divided. For the purposes of this next division, the *toomtoom* is included so that there are now four brothers, Ruven, the other two sons (Shimon and Levi), and the former *toomtoom*. Each, including Ruven, receives 18.75 percent of the estate. Ruven thus receives 43.75 percent of the estate.[25]

If the two portions to be received by the firstborn include items that are beneficial to receive contiguous to each other, the firstborn is entitled to select contiguous items. For example, if the firstborn is to receive two portions of the real estate owned by the father and the other sons are to receive one portion each, the portions received by the firstborn should be contiguous to each other if the firstborn so desires.

---

24. My friend Dr. Bernard Freidson of Jerusalem advised me that at the present time the sex can be determined without an operation by a sonogram or by a DNA test. The question that must be answered is how fast after birth this can be done and the result known. I suggest that if it is within a few moments of birth, then such *toomtoom* would not only share in the estate as a male and diminish the portion of the other sons, but might also diminish the primogeniture share of the estate. Thus Ruven would receive a primogeniture portion of one-fifth of the estate leaving four-fifths to be divided among the four sons. Ruven, Shimon, Levi, and the former *toomtoom*, receive one-fifth each. Ruven would thus receive two-fifths (forty percent) of the estate as distinguished from the 43.75 percent he would receive if the *toomtoom* is not included in the original calculation.

25. If the *toomtoom* were included for all purposes, Ruven would have received forty percent of the estate, and the three other heirs would have received 20 percent each.

Chapter 278

OBJECTS NOT INCLUDED IN THE PRIMOGENITURE PORTION

INTRODUCTION

Rabbi Yosef Karo calls this chapter "The Firstborn Does Not Take The Double Share of Loans [due to the father] And Not Of Improvements [made to the father's property] And If He [the firstborn] Sold His Share In The Primogeniture Portion."

He commences with a description of objects to which primogeniture does apply; in all of these situations the object is deemed to be in the hands of the father when he died. He then discusses other situations where the laws of primogeniture do not apply, such as debts or other uncollected receivables due to the father. One of these situations to which the laws of primogeniture usually do not apply is to improvements to the realty of the father made after his lifetime, although as is seen in the text below, even here it sometimes applies.

As can be seen from the title of this chapter in *Shulhan Aruch*, it also deals with situations where the firstborn sells his primogeniture portion to a third person, Aaron. Is such sale valid? The question arises because the extra primogeniture portion is a gift that the Torah confers upon the firstborn. Can a gift not yet received by the recipient be sold?[1]

Since this chapter deals with situations where the laws of the firstborn receiving his primogeniture portion do not apply, it concludes with a section on the firstborn waiving his primogeniture portion.

As in the previous chapter, Yaakov is the father and Ruven is the firstborn son.

TEXT

Objects deemed to be part of the estate for primogeniture purposes

When Yaakov, the father dies, he owes the *kethubah*[2] to his widow. If the widow then dies prior to having commenced the procedure to collect the *kethubah*, the amount of the *kethubah* is included in the primogeniture portion of the estate. However, once the widow has commenced proceedings to collect her *kethubah* from her deceased husband's estate, if she then dies before collecting the *kethubah*, the proceeds are not subject to the laws of primogeniture, but are divided equally among Yaakov's heirs.

Yaakov, the father, is a *kohen*[3] and as such is entitled to certain

1. Ordinarily, a donee of a gift cannot sell it until he takes ownership of the gifted object, but as stated in the text, this does not apply to the primogeniture portion.

2. See Glossary for definition of *kethubah*.

3. Aaron, the brother of Moses, was the first priest. Every descendant of Aaron, tracing through males only, is considered to be a priest (*kohen*) to this very day. There are not too many privileges reserved for priests (*kohanim*, plural of *kohen*) that are in effect today. A full list of such privileges is set forth in Maimonides, *Book of Agriculture*, Treatise VI, Laws Concerning First Fruits and Other Gifts To the Priesthood, chapter I, laws 1 – 10. The Torah grants twenty-four gifts to the priests: eight may be eaten by the priest only in the Holy Temple within the wall of the Temple Court; five may be eaten only in Jerusalem; five accrue to them only in the Land of Israel; five accrue to them both in the Land of Israel and outside the Land of Israel; and one accrues to them directly from the Temple.

Among the five that accrue to them both within the Land of Israel and outside the Land of Israel is the one derived from the commandment found in the Book of portions of every animal that is slaughtered. Naftali, one of the father's friends slaughters an animal and then the father dies. The portion of the animal that Naftali gives to Yaakov's estate is included in the estate for the purpose of determining the firstborn's primogeniture portion.[4]

Real estate held by the father at the time of his death is included in the primogeniture portion even if it is mortgaged.[5]

Personal property of the father held by others either on loan to them or leased to them, or being held for them by a bailee, whether paid or unpaid, is deemed to be owned and held by the father and is subject to the laws of primogeniture.[6] If a third party is holding an animal belonging to the father and the animal gives birth to a calf, there is a difference of opinion as to whether the firstborn has a primogeniture portion in the calf.

Animals left by Yaakov, the father, are subject to the laws of primogeniture, and if he left three sons when he died, the firstborn will have the use of the animal two days and each of the other brothers one day.

Business investments and shares owned in business are part of the primogeniture portion. However, wages owed to the father or rent due to the father are not deemed to be in his possession and are not subject to the laws of primogeniture.

Objects stolen from the father before he died and which he did not abandon hope of recovering are part of the primogeniture portion because his ownership never ceased. Similarly, real estate that is held by others by force against the wishes of the father are part of the primogeniture portion, since real estate cannot be stolen.

Deuteronomy (18:3) that anyone who slaughters an animal for food must give to the priest the shoulder, the two cheeks, and the maw.

The text refers to a person, Naftali, who slaughters animals for food and always gives these portions to Yaakov.

4. Naftali slaughters the animal while Yaakov is still alive. Since Naftali always gives the priestly portions to Yaakov, it is as if he had received it before he died, and thus it is deemed owned and possessed by Yaakov.

5. However, real estate mortgaged to the government for nonpayment of taxes that the government will sell is not part of the primogeniture portion.

6. Bailments are different than moneys loaned, which, as stated below, are not subject to the laws of primogeniture. Bailed objects must be returned to the bailor or lessor or lender of the object. However, money borrowed is to be spent by the borrower and he returns different moneys to the lender.

Primogeniture does not apply to the mother's estate

The firstborn receives a primogeniture share only if he is the firstborn to the father and only from the father's estate. He does not receive a primogeniture share of his mother's estate even if he is her firstborn and also the firstborn of his father. He receives a portion of his mother's estate equal to that of her other sons.

Objects not part of the estate for primogeniture purposes

The objects subject to the laws of primogeniture must be owned by the father at the time of his death and in his possession or constructive possession. It does not apply to any objects in which the father had only an expectancy.

If the father is survived by his father, and the father's estate inherits objects from the father's father,[7] these objects are not subject to the laws of primogeniture, since this was but an expectancy when the father died. Similarly, if the father had a debt owed to him that was not collected while the father was alive, and is repaid after the father dies, such moneys are not included in the laws of primogeniture since the moneys were not in the possession of the father; moneys are loaned for the purpose of being spent. However, if the thing loaned is an object rather than moneys, they are deemed to be both owned by the lender and to be in his constructive possession. Thus, if the father loaned a cow to a third party or it was hired by a third party, or was given to a third party to use and the father was to receive a share in the profits, or was grazing in a pasture, and after the father's death the cow gave birth to a calf, the firstborn takes his primogeniture portion in the cow and the calf.

The firstborn does not take a primogeniture portion in debts due to the father on the date of his death,[8] even if such debt is evidenced by

7. Isaac, Yaakov's father, died after Yaakov died. Yaakov's estate is one of the heirs of Isaac. The portion inherited from Isaac by Yaakov's estate is not subject to the laws of primogeniture by Yaakov's firstborn son, Ruven.

8. Anything that requires collection is not considered to be owned by the creditor, whether the debt is for wages due to the father, for money loaned by the father, or for goods sold that have not yet been paid for.

a note of indebtedness.[9] This holds true whether the repayment of the debt is by payment of money or personal property or real property. However, bonds issued by governmental agencies are considered money,[10] even though they may be provided for interest payments, and are subject to the laws of primogeniture.[11] There is a difference of opinion if the debt is due from the firstborn to the father, whether the firstborn has a primogeniture portion in such debt. The *halachah* resolves such doubt by permitting the firstborn a one-half primogeniture portion in such debt. The general rule that the firstborn does not have a primogeniture portion in the debts due to the father applies only to unsecured debts. However, if the father held collateral security,[12] the debts are deemed to have been collected[13] and the firstborn does have a primogeniture portion in such debts.[14]

Improvements to the estate property

The firstborn does not receive a primogeniture portion in improvements to property that occurred after the father's death. This law applies when the improvement occurred either (a) as a result of effort or money expended by the estate to bring about the improvement; or (b) there was an obvious change, such as green fruit that became ripe. However, if neither (a) nor (b) is present, the firstborn receives his primogeniture portion of the improvement, as where a small tree grew thicker.

Where the firstborn takes two portions of land that include improvements and he is not entitled to take the improvements on the

9. See Glossary, note of indebtedness.

10. That is true only if they are already due on the date of death.

11. The laws of this last sentence also apply to notes backed by governmental agencies and banks. The fact that they fluctuate in value does not make them less collectable than cash, since the value of money also fluctuates. However, notes issued by individuals are not part of the primogeniture portion.

12. Holding a mortgage on real estate is not the same as holding collateral security and the firstborn does not have primogeniture portion in such debt.

13. There is an opinion that if the borrower whose collateral security is held by the father is not Jewish, the holding of the collateral security does not place the debt within the scope of the laws of primogeniture.

14. This applies whether the father obtained the collateral security when the loan was made or sometime thereafter.

primogeniture portion, such improvements are appraised and he must pay the other brothers for such improvements.[15] However, since the firstborn will not take his primogeniture portion in the improvements if there is effort or expense to make such improvements, he can protest prior to their making such improvements and if he does protest and they nevertheless make such improvements, the firstborn receives his primogeniture portion in the improvements.

Sale of the primogeniture portion

If Ruven, the firstborn, sells his extra primogeniture portion before he receives such portion, such sale is valid.[16]

Waiver of the primogeniture portion

The firstborn may waive the primogeniture portion by an express waiver, or his waiver may be inferred by his conduct. For example, if only a part of the father's assets have been distributed to the sons and the firstborn did not take a primogeniture portion, he is deemed to have waived his right to receive his primogeniture portion on the rest of the estate. This applies if the firstborn does not protest or state that he intends to receive his primogeniture portion; but if he does protest in the presence of witnesses,[17] he is not deemed to have waived his right to receive the primogeniture portion.[18]

If the estate owes debts, the firstborn must pay a double portion of

15. For example, there are 5 acres of land that Yaakov owned when he died. The land was not divided among Ruven, the firstborn and the other three brothers, Shimon, Levi, and Yehudah until the there were improvements to the land which improvements were not part of the primogeniture portion. Each acre was worth $100 on the date of Yaakov's death. Each acre is now worth $110. The land is divided into five parcels (n+4) and Ruven receives two parcels. Those two parcels are worth $220. However, Ruven is not entitled to the improvements on the second parcel that is his primogeniture portion. He thus has to return $10 to be divided among all four brothers, including himself.

16. The reason is that the firstborn has a vested interest in the primogeniture portion even before the division of the property is made.

17. These witnesses need not be qualified witnesses as required in Volume I, Chapters 33, 34, and 35.

18. In each situation it is for beth din to determine the adequacy of the protest.

the debt as compared to the portion paid by the other sons. If the firstborn waives his primogeniture portion,[19] he need pay only the same portion of the debt as any other son.[20]

19. The firstborn owes money to Moshe, his creditor, and does not have sufficient funds to pay Moshe if the firstborn takes only a regular portion. However, if the firstborn takes his primogeniture portion, there will be enough money to pay Moshe. Moshe cannot collect his debt from the other portion if the firstborn waives such portion.

20. There is a difference of opinion as to whether an heir who is not a firstborn can waive his inheritance and avoid paying his father's debts to the extent of the inheritance.

Chapter 279

DECLARING WHO ARE AND WHO ARE NOT HIS HEIRS

INTRODUCTION

In Chapter 277 there is a section entitled "Proof that one is a firstborn." Regarding the firstborn there are times when the doctor (or midwife), the mother, or the father are believed to state who is the firstborn. This chapter discusses the general rule that one is believed when he makes a declaration as to who are his heirs or who are not his heirs. Thus if the decedent dies intestate (without a will), the person he names will or will not share in the estate of the declarant depending upon the law as stated below.

This chapter also discusses the topic whether a person who declared who or who are not his heirs may now recant the former declaration. The laws as stated in the Talmud incorporate over two thousand years of precedent and sometimes speak of slaves owned by the declarant. I have omitted these references to slaves and handmaidens stated in *Shulhan Aruch*. In the section dealing with recantation of former declarations, I have changed the references dealing with slaves to that of servant.

These declarations are made by a person who eventually dies intestate so that the person or persons named may be the sole heir or be included in the class of inheriting heirs of the declarant. This may be true even though when the declaration is made the person named was not a person who would otherwise inherit.[1]

(Yaakov is designated herein as the declarant of who are his heirs.)

TEXT

A person is believed when he states who his heirs are

Yaakov declares that Ruven is his son, or that Aharon is his brother, or that Moshe and Yehoshua are his cousins or have some other relationship. The person whom he names is a person who will inherit if Yaakov dies intestate according to the laws of intestacy in Chapter 276. The declaration of Yaakov is given full credence by beth din and such person will be an heir of Yaakov. This holds true even if it is not generally known that such person is so related to Yaakov; it holds true whether Yaakov so states when he is on his death bed or *halachikly* healthy.[2] The declaration may be in writing or he may make his intent known by nodding in response to a question put to him whether a certain person is his son or other relative.

His declaration applies to all his assets when he made the declaration and to assets that he later will acquire.[3] There is a strong line of authorities that this last sentence holds true only if the declared person as an heir is a son of Yaakov. However, if the declared person is a relative other than the son of the declarant, then he shares only those assets that were owned by Yaakov when he made the declaration.[4]

---

1. Yaakov has two sons, Ruven and Shimon. Yaakov declares that Levi is also his son. When Yaakov dies, Ruven, Shimon, and Levi inherit from him. Or Yaakov, who has a son, Ruven, makes a declaration naming Aharon as his brother from his father Isaac. Ruven predeceases Yaakov, leaving no offspring. Yaakov's father Isaac, predeceased Yaakov, leaving a known son, Pinchas. Pinchas and Aharon share Yaakov's estate.

2. See Volume VII, Chapter 250 for definitions of these terms.

3. It even applies to assets that he thereafter acquires while he is in a coma before he dies.

4. Assume that all of the facts stated in this note can be proved in beth din. Yaakov, on January 1, declares that Ruven is his brother from his father, Isaac. Isaac has two other known sons, Shimon and Levi, and if not for Yaakov's declaration, it was not

A person is believed when he states that a person is not his son

Yaakov is believed when he declares that Ruven, a person assumed by the community to be his son, is not his son; neither Ruven nor Ruven's son will share in the inheritance of Yaakov's estate.[5] However, if Ruven predeceases Yaakov, then Ruven's son will be an heir of Yaakov, since Ruven's declaration is not given credence when it applies to anyone other than his assumed son.

Yaakov states that a person who is not his brother or cousin, or other relative, his statement is not given credence, if it was assumed by all that such person was his brother or his cousin or other relative.

Recanting of a declaration regarding heirs

On January 1, Yaakov declared that Ruven was his son. On January 15,[6] Yaakov declares that Ruven is not his son, but is his servant.[7] Ruven's declaration of January 15 is not given any credence and Ruven is deemed to be his son for the purposes of inheriting from Yaakov.[8]

---

known that Ruven is Isaac's son. On January 1, Yaakov had assets worth $1,000. He thereafter on March 1 acquired assets of $500, making a total of $1,500 in assets that he possessed on April 1, the day of his death. Yaakov has no children or other descendants surviving him, and Isaac also predeceased him. Yaakov's estate is inherited by Isaac's sons. According to this view, Ruven would receive $333.33 or one-third of the assets owned by Yaakov on January 1, the date of the declaration; the other $666.67 is divided between Shimon and Levi. Ruven does not share in the other $500 since it was not owned by Yaakov on January 1. The $500 will be divided between Shimon and Levi.

5. Yaakov's statement that Ruven is not his son can be used only to defeat Ruven's right to inherit from Yaakov. It has no bearing upon the legitimacy of Ruven as a son of Yaakov for other purposes. Such a declaration by Yaakov cannot establish Ruven as an illegitimate son.

6. I purposely selected a time later than the original declaration. For had the recanting declaration been made within "a moment" of the first declaration, the latter declaration would have been given credence. There is a dissent that even within a moment Yaakov cannot recant. See Glossary for definition of "a moment."

7. Yaakov is not believed even if he gives a reason such as that he loves his servant so much that he refers to him as his son.

8. This in spite of the fact that Ruven performs those services usually performed by a servant.

However, if on January 1, Yaakov declares that Ruven is his servant and on January 15, he declares that Ruven is his son, his January 15 declaration is given credence by beth din.[9] Beth din must weigh all of the factors, for example, Ruven was always called the servant, the son of a handmaid.

Yaakov, while passing through customs or immigration authorities declares that Ruven is his son. Sometime later he declares that Ruven is his servant. His later declaration is believed since he obviously made the prior declaration to get Ruven through customs or immigration authorities, who permitted sons but not servants to accompany their fathers. The converse does not hold true. If Yaakov at the customs or immigration authorities declared that Ruven was his servant, and sometime thereafter declared that Ruven was his son, his second declaration is not given credence.[10]

9. This in spite of the fact that Ruven performs those services usually performed by a servant.

10. This law seems to contradict the law of the prior paragraph. In this case, however, the earlier declaration made in the presence of the customs authorities was a declaration made against his interest and would not have been made if not true.

Chapter 280

DOUBTFUL HEIRS

INTRODUCTION

Rabbi Yosef Karo calls this chapter "One [brother] Says 'He Is Our Brother'; Or Someone Comes Forward And Says 'I Am Your Brother.'" In Chapter 276 there is set forth a chart of the first twenty-eight categories of heirs of the decedent. It is stated there, "The heirs of the decedent Ruven inherit in the order set forth in the following list, always recognizing that the next category comes into effect only if there is no one to inherit under the category before it." Rabbi Karo in the title of this chapter deals with category 1, the sons of the decedent. But the results are the same regardless of the category of heirs.

Actually, this chapter also includes other situations that deal with the same types of legal problem, doubts as to who are the heirs of the decedent. The title given by Rabbi Karo indicates that there are those who are known as the sons of the decedent, and another person puts himself forward to also being a son of the decedent. There is a doubt as to the legitimacy of the claimant being an heir of the decedent. If the claimant is actually a son, the original division of assets will be rescinded and a new division will be made including the claimant.[1]

1. See Volume V, page 245, where it is stated:

Partition made in error

Unbeknownst to Ruven, Shimon, and Levi, Jacob left another son named Naftali. After a partition has been completed and the three brothers each

This chapter deals with four classes of doubts: (1) The doubt mentioned by Rabbi Karo in the title to this chapter, namely, is this claimant a legitimate heir of the decedent in the category of the other known heirs? (2) Is this person a male and therefore entitled to inherit? (3) Is the legitimate heir alive at the time of the decedent's death? (4) Did the heir die before the decedent?

Class (1): Is this person a legitimate heir? Ruven is designated the decedent in this chapter and leaves surviving him two sons, Shimon and Dan. They will inherit the entire estate of Ruven, even if Ruven left daughters surviving him.[2] However, another person, Levi, presents himself before beth din and claims that he too is a son of Ruven and therefore he is a brother of Shimon and Dan and he should receive a one-third interest in Ruven's estate. Assume that Shimon acknowledges Levi to be a brother. Dan has three alternatives open to him. (i) He may also acknowledge that Levi is his brother and since there is full agreement among Shimon, Dan, and Levi, there need not be a lawsuit to determine the heirs of Ruven. Or (ii) Dan may plead that he is in doubt whether or not Levi is his brother. Or (iii) Dan may plead that he is certain that Levi is not a son of Ruven. This chapter has two sections dealing with these last two alternatives of Dan's pleas, entitled "One heir denies knowledge of the claimant's claim" and "One heir denies the claimant's claim."

Class (2): Is the heir a male? Since the chapter deals with the doubts created by a person who may or may not be the legal brother of Shimon and Dan, it also deals with other doubts regarding a third person, not because there is any doubt that this third person is a child of Ruven, but rather whether he is a son. Most people are either male or female. The *halachah* recognizes other classes of human beings, the *toomtoom*[3] and the hermaphrodite. The former is a person whose sex is not apparent, and thus there is no certainty whether he is a male

---

operates his own part that he received on partition, Naftali appears on the scene and convinces beth din that he is indeed another son of Jacob. The original partition is rescinded, whether it was by agreement among the brothers or by casting of lots. Even if Naftali agrees to take a small part from each brother, any of the brothers can have the original partition rescinded and the property re-partitioned in four parcels. The law is the same in all situations where the original partition was made in error.

2. See Chapter 276.

3. See Chapter 277, note 7, for definition of *toomtoom*. Briefly, a *toomtoom* is one

and therefore he will not be able to be included in any class of males, such as the sons of Ruven in this situation.The hermaphrodite has the external features of both a male and a female; this person may also not be included in the class of those who are certainly males. The results will not be the same if the class of heirs are not males but rather females, such as the daughters of the decedent Ruven or his aunts, category 22 on the chart in Chapter 276.

In class (1) there is no doubt as to the claimant's (Levi's), sex, but there is a doubt as to his being a son of Ruven; in class (2) there is no doubt that the person is a child of Ruven; the doubt is what this person's sex is. Regarding class (1) the question is whether or not Levi is an heir of Ruven. The law is the same for every category, whether category 1, the sons of the decedent or, for example, category 8, the brothers of the decedent, or 28, the female descendants of the female descendants of the aunt of the decedent. However, regarding class (2), dealing with the sex of the child of Ruven, there may sometimes be a difference whether the category of heirs is that of males or females.

Class (3): Is the heir alive when the decedent dies? One example would be when Ruven dies and leaves no sons nor issue from sons, but he had an only daughter who went overseas and has not been heard from in a long time. If she is alive, then she is the sole heir; if she is dead, then Ruven's father is his heir. This doubt is also included in the section entitled "Doubt if the heir is alive."

Class (4): Who died first? This doubt deals with the situation where the decedent and a person who may be his heir died in what appears to be a simultaneous disaster. For example, the decedent and the first level of heir died in what appears to be a simultaneous occurrence and it is not known who died first. If the decedent died first, then the heir inherits the estate; if the heir died first, then the decedent's next category of heirs inherits the estate. This doubt is discussed below in the section entitled "Simultaneous deaths."

In Chapter 279, the person who dies leaving assets makes a declaration regarding who are and who are not heirs, something that he does not do in this chapter as it relates to Levi.

Does beth din have any presumptions when claims arise in these types of situations?

---

whose sex cannot be determined without an operation. On the other hand, a hermaphrodite has the outward signs of both sexes.

TEXT

Presumption regarding heirs

The general principle regarding heirs is that when an estate is to be divided, and if there are presumed heirs and doubtful heirs, those who are presumed to be heirs divide the estate and those who are only doubtful heirs do not receive anything. The presumption can arise when at least two witnesses testify before beth din that they know it as a fact or it was known to them and to the members of the community at large for a prolonged period of time that Shimon and Dan are the sons of Ruven.[4] Thus Shimon and Dan have inherited or are about to inherit their father Ruven's estate. Levi appears on the scene and pleads that he is also a son of Ruven, and therefore entitled to his share of Ruven's estate; Levi produces no proof or testimony to buttress his claim. Shimon and Dan plead that they do not recognize Levi to be a son of Ruven. The claim of Levi will be dismissed.

In those situations where it is not known whether Ruven had any heirs and now Levi and Yehudah claim that they are the sons of Ruven,[5] since both are doubtful heirs of the same category, they divide the estate.[6]

One heir denies knowledge of the claimant's claim

Ruven dies and Shimon and Dan are proven or reputed to be his sons. The community has no information one way or the other if Ruven left other sons. Levi arrives on the scene and claims that he is also a son of Ruven and demands to receive a one-third share of the estate of Ruven. Shimon acknowledges Levi to be a brother but Dan denies any knowledge whether Levi is a son of Ruven.[7] Dan receives one half of

4. As stated in the Introduction above, the same holds true in every category of heirs.

5. They could both have claimed that they were uncles of Ruven, if that is the earliest category of heirs to inherit Ruven.

6. It goes without saying that beth din will have to be convinced that these two persons are the heirs of Ruven for them to divide Ruven's estate.

7. Levi can compel Dan to take an oath that he really does not have any knowledge whether Levi is a son of Ruven.

Ruven's estate, Shimon receives one-third of the estate,[8] and Levi receives one-sixth of Ruven's estate.[9]

Thereafter Levi dies and leaves no children or other issue, and his father Ruven died before him resulting in his brothers Shimon and Dan (his father's sons) being his heirs. Assume that Levi, when he dies, still has the assets, the one-sixth that he received from Ruven's estate, or other assets that can be traced back to the assets that Levi inherited from Ruven.[10] Such assets are first returned to Shimon.[11] Then Shimon and Dan divide the balance of Levi's assets equally.[12]

Assume that when Levi dies, leaving no issue, he no longer has the assets that he inherited from Ruven nor can assets that he possesses when he dies be traced directly to assets that he inherited from Ruven.[13] One line of authorities holds that Levi's assets are divided equally between Shimon and Dan. Another line of authorities holds that Shimon receives a share of Levi's estate equal to the value of what he relinquished to Levi originally (one-sixth of Ruven's estate) and then Shimon and Dan share the balance of Levi's estate equally.

One heir denies the claimant's claim

Dan, instead of denying knowledge whether Levi is an heir of Ruven as in the prior section, pleads that he is certain that Levi is not an heir of Ruven.[14] Shimon admits that Levi is a son of Ruven. Dan receives one-half of Ruven's estate, Shimon receives one-third, and Levi receives one-sixth.

---

8. Shimon receives one-third because he acknowledges that there are three brothers to share the estate.

9. Levi receives one-half of that which Shimon acknowledges to be Levi's rightful part of the estate.

10. Beth din will determine if such assets are traceable to that which Levi inherited from Ruven.

11. Regarding improvements to those assets, if the improvements came about through Levi's efforts, they are deemed not to be part of what Levi inherited from Ruven. Beth din will have to determine who is entitled to such improvements.

12. Shimon admits that Levi is a brother to both Shimon and Dan. Therefore Dan shares in Levi's assets when Levi dies without issue.

13. In those cases where it is not clear to beth din if any of the currently owned assets of Levi are traceable to that which Levi inherited from Ruven, such doubt should be resolved in favor of Shimon.

14. Levi can insist that Dan take an oath that he is certain that Levi is not a son of Ruven.

If Levi dies leaving no issue, Shimon is his sole heir and Dan receives nothing from Levi's estate.[15]

Is the heir a male?

Ruven dies and leaves a son Shimon and also a *toomtoom* or a hermaphrodite. Shimon inherits the entire estate since he is surely a male, while the *toomtoom* or the hermaphrodite may or may not be a male. But if Ruven left no sons but just a daughter, Sarah, and a *toomtoom* or a hermaphrodite, Sarah and the *toomtoom* or the hermaphrodite equally[16] share the estate.[17]

If a man dies leaving both sons and daughters,[18] the sons inherit all of the estate and they must maintain their sisters until each sister reaches her majority[19] or becomes betrothed.[20] This only applies if the estate is ample, that is, there are enough assets sufficient to provide maintenance for both the sons and daughters until the last daughter reaches her majority. Ruven dies and leaves surviving him sons, daughters, and a *toomtoom* (or a hermaphrodite). (a) Assume the estate is ample. The sons inherit the assets of the estate, and the *toomtoom* is relegated to the class of the daughters to be supplied with maintenance until the *toomtoom* reaches majority.[21] (b) Assume that the estate is not an ample one. The daughters relegate the

15. This assumes that Levi left no closer relatives than his brothers.

16. There is an opinion that the *toomtoom* or the hermaphrodite inherits three-fourths and Sarah one-quarter. But this is a minority view that is generally not accepted.

17. The result is the same regardless of the number of definite heirs and the level of inheritance. Thus if Ruven left no sons or daughters and his father predeceased him, but he had brothers, Aharon and Moshe, and another member of his family was a *toomtoom* or a hermaphrodite, the brothers inherit all and the *toomtoom* or hermaphrodite inherits nothing. But if Ruven left no brothers but did have sisters, Sarah, Rivkah, and Leah, and a *toomtoom* or a hermaphrodite, Sarah, Rivkah, Leah and the *toomtoom* or hermaphrodite each receives one-fourth of the estate.

18. Assume he left no widow, since her rights may have priority.

19. That is, each is maintained until she reaches the age of 12 years, 6 months, and 1 day. (She reaches her majority at the age of 12 years and 1 day.)

20. See *Shulhan Aruch Eben haEzer*, Chapter 112.

21. I have not seen any commentaries on this point but I assume until the *toomtoom* reaches the age of 12 years, 6 months, and 1 day, rather than 13 years and 1 day, the age when a male reaches his majority.

toomtoom to the sons and the *toomtoom* does not share in the maintenance of the daughters.

Doubt if the inheriting heir is alive

Ruven dies and leaves no sons surviving him. Ruven is known to have an only child, a daughter, Sarah. Sarah went abroad many years ago and it is not known if she is alive. Ruven left a father, Yaakov, surviving him. If Sarah is not alive when Ruven dies, Yaakov is Ruven's heir. There is a presumption before beth din that Sarah is alive. Sarah is a definite heir of Ruven and unless it can be shown otherwise, beth din will presume that since Sarah was alive when she went abroad, she is still alive now. Yaakov is only a doubtful heir, depending upon whether or not Sarah is alive. Yaakov receives nothing and beth din holds the assets or appoints a conservator to conserve the assets. This follows what was stated above: "The general principle regarding heirs is that those who are presumed to be heirs divide the estate and those who are only doubtful heirs do not receive anything."

However, if Sarah was married to Naftali and she and Naftali went abroad and it is known that they died before Ruven, Sarah having died first, but it is not known if Sarah had any children, such children, if any, are doubtful heirs of Ruven; Yaakov, Ruven's father, is now a definite heir because he inherits from Ruven. Yaakov will inherit the assets of Ruven. Should issue of Sarah appear, then they will displace Yaakov as Ruven's heir and retrieve from Yaakov that which he inherited from Ruven.

Simultaneous deaths

Ruven is married to Sarah and they have a son, Shlomo. Sarah dies and Ruven marries Leah, who has assets of her own, and they have a son, David. Then Ruven dies. Leah and David perish in an automobile accident, and it is not known who, if either of them, died first. Shlomo, who is the closest heir of David, being his brother by a common father, Ruven, pleads that Leah died first and thus David inherited the assets of Leah; in turn, Shlomo inherits the assets of David. The heirs of Leah, such as her father, Pinchas pleads that David died first so that Leah's heir is Pinchas. The heirs of Leah will prevail since her assets belong to her estate until it can be proved otherwise, and Pinchas is certainly her heir. The heirs of David will not prevail because at best there is a doubt whether David survived Leah.

A similar situation will prevail if Ruven and his only child, his daughter, Penina, who is married to Aryeh, died in an automobile accident. The father of Ruven pleads that Penina died first and therefore he, the father, is Ruven's heir. Aryeh pleads that Ruven died first and thus Penina inherited the assets of Ruven, and Aryeh inherited the assets from her. The father of Ruven will inherit Ruven's assets, since the assets are presumed to remain where they were before, in the estate of Ruven. Thus his heirs, in this case, the father, inherit the assets, and Aryeh is considered to be a doubtful heir of Ruven.[22]

Yosef, who has considerable assets, has an only son, Asher. Asher owed money to Benjamin, and could not pay the debt. Yosef and Asher died in a plane crash and it is not known who, if either of them, died first. Benjamin pleads that Yosef died first so that Asher inherited Yosef's assets and now the estate of Yosef can pay Benjamin the debt owed to him. The other heirs of Yosef plead that Asher died first so that Yosef did not inherit from him and they, the other heirs, inherit from Yosef and Benjamin gets nothing. The other heirs of Yosef prevail since the money is in his estate and there is no proof to give the moneys to Asher.

22. Maimonides makes an exception to the law as stated in the text, and his view seems to be a minority view and is limited to the facts of the case of which he writes (*Laws of Inheritance*, chapter 5, law 7). A house collapsed on Yaakov and his daughter Sarah's son, Levi, and it is not known who died first in this occurrence. (Sarah had died sometime before.) If the grandfather Yaakov died first, then Levi is his heir and the heirs of Levi inherit Yaakov's estate. If Levi died first, Yaakov's estate belongs to Yaakov's heirs. Maimonides ruled that the estate of Yaakov is to be divided equally between the heirs of Levi and the heirs of Yaakov.

Chapter 281

DEVIATIONS IN NAMING BENEFICIARIES

INTRODUCTION

In Chapter 276 there are set forth the categories of natural heirs;[1] in Volume VII, Chapter 257 there is set forth a method of how a person may write a will that the *halacha* will recognize. The *halachik* will is framed in language of a gift and therefore need not comply with the laws of Chapter 276 (but the person is faced with the admonitions contained in Chapter 282).

The current chapter deals with those situations where a person writes a will, using only terms of a bequest or devise, and states how he wants his assets to be distributed after his death rather than stating that he wants his assets to be given as a gift to certain persons after he dies. Had he used terms of gift, then the provisions of this Chapter 281 do not apply to him. Using terms of bequest rather than terms of gift, he divides his estate among persons, some or all of whom may not be his natural heirs, or he divides his estate among his natural heirs in proportions other than those stated in Chapter 276, or leaves all of his

1. By "natural heir" is meant a person who would inherit the decedent if he died intestate, that is, without a will drawn, or without having made gifts, including gifts made in contemplation of death.

estate to less than all of his natural heirs, or he divides his estate neglecting to provide for his firstborn son in accordance with the laws of primogeniture. Is such a written document, or oral will where permitted, valid according to *halachah*? How much may a person deviate from the intestate order set forth in Chapter 276? Since most wills contain language of gift, such as "I hereby give, devise and bequeath," the applicability of this chapter is limited.

The laws of inheritance are specifically stated in the Torah and thus may not be tampered with. A person drafting a will must consider whether there is a Torah proscription against his wishes that will make his will ineffective.

The sequence of sections are: (i) that non-natural heirs may not be named as beneficiaries in a will; (ii) that one may not specifically disinherit or limit natural heirs in a will; (iii) the language that may be used to limit or to enlarge the bequest to a natural heir, (this (iii) differs from (ii) above where the declarant wants to cut a natural heir out of the will), while in this section (iii) the declarant wants to include all the natural heirs except that their shares would differ; in this the language is crucial; (iv) the declarant wants to limit which of his natural heirs shall inherit him, which declaration must conform to the valid language in (iii); (v) how the foregoing limitations apply to the firstborn male; and (vi) the applicability of the foregoing laws dealing with constraints imposed on the declarant.

"Yaakov" is designated as the testator, the one who writes the will. "Ruven" is designated usually as the son. When the son is a firstborn son, he is designated as "David."

TEXT

Non-natural heirs may not be named as beneficiaries in a will

The testator may at any time rescind or modify his will. Thus he may change his will provided that it conforms to the provisions of this chapter.

Yaakov, the testator, may not in his will name persons who are not his natural heirs as beneficiaries. The testator may not deviate from the intestacy progressions set out in the Torah and set forth in Chapter 276; all such deviations are of no effect. (If the assets are to be given as gifts to a non-natural heir, the proscriptions of this chapter do not apply.)

One may not specifically disinherit or limit natural heirs in a will

Yaakov, the testator, may not in his will specifically state that: (i) "Sarah, my daughter," a natural heir,[2] "shall not inherit me", (ii) "My firstborn son, David, shall not receive his primogeniture share."[3]

Language limiting or enlarging a bequest to a natural heir

The language of the declarant is determinative of whether or not the declaration in the will is effective. To be effective it must (i) be stated in the positive and (ii) specify the amount or percentage of the bequest. Some examples included in the codes are:

"My son Ruven shall inherit 50 percent of my estate and the other sons shall inherit the other 50 percent." This is a valid bequest since Ruven's bequest is stated in the positive and specifies the amount of the bequest.

"My son Ruven shall not inherit except 30 percent." This is not a valid bequest since it is couched in the negative regarding the bequest.

"Ruven my son shall inherit his portion of my estate and the portion of Shimon." This is not a valid bequest to Ruven regarding the portion of Shimon because the portion of Shimon is named as belonging to Shimon.

"Shimon shall not inherit but only Ruven." This is not a valid

2. Yaakov not having any sons, only daughters, including Sarah; or only one daughter Sarah.

3. Some of the examples given in the codes are "Ruven, my firstborn son, shall not receive his primogeniture share"; or, "Shimon my son shall not inherit me together with his brothers"; or, "My daughter shall inherit me" when he has a son; or, "My brother shall inherit me" when he has a daughter; or, "Gideon, [a nonrelative] shall inherit me" when Yaakov has a brother; or if he names anyone other than the persons who are of the first category eligible to inherit him.

bequest since the bequest to Ruven was not stated in the positive, nor was Shimon disinherited since regarding him it was stated in the negative.

"My son Ruven shall inherit me[4] and not Shimon." This is a valid bequest to Ruven since it is stated in the positive regarding Ruven and specifies the amount of the bequest.

"My son Shimon shall not inherit me, but Ruven shall inherit all of my estate." This is a valid bequest since it is in the positive and specific; but as to Shimon it is negative.

There is an opinion that all such deviations to be valid must be declared during the daytime[5] before beth din.

One may limit which of his natural heirs shall be his beneficiaries

Yaakov may specify that some or even one of his natural heirs be his beneficiaries. Thus if his natural heirs are his daughters[6], Sarah, Rivkah, Rachel, and Leah, Yaakov may state, "Sarah and Leah shall inherit me," or, "Rachel shall inherit me." These statements are declared in the positive and thus the natural heirs, while omitted as beneficiaries, are not specifically excluded as beneficiaries.

The limits may be stated as percentages or fractions of the estate that the natural beneficiaries will receive and still be effective. Thus in the prior paragraph[7] Yaakov writes in his will, "I bequeath to Sarah 50 percent of my estate and 30 percent to Leah and 20 percent to Rivkah."[8] Since this is all written in the positive, the will is valid.

There is an exception to this procedure as stated in Volume VII, Chapter 246. If the person making a written will[9] states that all of his

4. Or Yaakov states, "My son Ruven shall inherit all of my assets, and not Shimon."

5. See Volume I, page 41.

6. Yaakov had no sons.

7. By the laws of intestacy, Sarah, Rivkah, Leah, and Rachel should each inherit 25 percent of the estate.

8. Or Yaakov can write, "I bequeath 50 percent of my estate to Sarah and the balance to be divided among my other daughters."

9. If the bequest is an oral one, such as by a person giving a gift in contemplation of death, then the bequest is valid even if given only to one son.

assets are to be given to one son, then that son is deemed a trustee for all of the heirs.[10]

The bequest to the firstborn son may not be limited

All of the aforestated limitations do not apply to the firstborn son, David. Yaakov cannot declare any bequest involving David that provides that David shall receive less than his primogenitor portion, or shall receive the same portion as the other brothers.[11]

The foregoing applies even if there is some local custom that the firstborn male does not receive a full primogeniture portion. The local custom is to be disregarded.

There is an opinion that if Yaakov bequeathed more than an equal share to one of the brothers who is not a firstborn, this is not a valid bequest, since this will diminish the primogeniture portion of the firstborn son. There is an opinion that such a bequest is nonetheless valid, and all of the brothers will have to give up a proportionate amount of what they inherited to give to the firstborn son to make up his double portion in his father's estate. There is an opinion that a non-firstborn cannot be given a double portion even if that does not detract from the double portion given to the firstborn.[12]

Applicability of the foregoing laws limiting the declarant

All that has been said above restricting the ability of the declarant to make certain bequests applies only to wills or declarations in the nature of a will. As is seen in Volume VI, Chapters 250 and 257, gifts can be made that deviate from the sequence of intestate inheritance. The declarant may increase the gift to one and decrease to another, he may vary the gift to any of the natural heirs including the firstborn son, he may omit to give them a gift or give a gift to a person who is not

10. See Volume VII, page 141.

11. Yaakov can by gift give away his assets to others so that David, his firstborn son, will not receive his primogeniture portion. Yaakov cannot do this by a will.

12. For example, Yaakov has five sons, including David his firstborn son. Thus David should receive one-third (2 portions of 6, n+1=6). Yaakov can provide that David receive two-sixths and that Ruven receive two-sixths, and that the other one-third be divided among the other three sons.

a natural heir. A person may give a gift of all of his assets to non-natural heirs and completely leave out his natural heirs, since this is not an inheritance but rather a gift. This may be a gift *causa mortis* or the gift of a healthy person made binding with a *kinyan*. There are times that the language of the gift is interspersed with words that make it seem like a will. Beth din should attempt to construe the declaration to be a gift if the declarant used words of gift,[13] although he also used words of bequest.

Sometimes the declarant is ambiguous in his choice of words and they can be construed as either a gift or a bequest after death. If the former, all of the laws of intestacy do not apply; if the latter, then all of the laws of these chapters do apply. Beth din will have to examine the exact words and determine what was the intent of the declarant. Local usage will aid beth din.

The codes emphasize that the natural heir is not disinherited unless the language of the declarant leaves nothing to be disposed of to such heirs. But if the declarant by gift did not dispose of all of his assets, the non-disposed-of assets will be divided by the natural heirs in accordance with the laws of Chapter 276. For example, Yaakov, the declarant had a nephew, Ruven, his sole natural heir, and a niece, Sarah. Yaakov gave a gift for a certain sum to Ruven, and said this gift was to be given to Ruven in lieu of all rights Ruven may have in Yaakov's estate. Yaakov died without disposing of his other assets. It was held that Ruven will obtain the balance of Yaakov's estate since he is still Yaakov's heir, although it was obvious that Yaakov wished that his niece would inherit the balance.

There is a major practical difference between a valid gift and a bequest. If the gift is valid, then creditors of the donor[14] cannot seek their payment from the gift if there are no assets in the estate to pay the debt. If the declaration, whether written or oral, is construed to be a will, then the creditors can obtain their moneys from the estate of the debtor.

13. Although the codes give examples of what can be construed by beth din to be words of gift, I have omitted such references, since each beth din will have to construe the words according to its then local usage.

14. The donor's wife is also a creditor to the extent of her *kethubah*. See Glossary for definition of *kethubah*.

Chapter 282

A PERSON SHOULD NOT DEVIATE FROM THE TORAH LAWS OF DESCENT

INTRODUCTION

Caveat: All that is said in this chapter permitting certain deviations from the laws set forth in Chapter 276 is not to be done in the first instance.

Thus the fact that the wills and certainly the gifts made by the declarant, Yaakov, that deviate from the laws of Chapter 276 are valid does not mean that it should be done. If anything the Torah scheme of distribution of assets should be followed where possible. There are exceptions for charity.

A person is given a power of appointment in a will; may he deviate from the Torah laws of intestacy as regards the heirs of the testator?

TEXT

Not to deviate from the laws of intestacy

When a person disposes of his assets other than as is stated in the Torah laws of intestacy, although such gifts and some such bequests are valid, the Sages of Israel are displeased with such actions. This applies even if it transfers the bequest from a son who is not of a high moral quality to a son who is a great sage and pious.

There are authorities that hold that the statement of the prior paragraph applies only if the declarant had sons, but that if he had no sons, then the declarant may dispose of his assets as he pleases. Most authorities, however, hold that the law of the prior paragraph applies to all heirs.

It is the characteristic of a pious person that he will not be a witness to a will that bequeaths assets other than as is stated in the Torah laws of intestacy.

Maimonides writes,[1] "The Sages have decreed that a person, during his lifetime, should not make a distinction between his sons, even regarding minor matters, in order that there should not be any jealousy even as was the situation of Joseph and his brothers."[2]

Exceptions for charity

All that has been said in the prior section does not apply if the gift or bequest is to charity.

This is especially true if the charity will perpetuate the memory of the decedent by enshrining his name on a plaque and will commemorate the anniversary date of death of the decedent.

The declarant may and under certain circumstances should deviate if, for example, his closest natural heirs are all wealthy and he has a more distant category of heirs who are poor.

Powers of appointment

Yaakov, in his will, states that his assets should be disposed of as his friend Menachem shall deem best. Menachem should dispose of Yaakov's assets as set forth in the Torah laws of instestacy.[3]

However, if it is obvious to beth din that the intent of Yaakov was for Menachem to distribute the assets to others, he should be permitted to do so.

1. Maimonides, *Laws of Inheritance*, chapter 6, law 13.
2. See *Genesis*, chapter 37.
3. Since the Torah set up these laws of descent, this is obviously the best.

Chapter 283

INHERITANCES OF GENTILES, PROSELYTES, AND APOSTATES

INTRODUCTION

All that has been said in the previous chapters applies when the testator is Jewish. Assume that beth din has control of the judicial system of a community or the nation of Israel and the Gentiles living within its confines are subject to the *halachah*.

Or assume a situation where a person who was born Jewish, and is therefore always recognized as a Jew by *halachah*, converts out of Judaism to another religion. Leaving aside voluntary conversions by such apostate Jews to other religions, there were and still are many instances where Jews are forcibly converted.

Regarding the proselyte, there is already a chapter devoted to the property of a proselyte who dies without heirs, Chapter 275. This chapter discusses the relationship between the proselyte and his parents who are not Jewish. Assuming that under the laws of the land he would inherit from his father, does the proselyte inherit from his father according to *halachah*?

TEXT

A Gentile wishes to bequeath his assets

According to *halachah*, a Gentile, Timothy, inherits from his father, Christopher, according to their customs. Thus, if the Gentile is a Christian, he would conceivably follow the canon law of his particular denomination, if any; lacking such laws, he would follow local custom, or in lands where the secular authorities have laws of descent, such laws would be followed.[1]

The proselyte inheriting from his non-Jewish relatives

According to Torah law, a proselyte does not inherit from his non-Jewish relatives.[2] But by Rabbinic decree, a proselyte inherits from his non-Jewish relatives according to the law of the land as if he were a Gentile inheriting from a Gentile.[3] It is to be noted that the law is the same if his relatives also converted. According to Torah law he would not inherit from them since each new convert is legally a newborn person without relatives. The law would be the same if the proselyte has a Jewish father and a Gentile mother. When the son converts he is not related to his father or his mother.

The Gentile is not bound by any of the *halachah* laws of intestacy and may bequeath his assets to whomever he wishes, including the proselyte, in any manner he deems fit. He is not bound by the laws of the last few chapters limiting the authority of a person to bequeath his assets.

In inheriting from his father together with other children of the non-Jew, the proselyte should ask for a division of the father's assets in such a way that the proselyte does not inherit things that are

1. Assume that a Jew owes money to a Gentile who dies. The Jew must pay the money to the heirs of the dead Gentile creditor. This will cause the Gentile to respect the laws of the Jews.

2. The proselyte is considered as a newborn person with no legal ties to his former family, including his father and his mother. The *halachah* does not consider them to be his relatives. See Chapter 275.

3. The reason for the Rabbinic decree is to prevent the proselyte from having second thoughts if he cannot inherit some or all of the assets of his relatives.

prohibited to a Jew, such as non-Jewish religious objects, or non-Jewish wine.

The Gentile does not inherit from his proselyte relative, such as a Christian not inheriting from his father who became a proselyte. Nor does a proselyte inherit from a proselyte.[4] A child born to a proselyte but conceived before the father converted is considered a nonrelative for the purposes of inheritance, even if the child was born to a Jewish mother after the father converted.

The Jewish apostate

An apostate Jew inherits his Jewish relatives. However, beth din may deprive him of his inherited property in order to discourage him from continuing his apostasy. If the apostate's father dies and the apostate has children who are loyal to Judaism, beth din may turn their grandfather's assets over to the grandchildren. If the apostate attempts to circumvent the implementation of the prior sentence by giving a gift to a third person, beth din can void such a gift.

There is an opinion that instead of transferring that which the apostate inherited from his father to his children, the assets should be sequestered in beth din and if he repents, the inheritance should be given to him.

A Jew does inherit from a relative who is an apostate Jew. This holds true even if the assets of the apostate was held by others, including Jews, and even if the apostate had children during the period of his apostasy; they are not his heirs. There is an opinion that if a third person held the money of the apostate Jew and expropriated the money for himself, then the relatives of the apostate Jew cannot recover the money from the third person.

The following incident is related in some of the codes: Leah was kidnapped and her mother collected moneys from members of the community to ransom her. The mother was informed that Leah had become an apostate. It was held that if the mother can return the

4. For example, if a father, Christopher, and his son, Timothy, both non-Jews, converted to Judaism, whether separately or even simultaneously, they are no longer related according to *halachah*, each being a newborn person.

moneys to the contributors, she should do so. If she is not able to return the moneys,[5] then the moneys should be deposited into a fund for ransoming prisoners. The money can be used to ransom Leah if she gives up her apostasy.

5. Some contributions may have been given to her anonymously, or she lost the list of contributors or for some other reason.

Chapter 284

PROOF REQUIRED TO ESTABLISH HEIRSHIP

INTRODUCTION

Chapter 280 discusses some of the problems in establishing whether a person is an heir of the decedent and entitled to inherit all or part of the assets of the decedent. There were certain presumptions based on testimony of witnesses; there may not have been certainty beyond any doubt that this person is the heir of the decedent. The presumptions based on the testimony of the witnesses that they know that for many years the decedent held certain persons out to be his heirs, such as his sons, or his brothers, or sister, or uncles, established such fact before beth din and such person was included as an heir of the decedent. Thus if beth din at the moment feels that the person testified about are the closest heirs, it does not have to delay their decisions and wait to ascertain whether perhaps other heirs of equal degree of closeness or even closer to the decedent will appear.

A situation may arise where two (or more) persons appear before beth din, each claiming that he is the closest heir of the decedent and beth din is not able to decide who should be declared the closest heir. What is the result? What if there is subsequent proof that beth din accepts after they have rendered their decision of not being able to decide?

This chapter also discusses what matters must be proved. Did Yaakov die and thus his assets may be divided among his heirs? Under certain circumstances certain statements that a person died permit his wife to remarry based on such statements but do not permit the heirs to inherit; on the other hand, some statements permit the heirs to inherit but do not permit the wife to remarry.

TEXT

Heirs are usually declared based on presumptions

Beth din, in deciding whether a person claiming to be an heir of the decedent really is an heir and whether he is the closest heir, must rely on testimony of at least two[1] competent witnesses[2] who can only testify as to what they know from their observation over an extended period of time. The witnesses will rarely be the person who attended their birth and saw them grow up as the relative of the decedent that the person claims to be. They will usually testify as to what the community perceived them to be, or as to what the decedent or his other relatives acknowledged to persons in the community, or as to documents that show the relationship of the decedent to the person claiming to be his heir.

Beth din unable to decide if someone is truly an heir

Ruven and Shimon appear before beth din and each one pleads that he is the only brother of Levi, the decedent. Neither offers proof upon which beth din can render a decision. Beth din may decide to leave the parties to adjust the matter between themselves, knowing that the person who is stronger may employ self-help[3] and prevail.[4] If the party who employed self-help to seize some or all of the assets of the

1. The testimony of one witness is not sufficient to establish heirship.
2. See Volume I, Chapters 34, 35, and 36.
3. See Volume I, Chapter 4, regarding self-help.
4. This is not a viable option nowadays when so many of the assets are not personal property that one party can seize to the legal detriment of the other. Most assets, such as bank accounts, real estate, automobiles, stocks and bonds, pension

decedent admits that he is not really the closest heir, or if proof satisfactory to beth din is later produced by either Ruven or Shimon or perhaps by a third party that one of the two is the true heir of the decedent,[5] the assets are returned to beth din and given to the party that beth din now determines is entitled to the assets.[6] The assets must be returned together with any profits made thereon.

There must be proof that the owner of the assets is dead

Ruven, who is known to be the son of Yaakov, appears before beth din and pleads that he is entitled to the assets of Yaakov, since Yaakov died and he, Ruven, is Yaakov's sole heir. Ruven must prove to beth din that Yaakov is dead before beth din can permit Ruven to take to himself the assets of Ruven.

There must be cogent proof by two competent witnesses.[7] The proof that permits Sarah, a married woman, to remarry because it has been testified that her husband, Yaakov, is dead may not be adequate in this case.[8] If the proof of her husband's death is the statement of the wife, she may remarry and collect her *kethubah*, but his heirs cannot

---

funds, and so forth, are registered or stored on computers or in the records of those institutions that hold the assets.

5. The proof need not be that one is the heir and that the other is not an heir. It is sufficient to offer proof that one is an heir.

6. If the other party then proves that he is a closer heir, beth din will take the assets from the first person and transfer them to the second person who is closer to the decedent.

7. The testimony of one witness is not sufficient to establish death of the person.

8. For example, if it was rumored that Sarah's husband was dead, or if a Gentile came and in a casual conversation stated that her husband was dead, or if a person states that he just came from his funeral, or that he killed the husband, to name but a few examples. See Maimonides, *Laws of Divorce*, chapter 13. In all of these situations Sarah may remarry and collect her *kethubah* from the estate of her husband. But her husband's heirs cannot divide his assets based on such testimony or statements. See Glossary for definition of *kethubah*. For the purposes of the woman being able to remarry the Rabbis wanted to avoid preventing her from being forever prohibited to remarry as might be the case if beth din has to wait for adequate proof. However, if she relies on this leniency and does remarry, she takes a major risk, for if her husband was not dead, then she must leave her second husband, her first husband must divorce her, she receives no *kethubah* from either husband, and the children she has from the second marriage are bastards. Therefore the woman will be more demanding of proof that her husband is indeed dead.

inherit his estate. An exception is made if Sarah, the wife, states that based on her statement that after Yaakov, her husband died she entered into a leviratical marriage with her brother-in-law, Shimon, Shimon takes the inheritance of Yaakov based on her statement.

Conversely, there are situations where the heirs can inherit but the wife cannot remarry. For example, witnesses testify that Yaakov went down in endless waters in their presence, and all trace of him was lost, and Yaakov has disappeared, the heirs inherit Yaakov's estate but his wife may not remarry. Or witnesses testify that Yaakov fell into a den of lions or tigers, or that they saw him hanging and birds were eating his flesh, or that he had been murdered but they did not recognize his face but did recognize distinctive marks on his body. The heirs inherit, since for the purpose of inheritance there are two combined factors, Yaakov's disappearance with death a plausible explanation why he has disappeared. This is adequate proof that Yaakov is dead for the purpose of inheritance. But regarding his wife's ability to remarry, there has not been any statement that says that Yaakov is dead; the statements indicate a likelihood that he would be dead. Since the word that Yaakov is "dead" has not been used, his widow Sarah cannot remarry.[9]

9. In the prior paragraph the word "dead" was used to describe Yaakov. In this paragraph there were facts testified to that would tend to show Yaakov is dead, but there is no mention of anyone by rumor or otherwise that Yaakov is dead.

Chapter 285

HEIRSHIP REGARDING CAPTIVES

INTRODUCTION

This chapter continues the topic of the last chapter regarding the proof required so that those who would be the heirs in case of Yaakov's death can take possession of his assets. Yaakov has been missing for a long period of time. Is he dead? If he is not dead, where is he? Should beth din intervene in any of these situations?

In the prior chapter there is a distinction between (i) the situation where it is rumored that Yaakov died, and (ii) the situation where it is testified that he drowned, but his body has not been found. In (i) there is just the rumor and this is not proof; in (ii) there is competent testimony to state a fact from which it can be deduced that it is nearly certain that Yaakov has died, which testimony is coupled with his failure to reappear. In (i) the heirs are not entitled to claim the assets while in (ii) the heirs can claim the assets of Yaakov, who is probably dead.

In this chapter, instead of the missing person having probably drowned, the missing person was taken captive. Once again there must be these two factors present: the disappearance of Yaakov (or Isaac, as defined below) together with facts that tend to show that he may not reappear. It should be remembered that the only consequence is to permit his closest relatives (as defined below) to divide his assets.[1] If the news of Yaakov's demise is premature, beth din can always recover the assets from the heirs who divided them, unless they have been dissipated.

There is a difference if Yaakov's disappearance results from (i) his being captured, kidnapped, or he fled because he was afraid for his life; or (ii) having gone off on his own volition, leaving his assets behind, and without having returned.

Capturing individuals and incarcerating them and killing them has been a scourge of mankind through the ages; for example, being sent to concentration camps and death camps. Who does not know what the consequences are of such incarceration! The current century is the most illustrative of such capturing of individuals and murdering them. Once a person has been placed in such a position, what should be done with his assets? What is said regarding captured persons applies equally to persons who flee their homes due to fear of being arrested and killed without justification, and now have disappeared.

This chapter discusses what is to be done with the assets of the following individuals: (i) a person who is held captive or flees because of danger to his life; (ii) a person who is held captive or flees because of danger to his life, and he is reported dead (but not with the usual requisite proof); and (iii) a person who left on his own volition.

Beth din has several options available to it in these types of situations. (a) It may decide to do nothing, or (b) it may appoint a person to take possession of the personal property and/or real estate of the missing person and conserve them until the further order of beth din (such appointed person is designated as the "conservator"[2]), or (c) it may appoint a person to operate the property, collect the profits and rents of the property of the missing person (such appointed person is designated as the "receiver"), or (d) it may transfer the assets to the closest relatives of the missing person (the persons designated as the "closest relatives" are the same persons who are the natural heirs of the missing person when it is ascertained with

1. This type of proof does not permit Yaakov's wife, Sarah, to remarry. See Chapter 284.

2. The codes use the term "trustworthy person" to describe what is herein designated as the "conservator."

proof that he is dead).[3] The conservator just takes control of the assets, but does not operate the assets for profit; the receiver operates the assets and takes control of the profits and under the control of beth din takes a share as would any manager or sharecropper. The balance is delivered to the conservator for safekeeping or to the owner if he returns. There are times when the conservator or receiver is the closest relative and other times when the closest relative is deliberately not made the conservator or receiver.

The situation where the minor is a conservator or receiver is also discussed. The converse, where the missing person is a minor, is also discussed. There are certain inherent dangers in appointing some persons, especially relatives, as conservators or receivers for a minor. They may later plead that the property[4] belongs to them and base their proof on an alleged purchase or inheritance by them and that they were on the real estate for the requisite period to raise the presumption that they own the property.

The person who is taken captive or flees because his life is in danger is designated as "Yaakov." The person who disappears after leaving on his own volition is designated as "Isaac."

TEXT

Guarding the assets of a captive or one who fled for his life

The ideal situation is that in which beth din, where the assets of a person is taken captive are located, takes all steps necessary to preserve his assets during his absence. Beth din might not give possession of the real estate to a tenant farmer since there is no one to supervise him. He might, if supervised, increase the yield at the expense of the land. Therefore if there is an individual who is willing to act as a guardian of the real estate of the captive, he can lease the real estate to a tenant farmer and supervise him. But a person who will spend so

3. The closest relatives automatically become the natural heirs when the missing person dies. The order of the natural heirs is set forth in Chapter 276.

4. See Volume V, Chapter 140.

much time supervising tenants for a person who is not present is almost impossible to find. Such guardians are seldom appointed even if one can be found. Instead there has evolved the system of laws described below.

Yaakov has been captured and is being held in a prison where the chances of his ever being freed are unlikely because of the nature of his captors, or he has fled his home because the authorities have fabricated some spurious accusations against him and such accusations will result in his being put to death.[5]

Assume there is no rumor or hint that Yaakov is dead.

Beth din must take control of his assets.

The personal property is deposited with a conservator, who may hold it or turn it over to beth din according to the instructions of beth din.

The real estate, such as vacant fields, gardens, vineyards, and the like, is to be transferred to the closest relatives as receivers[6] so that they may cultivate the land and take care of it until Yaakov returns or until it is known if he is dead.

However, the real estate may sometimes consist of growing crops ready to be harvested, or fruit, or grapes ready to be cut, and the like, or houses, stores, hotels, and other real estate, which are designed to be leased for a rental and do not require labor, and are not given out to participants in the operation of the facility. In such instance, beth din takes possession of the land and appoints a receiver of the income (other than a close relative) who harvests the crops, picks the fruit, and sells the produce or fruit; and deposits the money with the conservator appointed by beth din or to beth din, which holds it together with his personal property. If the property is of such a nature that operating it would not cause it to deteriorate, then the real estate is transferred to the closest relatives as receivers upon the same terms as stated in the prior sentence; if not, the nonrelative receiver continues to operate it.[7]

Should Yaakov return, the relatives who possessed the real estate

5. If it is only his money that is in danger, the laws of this chapter do not apply.

6. If there are several closest relatives, some of who are capable of operating the farm or other business, and the other closest relatives are not capable, the ones who are capable of running that farm or business are appointed.

7. The real estate is not transferred to the closest relatives at the outset instead of

have their work appraised in accordance with the local custom of wages paid to sharecroppers regarding real property or as workers regarding other types of property, taking into account the profits they have taken from the land.

Guarding the assets of a captive who is rumored to be dead

Yaakov was taken captive or fled to safe his life, and he is rumored to be dead. The closest relatives (i.e., those who would inherit the estate) may take possession of the real estate and treat the assets of Yaakov as their own.[8]

The missing person who left of his own volition

Isaac, leaving his property behind, voluntarily walked out and traveled to a distant place, far from his home, to a place where there is not much regular traffic,[9] and has disappeared. It is not known where he went or what happened to him. The beth din does not appoint anyone to take care of his property, whether real property or personal property. However, if Isaac's closest relatives take possession of the property, beth din will not remove them.

Assume that Isaac's closest relatives do not take possession of the property. Beth din will permit the personal property to remain in the possession of anyone, including strangers who take possession of it until the owner returns and claims it, or until he dies and his heirs claim it. Regarding real estate, if there is a tenant in a house or on land, the tenant may continue to live there and pays no rent until Isaac

---

to the outside receiver because the relatives might remove the fruit or produce ready to be harvested and use it themselves.

8. There are some authorities who state that if the closest relatives, without permission from beth din, have already taken possession of Yaakov's real estate, they are not dislodged, although they should not have done so in the first instance. However, the prevailing view is that they may take possession and divide the real estate in the first instance.

9. Isaac, traveling to such a remote place, would have left instructions how to manage his assets until he returns. Since he left no instructions, it was apparently his intent that his assets not be supervised. But if he left for a place not far away where he could easily return, his failure to return indicates that he met with an accident.

returns; if a vineyard or a field is in the possession of a tenant farmer, it remains in his possession.[10]

If it is rumored that Isaac is dead, and the closest relatives take possession of his real estate and divide it as their own, they are dislodged from the land until they produce credible proof that Isaac is dead. Pending such proof, beth din takes possession of Isaac's assets. The personal property is placed in the hands of a conservator; the real estate is delivered to the closest relatives who hold it as tenants who share the income until proof is produced that Isaac is dead or until he returns.[11]

The minor as the conservator or receiver

A minor should not be appointed a conservator or receiver as described in this chapter.[12]

The conservator or receiver of the assets of a missing minor

A relative may not be appointed a conservator or a receiver for the real estate[13] of a missing minor.[14] Such relatives may later plead that the real estate is his by stating it was his share of an inheritance. The claim of persons not so appointed is enough to prevent any such person from pleading that the real estate is his by virtue of an inheritance, or gift, or purchase from some prior owner. For example there were two brothers, one an adult and one a minor. The minor was taken captive. The adult may not be a conservator of the minor's real

10. Regarding the tenants in this paragraph, they will pay rent to Isaac if he returns; they will not pay rent to the closest relatives if Isaac does not return and the closest relatives turn out to be Isaac's heirs.

11. In the first sentence of this paragraph the closest relatives took possession of Isaac's assets to keep them for themselves as their own; they are dislodged. In the second sentence beth din delivers the real estate to the closest relatives to act as conservators.

12. A minor may permit the property to deteriorate.

13. There is an opinion that this law applies to any assets of a minor.

14. There is an opinion that this applies where the family is no longer a unit keeping house together. But if they are no longer being supported from the assets of the father, a relative can be appointed to protect the interests of the captive who is a minor.

estate, since the minor cannot make a formal protest, and the adult brother may later plead that the real estate is his since he held it the requisite amount of years without protest from the minor brother. The older brother may plead that he obtained the real estate as part of his own inheritance from their father. Not even the captive's brother's son is to be appointed.

The codes relate the following incident: Sarah, who had three daughters, Rivkah, Rachel, and Leah, was taken captive together with Rivkah. Her second daughter, Rachel, died leaving a minor son, Pinchas. It was held that Leah should not be appointed the receiver of the assets of Sarah, since if Sarah is dead, part of the assets belongs to Pinchas, through his mother Rachel. Pinchas cannot be put into possession of the real estate since it is possible that Sarah is alive, and a minor is not put in charge of a captive's property. Since it is required to appoint a conservator to protect the interests of Pinchas, the same conservator will conserve all of the assets of Sarah.

Chapter 286

ADULTS AND MINORS SHARING AN ESTATE

INTRODUCTION

In Volume VI, it is stated on page 30:

> "When a person dies his heirs are considered constructive partners in a constructive partnership that consists of the assets of the estate, which may include an ongoing business operated by the deceased father. This constructive partnership continues until the assets of the estate are divided."

On page 11, it states:

> "Unless otherwise agreed upon, the partners may take funds from the partnership for their own personal use for clothing, food, and other items until any of the other partners object. Such money taken from the partnership is not deemed part of the share of the partner making such withdrawals."

When the decedent dies and his heirs have not yet divided the estate and certain heirs need more money to meet their demands than do the others, should the estate pay for each of them regardless of his expenses? If the estate is divided, then each heir pays for his own expenses. What if one of the sons of Yaakov makes a wedding for himself and the estate pays for it? May the other brothers demand the same type of wedding? What if the father made a wedding for one son before the father died and then the other sons are to get married after the father dies, does the estate pay for such weddings? It was customary in some communities for the wedding guests to send gifts with the understanding that the gifts will be reciprocated when the giver's family makes a wedding. Usually, the father of the groom would reciprocate the gifts to the giver. The father dies before he can reciprocate gifts that were given to Ruven, who got married while Yaakov was yet alive. After the death of Yaakov, must the estate reciprocate the gifts that were given to Ruven? What about gifts that were given by Yaakov while he was alive and the father of the recipient's groom wants to reciprocate at a wedding of one of Yaakov's heirs? Who gets such gifts, the groom or the estate of Yaakov?

TEXT

The heirs of the decedent make equal withdrawals from the estate

Yaakov dies without leaving a will, and leaves four sons, two adults, Ruven and Shimon; and two minors, Levi and Yehudah.[1] For any variety of reasons, beth din does not at the present time wish to divide the estate and the estate will for some time be operated as a constructive partnership, all of the brothers being supported from the assets of the estate.[2] The older sons, Ruven and Shimon, spend more money on clothes than do Levi and Yehudah, while Levi and Yehudah spend more money on food than do Ruven and Shimon. Assume that they all live in Yaakov's home and there is enough money in the estate to pay their everyday necessities. The *halachah* recognizes two possibilities: (i) If none of the brothers protests, each brother may take as much as he requires for his food, clothing, and other personal

1. The law is the same for any heirs of the same class. Thus the same result would occur if Yaakov dies and leaves no sons, but does leave four daughters, Sarah, Rivkah, Rachel, and Leah. Also, the number four has no significance, but is used for illustrative purposes.
2. See Volume VI, Chapter 177.

items.[3] (ii) If any brother protests, all the brothers share equally in the estate and pay for their own expenses.[4]

Ruven takes a large sum of money for his clothing and Levi and Yehudah, the two minor brothers, protest. Their protest will be recognized by beth din. However, their protest will be disallowed if Ruven is required to be well-groomed and to wear new types of clothing that he wears when he represents the interests of the minor children in dealing with others. In such event Ruven may[5] take a larger share of the estate for his clothing purposes.[6]

Wedding expenses of the heirs

After Yaakov dies, Ruven gets married and pays for the wedding expenses out of the assets of the estate.[7] The other sons, when they get married, may get married in the same manner and style as did Ruven at the expense of the estate.

If the older brothers got married at the expense of Yaakov while Yaakov was still alive, the other brothers cannot, after Yaakov dies, demand that the estate provide similar weddings for them.

Ruven becomes engaged to be married, and his father Yaakov tells him that he will give him a dowry of $1,000 to be paid when he gets married. Yaakov dies before Ruven gets married. The estate is not obligated to pay to Ruven the dowry, unless Yaakov had segregated the $1,000 into a special fund held by an escrowee. Daughters are treated

---

3. It is assumed that if any brother takes more than his proportional share and the others have not protested, the other brothers have waived their right to protest. There is a dissent that holds that silence is not a waiver, and that the brothers who received less than another brother who took a larger share than he was entitled to can always claim such share that is rightfully theirs.

4. The protest is effective even if all of the brothers have reached their legal adulthood of 13 years and 1 day. The protest may be made by a brother who does not reside and share in the daily expenses with the other brothers.

5. Although the *halachah* permits the use of such funds, it admonishes the older brother not to waste the money of the estate on the pretext that his spending is for the benefit of the estate.

6. The *halachah* takes cognizance of the axiom that sometimes clothes make the man.

7. The expenses are those that are customary according to the locality where the wedding takes place, and would usually include clothes, dowry, caterer, hiring of a wedding hall, wedding invitations, and so forth.

differently in the *halachah*. Had the promises by Yaakov been to a daughter, the estate must deliver such gift after Yaakov dies. Also, if Yaakov made a wedding for one of his daughters and after he died another daughter is to be married, she may insist that the estate provide a similar wedding for her.

Yaakov, at his own expense made a wedding feast for Ruven. Wedding gifts were given to Ruven while Yaakov was still alive. After Yaakov dies persons who gave gifts to Ruven make weddings for their sons. The estate of Yaakov makes the reciprocal gifts.[8] If Ruven made his own wedding at his own expense, then Ruven must make the reciprocal gifts from his own funds.

Yaakov, in the name of his son Ruven, sent a wedding gift to a son of his friend Moshe. After Yaakov died, Ruven got married, and Moshe sent a gift to Ruven. The gift belongs to Ruven. However, if the original gift from Yaakov to Moshe's son was sent in the name of Yaakov or all of Yaakov's sons, the gift from Moshe[9] belongs to the estate of Yaakov.

Ransoming of the heirs

Ruven is taken hostage and Yaakov pays $1,000 to ransom him[10] and then Yaakov dies. Under certain circumstances, for example, if Ruven's conduct was partially responsible for his being taken hostage, Ruven's share of the estate is reduced by the $1,000,[11] unless it is clear that Yaakov meant it as a gift.[12]

8. The basis of these laws dealing with gifts is found in the Talmud. It was a debt that had to be repaid, and that is why the estate may be required to make such reciprocal gifts.

9. Even if Yaakov sent the gift in the names of all his sons, Moshe need reciprocate only to those sons who attended his own son's wedding.

10. The laws of this paragraph apply only if Ruven was kidnapped because of his conduct, such as cavorting with the wrong types of people, for example, drug pushers who kidnap him for money owed, or gamblers to whom he owes money. But if he is kidnapped not because of his own conduct, the money paid by Yaakov is a gift.

11. Ordinarily, the gifts that a father made to a member of the family during the father's lifetime do not reduce the donee's share of the estate. That is when the gift is given voluntarily by the father to the child. In this case the father would rather that the son was not kidnapped and have to be redeemed; in that sense the paying of the ransom is not similar to a gift.

12. Unless it is clear that Yaakov meant the $1,000 as a gift, the ransom money is considered a loan and not a gift.

Chapter 287

SOME OF THE HEIRS BENEFIT THE ESTATE

INTRODUCTION

Yaakov dies[1] and leaves as his sole heirs four sons: Ruven and Shimon, who have reached adulthood; and Levi and Yehudah, who are still minors.[2] For some reason beth din is not ready to divide the estate and as stated in Volume VI, at page 30, cited at the beginning of Chapter 286, the four sons are thus constructive partners in the estate. Assume that the bulk of the value of the estate is in a business that sells men's clothing. Shimon runs the family business and the others do not participate in running the business.

This chapter differs from Chapter 177 in Volume VI, in that the latter discusses the income from the constructive partnership, while this chapter discusses the enhancement in value of the assets of the partnership. For example, the constructive partnership had a net worth of $1,000 on January 1, the date of death of Yaakov. Each year the men's store that is being run by Shimon earns $100. The first-year profits are invested in an addition to the building. On December 1, the

---

1. Yaakov dies without leaving a will. If he leaves a will, the questions raised and answered in this chapter may be academic, since the will provides for these matters.
2. Males reach adulthood at the age of 13 years and 1 day.

net worth of the partnership is $1,100.[3] Who shares in the appreciation of the net worth? How was the building enlarged, and with whose funds and by whose work? Did Shimon state that he was going to retain all enhancement of the net worth of the business for himself?

Chapter 177 discusses the heirs taking certain expenses from the estate, and there is a discussion of medical expenses, which may be taken from the estate and which must be paid for by the heirs from their own account. This chapter discusses disposition of some of the assets of the estate by some of the heirs without the initial consent of the others; is it binding on the estate?

Chapter 285 discusses owners of assets who have fled or were captured and are not here; they may return or never return. There they were known to be the owners.

Chapter 280 discusses heirs who show up and declare that they are heirs. If they are truly heirs, they share in the estate by having each of the heirs who inherited assets give a proportional share to the newly found heirs. Assume that such heirs arrive on the scene and demand their share of the estate of their father Yaakov. Do they share in the enhancements made by Shimon?

The question sometimes arises as to how long an estate can be kept open and run as a partnership. It has been said that it can be so run for three generations, that is, Ruven, Shimon, Levi, and Yehudah, and their children who are first cousins to each other, and their children who are second cousins to each other.[4] There is an opinion that it can last even beyond three generations until such time that the heirs or their descendants wish to terminate the constructive partnership.

TEXT

Who shares in the increase in value of the partnership?

Yaakov dies and leaves no will and the assets of Yaakov consist of a men's furnishings store. Shimon works in the store, Levi and Yehudah

3. This came about by Shimon enlarging the building where the store is housed and the real estate is now worth more. There is no additional income but the building can now be sold for more money.

4. See Jerusalem Talmud, *Baba Bathra*, chapter 9, law 3.

are too young to work in the store, and Ruven has outside employment and cannot work in the store.[5] Due to Shimon's ideas and supervision, the net worth of the business has increased in value from $1,000 to $1,100, the additional $100 having been invested in additions to the building. All of the brothers share equally in the increase in value of the partnership; when the partnership assets are divided, each brother will receive $275. Shimon does not receive a larger share of the enhancement, nor does he receive any fees or salary for the enhancement of the partnership assets.[6] Shimon did not do any extra work or put up his money to construct the addition to the building. Nor did he announce that he would retain for himself the enhancement value. The funds for the enlargement of the building were generated by income from the business and the construction work was done by outside workmen.

Assume the same facts as in the prior paragraph with two changes. (i) Shimon did the construction work himself[7] or worked extra hours to supervise the construction work and/or he paid for the construction work from his own funds. Shimon did such work or expended such moneys without informing the other partners, or (ii) Shimon informed the other partners that he will retain for himself the entire enhancement of the enhancement value. The announcement is made to beth din[8] regarding the interest of the minors, and to Ruven, the adult, in the presence of witnesses,[9] that he (Shimon) will increase the value of the business and that he will keep the entire enhancement for himself. According to the majority view if either (i) or (ii) is present the entire enhancement of the building belongs to Shimon. In dividing the partnership assets, Ruven, Levi, and Yehudah receive $250 each and Shimon receives $350. According to the minority view,

---

5. The laws that are stated in this paragraph are the same if all of the brothers are adults.

6. See note 3 above.

7. Or members of his family did the work. Shimon cannot plead that since they did the work they should be compensated by retaining the enhancement of the value. They stand in the same place as does Shimon.

8. Beth din may appoint a guardian to protect the interest of the minors Levi and Yehudah.

9. There is an opinion that regarding Ruven, who is an adult, the announcement need not be made in his presence if made in the presence of two competent witnesses.

Shimon can retain for himself the entire enhancement of the value only if both (i) and (ii) are present. Even according to the majority view, if neither (i) nor (ii) is present, Shimon must share the enhancement with the other brothers.[10]

According to the majority view, if Shimon relies on (i) and does work in supervising the construction that could conceivably have been done by the minors, then Shimon is not entitled to the enhancement but must share it with Levi and Yehudah.[11] It is the function of beth din to determine if Shimon is to keep the entire enhancement in value or if any of the other or all of the brothers share in such enhancement.

All that has been said regarding males applies if the heirs are females.

When no announcement need be made

If Shimon is a scholar and would ordinarily not forsake his Torah studies and in this instance does forsake his Torah studies and enhances the value of the partnership assets, he retains the entire enhancement as if he complied with (i) or (ii) or both as required in the prior section. There is authority that this law does not apply at the current time. Beth din must examine each case on an individual basis.

Acquiescence of expenditure of partnership funds

One of the heirs of the estate gives away assets from the estate and the other heirs are aware of the gift and do not protest. Any other disposition of estate assets made by any of the heirs and known to the others who do not protest is deemed as acquiesced to by the others.

Newly discovered heirs

When Yaakov died it was thought that Ruven, Shimon, Levi, and Yehudah were his sole heirs. It now turns out that Yaakov had another

10. However, see the next section.

11. They need not share the enhancement with Ruven since his outside employment precluded him from supervising the construction.

son, Naftali.[12] Assume the same facts as above that the estate was valued at $1,000 when Yaakov died and that Shimon enhanced the estate so that it is now worth $1,100.

If Naftali is a minor, then he shares in the enhancement with the other brothers or with Shimon alone, depending upon the facts as described above. If Naftali is an adult, then the work of Shimon is appraised similar to that of a sharecropper who enhanced the assets consisting of farming real estate, or as an employee of the estate. Shimon is paid such amount before giving Naftali his share.

12. Assume that the adult brothers admitted that Naftali is an heir and/or beth din so decided.

Chapter 288

MISCELLANEOUS LAWS REGARDING DIVISION OF THE ASSETS

INTRODUCTION

Rabbi Yosef Karo calls this chapter "How Is The Appraisal Made Regarding The Clothes On The Backs Of The Sons And Daughters When They Divide [the estate]?"

It has been stated in Volume VI, page 11,

> "Unless otherwise agreed upon, the partners may take funds from the partnership for their own personal use for clothing, food, and other items until any of the other partners objects."

The estate of Yaakov, the decedent is about to be divided among his four sons, Ruven, Shimon, Levi, and Yehudah. If there are any questions as to how to divide the estate, beth din will resolve such questions. There are sometimes minor items that have to be taken into account. Unfortunately, sometimes these minor things are fought over because the siblings do not get along or are under pressure from others, such as wives, to make sure that the other does not get "one cent more than you do." Or sometimes, unfortunately, all or some of the sons are so poor that they really need every last cent, not because they dislike each other. Or else they want to do that which the *halachah* provides as a matter of principle.

Another topic discussed in this chapter is that of the father Yaakov giving instructions to his sons to give a gift to Eliyahu, a friend of Yaakov, and the sons divide the estate without making such a gift. What are the results of such action?

TEXT

Appraising the wardrobes worn by the heirs

The things that are purchased by an heir from the assets of the estate as discussed in this section deal only with clothing, food, and beverages. It does not apply to luxuries such as jewelry, automobiles, artworks, and other things of value. Beth din will advise the heirs what they may and what they may not purchase with estate funds.

The heirs are dividing the assets of Yaakov, their deceased father. After all of the other assets have been appraised, there is the question of the wardrobes worn by the heirs, their wives, and children, which have been purchased with funds from the estate.[1] Is it to be included in the share of the heir who made the purchase with estate funds, or is it to be borne by the estate and not to be part of the share of that heir?

When the appraisal is made for dividing the estate of Yaakov, an appraisal is made of the value of the wardrobe purchased with estate funds by Ruven, Shimon, Levi, and Yehudah for their own use as at the time of the appraisal.[2] There is an opinion that the wardrobe purchased by the oldest son with estate funds is not appraised or included in his share of the estate.[3]

The wardrobes that the sons of Yaakov purchase and give to their wives, sons, and daughters with estate money are not appraised.[4]

1. It may be that Ruven and Levi took out $1,000 each to buy expensive suits, while Shimon and Levi were satisfied to take out only about $200 for their suits or coats.

2. Clothing that has been lost or worn-out is not appraised.

3. Since he may now be the new head of the family the other siblings recognize the necessity for him to be well-dressed.

4. It would be degrading to have the wives and children have to appear in beth din to have their wardrobes appraised.

The foregoing applies to the everyday clothes of the wives, sons, and daughters of the heirs. But if they purchased Sabbath clothes with estate money, such clothing is to be appraised.

Failure to make a specific gift

Yaakov, before he died, instructed that a certain item of his be given to a friend, Eliyahu. Ruven, Shimon, Levi, and Yehudah divided all of the assets of the estate without giving that certain item to Eliyahu. Their division of the estate is null and void. They must make the gift and then redivide the estate. However, any of the sons, for example, Shimon, may insist upon making the gift from his part of the estate and the other brothers must reimburse him, and no redivision need to be made; or he may insist that one of the other brothers make the gift and he will reimburse such other brother.

Eliyahu may waive receiving the specific item and the heirs may make the gift in some other way.

Chapter 289

ADDITIONAL LAWS OF ESTATE DIVISION

INTRODUCTION

This is the penultimate chapter dealing with the laws of inheritance and serves as an introduction to the last such chapter, which deals with the function of the guardian. It deals with the situation where there are adult and minor heirs surviving the death of Yaakov, the decedent. Theoretically, beth din, which is the true guardian of the minors, can act as guardian. However, it is not practical for beth din to attempt to do so for it cannot pay sufficient attention to the needs of all the minors in the community.[1] Beth din may appoint a guardian to protect the interests of the minor heirs, and the appointed guardian can more particularly protect the interests of the minors, subject to their actions being approved by beth din. What is the legal effect of the decisions made by the guardian?

May beth din exercise the "Buy or Sell Option" described in Volume V, Chapter 171? Aharon and Pinchas, who are partners, own real estate

1. Also, if there would be a dispute between the adult heirs and beth din as to the best way to divide the estate, beth din would find itself acting as the lawyers of the minors, and this would present a conflict between its duty as guardian and its function as beth din.

that does not lend itself to partition because of the size of the real estate or configuration. Either partner may make an offer to the other giving the other the right to either buy out the offeror's interest for $100 or to sell the offeree's interest in the real estate to the offeror for $100, obliging the offeree to elect one alternative or the other. May the guardian or beth din engage in such a transaction? This is discussed in Volume V at page 228, which section is recopied below in the section called "Minors in partition or demand situations."

In *Shulhan Aruch* the last four paragraphs are as follows:

"2. If all of the brothers are not present [before beth din], but those that are present seek to divide [the estate], or did already divide and another brother or a creditor arrives and seizes one portion is discussed in chapter 175."[2]

"3. One of the brothers commences a job and gets ill, or he desires to go off to study is discussed in chapter 177."[3]

"4. One of the brothers holds instruments of indebtedness and he claims that they are his, is discussed in chapter 62."[4]

Paragraph 5 in *Shulhan Aruch* discusses the situation where some of the heirs seized part of the assets of the estate before the decedent was buried and is discussed in the section entitled "Seizure of estate assets."

TEXT

To appoint a guardian to protect the interests of minors

Yaakov dies leaving adults and minors as his heirs.[5] The adults wish for beth din to divide the estate so that they may manage their own property without having to contend with simultaneously managing the affairs of the infants subject to the restrictions found in the last few chapters. Beth din appoints a guardian for the minors to protect their interests in the division of the estate of Yaakov. The guardian

2. See Volume V, page 245.
3. See Volume VI, page 30.
4. See Volume II, page 167.
5. It may be the sons of Yaakov, or his daughters, or his brothers, or his sisters, or his cousins. The level of heirship is not determinative, but rather when the class of heirs is reached, the level consists of at least some minors, or all minors.

selects for the minor what he considers to be the fairest shares, which selection must be approved by the beth din. When the minors reach adulthood, they cannot request beth din to rescind such selection, since it was approved by beth din.

If there is some doubt as to which is the better portion, the guardian has the choice and the adults are deemed to acquiesce in their selection.

There are authorities who hold that the estate should be divided in equal portions and then there should be a drawing as to who gets which portion.

When the division made by the guardian can be rescinded

If the guardian made an error in the division of Yaakov's estate, which beth din approved, giving to the minors at least one-sixth less than they should have received, the minors when they become adults may petition beth din to rescind the division. Beth din may annul the division and order a new division of Yaakov's assets to be made. This holds true even if the mistake in appraisal applied to real estate that is not ordinarily subject to the laws of overreaching.[6]

Minors in partition or demand situations

Levi died, leaving his sons to inherit his estate, some of whom are minors and some of whom have attained their majority. The sons who have reached their majority may make a demand for partition and beth din will appoint a guardian for the children in the partition lawsuit.

If the property inherited from Levi does not lend itself to partition and those who have attained their majority wish to make a demand that the minors exercise their right to sell or to buy their share of inherited property, there is an opinion that beth din will appoint a guardian to protect the interest of the minors and determine whether it is in their best interest to sell or to buy on behalf of the minors. Similarly, if beth din determines that it is not beneficial for the minors to remain as joint owners with their older brothers, beth din may

6. See Volume VII, Chapter 227.

appoint a guardian to make the demand that the older brothers either sell to the minors or buy the interest of the minors. Beth din may determine that the minor need not sell or buy.

There is also a view that the guardian and beth din may not exercise the sell or buy option on behalf of minors, but this seems to be a minority view.

Seizure of estate assets

Yaakov dies and leaves sons: Ruven, Shimon, Chaim, and Shlomo. Before Yaakov is even buried and before there is any division of the assets of Yaakov among his sons, Ruven and Shimon seize some of Yaakov's assets; Chaim and Shlomo seized nothing. David, a nonrelative, holds some assets belonging to Yaakov. Ruven and Shimon request that David give them these assets so that they will have money to bury Yaakov. Chaim and Shlomo resist this transfer and plead that if David gives these assets to Ruven and Shimon, there will not be any assets left to them from the estate of Yaakov since they anticipate that it will be difficult for them to retrieve anything from the assets that were seized by Ruven and Shimon. They plead demanding that all of the four brothers should now each pay one-quarter of the expense of the burial and that beth din can later decide what should be done with the assets held by David. It was held that the pleas of Chaim and Shlomo are correct and that the burial should be paid by all four brothers immediately, even if this will result in a slight delay in the burial of Yaakov. The same applies if Yossi, a creditor of Yaakov, demands that the funeral be delayed so that he can collect his debts from the estate. Beth din has the authority to delay the burial and order the brothers to pay the debt, if it appears to beth din that it will be difficult for Yossi to collect the debt once Yaakov is buried.

Chapter 290

GUARDIANS

INTRODUCTION

Maimonides ends the *Laws of Inheritance* with the laws of the guardian. His last paragraph states:[1]

> Although the guardian is not required to render an account, as we have stated, he must make reckoning to himself privately with great care and beware of the Father of these orphans who rideth the skies, as it is written Extol Him that rideth upon the skies . . . A father of the fatherless (Ps. 68:5–6).

Throughout this work, when minors are mentioned, the term often associated with the minors is the person who is called a guardian. In Hebrew the term is *Appotropos*, from the Greek meaning "the father of the minors." In this chapter, I have referred to the minor child in the singular, but all of the laws apply equally regardless of the number of minors involved.

The guardian is appointed not only for minors, but also for other persons who are not capable of taking care of their fiscal affairs.

The guardian may be appointed by the father of the minor and/or beth din.

1. Maimonides, *Laws of Inheritance*, chapter 11, paragraph 12.

This chapter will examine who should appoint the guardian, the method of his appointment, who may be appointed, how the guardian commences his duties, the powers and duties of the guardian, the compensation of the guardian, the method of his completing the task and removing a guardian, and other matters dealing with the guardian. There is also a section dealing with a person (Shlomo) who takes care of a minor without being officially appointed as a guardian. I have designated him (Shlomo) as an "unofficial guardian." (There are laws dealing with slaves belonging to the estate, and how the guardian should handle their upkeep and sale; these laws are omitted here.)

The father of the minor children is designated as "Yaakov" and the guardian of the minor is designated as "David."

TEXT

Who should appoint a guardian

The term "beth din" as used herein is the official beth din of the community, or if the community has appointed a rabbi to be the sole judge of the community, the term beth din will include such rabbi.[2] It does not refer to any three persons who decide to constitute themselves as a beth din. If there is no beth din in the community, then the beth din of a closest town will have jurisdiction over the matters discussed in this chapter. Beth din is the guardian of all minors; it is not the guardian of adults.[3]

Yaakov, a person who has a minor child[4] who will be his heir, or a pregnant wife,[5] whose child may or will be his heir, should appoint a guardian[6] (David) in his lifetime or by a last will and testament to

---

2. See Volume I, page 30.

3. Unless the adults are incompetent as stated below.

4. Whether just minor child or children, or a combination of minor children and adult children. Male minors become adults when they attain their 13th birthday plus 1 day; female minors become adults when they attain their 12th birthday plus 1 day.

5. The child to be born, if a son, will be an heir if there are no other sons, and if there are other sons, will share in the estate with the other sons; if there are no sons, then the child to be born, if a daughter, will be an heir, and if there are other daughters, will share the estate with the other daughters.

6. Yaakov appoints David as a guardian for his minor son, Naftali. Yaakov's wife,

protect the interests of the minors in the case of his death. If Yaakov has a minor child and adult children, his appointment of a guardian is effective only insofar as it applies to the minor child or children. However, if Yaakov does appoint David to be the guardian of the minor child and the adult children, David may so act on behalf of all if there is no objection from the adult children. If any of the adult children object, then David cannot act as the guardian of the shares of the adult children in Yaakov's estate. The reason is that the moment that Yaakov dies, his estate belongs to his heirs, and beth din has no jurisdiction over the adult, only over the minors who are always wards of beth din. Yaakov can during his lifetime by a trust document or by a will set up a trust of his assets and the trustee of the trust will administer the shares of the minor children and the adult children as provided for in the trust. The guardian will oversee the minor's interests until he reaches adulthood. The father may decide that he does not want to appoint a guardian for his minor son and may declare that his minor son be given his share outright without the appointment of a guardian; the father's desire must be adhered to. The father may not grant David, the guardian whom he appoints, the power to appoint another guardian, even if Yaakov names the other person whom he wants David to appoint as a guardian, whether the exercise of such appointment is to take place prior or subsequent to the death of Yaakov. If David asks Yaakov, who is on his death bed, if he wants David to take charge of Yaakov's assets,[7] and if Yaakov assents, David is appointed a guardian of the minor child of Yaakov. If David was the manager of the assets of Yaakov for an extended period of time before Yaakov's death, and then Yaakov dies, David will not necessarily be appointed by beth din to be the guardian of the minor child.[8] However, if Yaakov appointed David the manager of his assets close to the time of his death, beth din will appoint David the guardian of the minor child, unless beth din determines that he is not

who is pregnant at the time Yaakov dies, thereafter gives birth to a son, Aharon. Thereafter Naftali dies. It has been held that David will be the guardian for the newborn son, Aharon.

7. Or other language recognized by beth din to be effective to appoint David the guardian of Yaakov's minor children.

8. If may be that Yaakov felt confident that he could adequately supervise David, but does not have confidence in others supervising the activities of David.

qualified to be the guardian; beth din may appoint another since Yaakov did not actually appoint David the guardian.

If Yaakov fails to appoint a guardian for the minor child, then beth din may appoint itself as the body to protect the interests of the minor.[9] If beth din does not desire to exercise such authority, then beth din must appoint a guardian. However, if beth din determines that the adult brothers can manage the affairs of the estate including the protection of the minor, then beth din will not appoint a guardian but will designate the adult brothers to manage the affairs of the estate.[10]

If Yaakov appoints two guardians and they cannot make decisions because of disagreement, then beth din should appoint a third guardian acceptable to the other two, who will also vote on the decisions to be made. In all events, if there is still no way to resolve their conflicts, the decision of the guardian appointed by the beth din will be controlling.

Assume Yaakov appoints two guardians, and one dies. There are two opinions. One holds that beth din shall appoint another guardian to replace the deceased guardian, and the other opinion holds that beth din should not appoint a second guardian and the remaining guardian functions by himself.

All that is said about the guardian of a minor applies to a situation where the beth din appoints a guardian to protect the interests of a person who needs protection, such as a deaf-mute or a mentally deficient person.[11]

Who may be appointed a guardian

The father may appoint any person he wants to be the guardian of his minor child. He may appoint a Jew or Gentile, a woman or a minor, a mentally deficient person, or a deaf-mute.[12]

9. If beth din perceives that there will be litigation in which the judges will have to testify or act on the dispute, then they will not appoint themselves to protect the interests of the minors.

10. See Chapter 287.

11. These three persons, the mentally deficient, the deaf-mute, and the minor, are very often grouped together in *halachah* as persons who are not capable of managing their own affairs.

12. The Talmud and some of the codes also discuss the father appointing a slave as the guardian.

Beth din should not appoint a Gentile, a woman, or a minor [nor a slave] as a guardian nor anyone who is not qualified, even if he is in possession of Yaakov's assets, unless it is proved that he was appointed by Yaakov.[13] It is presumed that if someone is unlearned he is not qualified.[14] Beth din should appoint someone who is reputable and trustworthy, who will know how to protect and assert the rights and interests of the minor and to plead his cause, and who is knowledgeable in worldly affairs, in order to protect the assets left to him by Yaakov and to turn a profit from the operation of the estate. As stated below, the guardian appointed by beth din will have to take an oath regarding his stewardship of the assets belonging to the minor when the term of the guardian ends upon the minor achieving adulthood. If beth din cannot find a guardian who is willing to take such oath, they may dispense with the oath.

The guardian need not be a relative to the minor, but may be, except that if he is related to the minor, he may not take possession of his real estate.[15] Also, beth din should not appoint someone related to any of the judges if the guardian will be compensated for his stewardship.

A guardian may not be appointed without his consent.

Until the guardian takes up his duties by taking possession of some of the assets of the minor or commencing to work on his behalf, he may refuse to embark on the role of a guardian. Once he has taken possession of some of the assets of the minor or commenced working on his behalf, he may no longer refuse to continue the task of the guardian, unless he receives permission from beth din, whether or not he receives compensation.[16] This is true if the guardian continues to reside within the community. However, if he moves to another

13. And that is why he is in possession of Yaakov's assets.

14. It is stated in Mishnah 6, *Ethics of the Fathers*, chapter 2, "A boor cannot be fearful of sin, an unlearned person cannot be scrupulously pious."

15. The relative may claim that the real estate is his by the right of a presumption. See Volume V, Chapter 140.

16. Ordinarily, an employee may terminate his employment at will (although he may be liable for damages to the employer). That is because a person can be a slave only to God and not to men. A guardian is not a slave to any employer but is an employee of God because he does His work in taking care of the minor.

community,[17] he may gather all of the assets of the minor, bring them to beth din, and terminate his role as the guardian. Beth din will appoint another guardian to take his place.

Compensation of the guardian

Beth din may agree to compensation for the guardian it appoints to be paid from the assets of the minor, if the guardian cannot take up his function as guardian because he cannot afford not to receive compensation. Beth din has to determine if persons who will serve without compensation can act as capably as the persons who cannot afford to act without compensation. If the guardian is to be compensated, it has been suggested that the relatives of the judges should not be appointed; if the guardian is related to the minor, he may be compensated.

The guardian may purchase clothes for himself from the assets of the minor if it is deemed essential to be dressed properly so that he may be respected when he negotiates to enhance the assets of the minor. There is authority that the minor can protest such action on the part of the guardian.

Taking up the role of a guardian

When beth din appoints the guardian, he and beth din should take an accounting of each and every asset that is being transferred to the guardian. Two written copies of such accounting are made and beth din must keep one and the guardian keeps the other. The purpose is so that beth din will know what the guardian has to return when his stewardship is over.

Beth din divides the assets of the estate into three component parts.

(1) The cash is invested with Yitzchak, a trustworthy person,[18] to do

17. Whether he moves to the other community permanently or for a protracted period of time.

18. The person is described in the codes as one who owns high quality real estate, is trustworthy, learned in Torah studies, and has never been excommunicated. If he does not own real estate, he gives a pledge of broken pieces of gold that are not distinctive. The reason for their not being distinctive is that no person can later come forward and plead that the gold pieces belongs to him. Since the pieces are broken and not distinctive, he cannot prove his allegation.

business with the money and to share in the profits with the minor,[19] but not to require that the minor bear any of the losses if such ensue. One opinion holds that this person is technically not a guardian; the other opinion holds that he too is a guardian. Beth din sets the percentage of profits that Yitzchak must turn over to the minor and retains the balance for himself. If beth din cannot find a person who is willing to share profits but not require the minor to bear a part of the losses, then beth din purchases essentials, such as food for the minors, and real estate is purchased with the balance and delivered to the beth din-appointed guardian.

The beth din turns over to the guardian everything except for the cash of Yaakov, the decedent.

(2) The personal property is appraised and sold in beth din, or in the closest market place, and the money realized from the sale is added to the other money belonging to the minor to be used as designated in (1) above. The real estate, all unsold personal property, and accounts receivable are transferred to the guardian.

Duties and powers of the guardian

The guardian has the same responsibility for the assets of the minor as does a gratuitous bailee.[20] That is, he is not liable if any or all of the assets were stolen or lost, or lost or destroyed by *force majeure* or for reasons not considered his negligence.[21] The guardian is liable if there were losses of some or all of the assets due to his negligence.[22]

The guardian must keep accurate books and records of the assets of the minor, including expenses, income, and other matters that are usually kept by persons managing the property of others.

The guardian may do anything if he first obtains the permission of beth din. Absent such permission, what may he do? The guardian must

19. The agreement is to give the minor a percentage of the profits, such as a quarter or such other percentage as beth din shall negotiate with the guardian.

20. See the chapters commencing 291 until the end of this Volume.

21. An example given in the codes of *not* being negligent is that the guardian purchased an ox and sent the ox out to graze with the other oxen and he did not notice that the ox had no teeth and could not eat, and the ox died of starvation.

22. There is an opinion that if the guardian was appointed by the father he is not liable even for losses caused by his negligence. Otherwise, it may be difficult for the father to find a guardian.

manage the property of the minor as he would manage his own property. It has been stated that this applies if either of two courses[23] would pose a danger to the assets of the minor. However, if only one course would pose risk or a danger to the assets of the minor, then the guardian must pursue the safe course (although he might have pursued the more doubtful course for himself), or obtain advice from the beth din.[24]

The guardian manages all property that has been transferred to him, pays all of the expenses of the property, and receives all of the income; he may construct things on the real estate and he may raze structures, hire employees, and do anything he deems to be in the best interest of the minor. He provides him with the necessities of life for food, clothing, and shelter in conformity with the amount left by Yaakov for the minor and with the amount of money he earns on their behalf, and what is fitting for him, neither too miserly or nor overly generous.

The guardian may not lend funds belonging to the minors to third parties. If he has done so, beth din may recover the money from the borrower. If the borrower does not have the money to return, the guardian is held liable to the minors for such amount. If a loan is made, it should be evidenced by a note of indebtedness. This will obviate the oaths as set forth below in this section.

The guardian may sell assets of the estate[25] to provide food for the minor, but he may not sell assets to let the money lie without being invested. He may sell a field in order to purchase a tractor for other fields.[26]

The guardian may not sell real estate that is distant in order to

---

23. An example given in the Talmud and continued in the codes: If a guardian had some beer belonging to the minor and if he would keep it until he can sell it where he is, the beer might deteriorate, or if he goes to the market to obtain the best price, there is the danger of the beer being lost on the way. He should do with the beer that which he would do with his own beer.

24. There is authority that the guardian must obtain the advice of beth din in all events if there may be some danger in his conduct of selling or investing the assets of the minor.

25. While the *halachah* provides for the order of sale of the assets, it concludes that the guardian should use his judgment as to what is best for the minor.

26. The codes speak of selling a field to purchase an ox for plowing. The codes also speak of selling slaves to purchase food for the minor.

purchase real estate that is closer to where he is located; nor can he sell real estate that is of poorer quality to acquire real estate that is of superior quality, the reason being that he may have made a wrong choice.

Similarly, David, the guardian, may not litigate as a plaintiff on behalf of the minor in order to attempt to acquire a right for the minor, when it may turn out that he will lose the lawsuit and the minor will lose such right; the guardian should wait until the minor comes of age and litigates on his own behalf. A party who has a claim against a minor should not sue because if he does and the guardian defends the lawsuit and wins, the judgment in favor of the minor is binding on the other party; if the guardian loses the lawsuit, the minor can have the judgment against him set aside. The guardian may be a witness in a lawsuit in which the moneys of the minor are involved since the guardian has no interest in the outcome of the lawsuit.[27] For example, the guardian loaned money[28] to Shimon, Shimon pleads that he repaid all or part of the loan to the guardian, and the guardian pleads that Shimon did not repay the loan; if it is admitted by Shimon that the moneys belonged to the minor, then the guardian is believed without having to take an oath. However, if Shimon does not admit that the moneys belong to the minor, and if it is not proven that the moneys loaned belonged to the minor, then the guardian must take an oath that the loan was not repaid.

The guardian may set aside tithes[29] from the property of the minor in order to make the food fit for consumption. However, he may not set aside tithes so that they can be sold as tithed produce and he

27. The question is raised that if the guardian litigates and loses he may be liable to make good the losses when he renders his final accounting to the minor when he becomes of age. One of the answers given is that the guardian is not liable in a situation where it was the father who appointed the guardian and he does not have to account.

28. David personally made the loan, and not through an agent. If David did not personally lend the money to the borrower, David is believed to the same extent as any other sole witness who testifies in a lawsuit. He obligates the defendant to take a Torah oath of denial or lose the lawsuit. See Volume III, Chapter 87.

29. See Volume II, pages 206 and 207.

cannot set aside tithes so that the produce will be ready when the minor reaches his majority.[30]

The guardian may purchase for the minor religious objects so that the minor can train to fulfill his religious obligations.[31] He may purchase textbooks and pay tuition for the minor. The reason that the guardian is permitted to purchase these objects is that they have a fixed cost, depending upon where they are purchased. Without the permission of beth din the guardian may not make charitable contributions nor be taxed to make a charitable contribution on behalf of the minor, even for the redemption of captives,[32] since there is never a fixed amount of charity that a person should give.[33] However, if it is a fixed sum and the minor's reputation will be enhanced by the giving of such charity on his behalf, it may be done by the guardian with the permission of beth din.[34]

Completing the role of guardian

When the minor reaches his majority, beth din has no discretion but must terminate the guardianship and turn over to the minor all of his

30. The minor will be able to tithe the produce when he attains his majority and will benefit by giving the tithes to the *kohen* or Levite of his choice.

31. The minor is not obligated to fulfill the religious obligations. There is, however, an obligation on the guardian to fulfill the role of the parent to train the minor in the fulfillment of the Torah commandments.

32. As stated by Maimonides, *Gifts to the Poor*, chapter 8, paragraph 10:

> The ransoming of captives has precedence over the feeding and clothing of the poor. Indeed there is no religious duty more meritorious than the ransoming of captives, for not only is the captive included in the generality of the hungry, the thirsty, and the naked, but his very life is in jeopardy. He who turns his eyes away from ransoming him, transgresses the commandments *Thou shalt not harden thy heart, nor shut thy hand* (Deut. 15:7), *Neither shalt thou stand idly by the blood of thy neighbor* (Lev. 19:16), and *He shall not rule with rigor over him in thy sight* (Lev. 25:53). Moreover, he nullifies the commandments *Thou shalt surely open thy hand unto him* (Deut. 15:18), *That thy brother may live with thee* (Lev. 25:36), *Thou shalt love thy neighbor as thyself* (Lev. 19:18), *Deliver them that are drawn unto death* (Prov. 24:11), and many other admonitions like these. To sum up, there is no religious duty greater than the ransoming of captives.

33. But beth din may make a charitable contribution on behalf of a person who has become mentally deficient or a deaf-mute.

34. There is an opinion that this may be done even without the permission of beth din.

assets.[35] However, if the father of the minor before he died provided that the guardian should continue to function until the minor reached a specified age beyond his attaining his majority, or having certain admirable qualities, the wishes of the father will be adhered to by beth din.

When the minor reaches adulthood,[36] the guardian must turn over to him all of the assets of the minor that the guardian has in his possession. If any assets are missing because they were stolen or lost or lost or destroyed by *force majeure*, the guardian takes the same oath as does a gratuitous bailee. The oath consists of 3 parts: (i) that the guardian was not negligent in causing the loss of the asset; (ii) that he did not make unauthorized use of the asset before it was lost or stolen; and (iii) that the asset is not in the possession of the guardian.[37]

If the guardian is appointed by beth din, he is not required to render an accounting of the receipts and disbursements. He may tell the minor that he is turning back to him that which remains from his assets. In such event he must take an oath[38] while holding a sacred object that he did not rob the minor of anything.[39] If as stated above the guardian was appointed upon condition that he does not take such an oath, such condition will be upheld. However, if the guardian was appointed by the father of the minor or by another ancestor of the minor, he is required to render an accounting, but he is not required to take the oath unless it is pleaded with certainty that the

35. Beth din can, however, provide for training the former minor so that he will be a productive citizen.

36. In the case of boys who are the heirs, the age of 13 years and 1 day; in the case of girls who are the heirs, 12 years and 1 day.

37. Another way of putting this part (iii) of the oath is that the asset was stolen (or lost) as the guardian alleges.

38. See Volume III, page 132, wherein it states:.

20. Oath of a guardian.

a. The guardian has been appointed to manage the affairs of orphans.

b. The guardian/defendant takes the oath.

c. The guardian swears that his report is true.

d. If the guardian takes the oath, his report is accepted as accurate.

e. Chapter 93.

See also Chapter 93.

39. This is not the same oath referred to in the prior paragraph. In that paragraph there are assets missing, which is not the case in this paragraph.

report of the guardian is not accurate. The current practice is for the guardian to render an accounting even if he was appointed by the father of the minor since the guardian does not take an oath.[40] If there are two competent witnesses that the guardian has not accounted accurately or turned over all of the assets of the minor, or is guilty of misconduct, the guardian must pay such damages. If the guardian was appointed by a secular court he must render an accounting since this is usually the practice in secular courts.

In all situations where the guardian has a monetary interest in the outcome of the gain or loss of the assets even if appointed by the father of the minor, the guardian must take an oath when he returns the asset to the minor upon his achieving his majority.

In all situations beth din proclaims a ban on any person who is a guardian of minors who has taken assets belonging to minors.

As stated at the commencement of this chapter, the major responsibility of accounting for the assets of the guardian is to the true Father of the orphans.[41]

Levi pleads that Yaakov gave him money with instructions to distribute the money to the sons of Yaakov. Levi may distribute such money to all of Yaakov's sons and need not take an oath, since he is similar to a guardian appointed by a father of a minor. However, if Levi asserts that he is distributing the moneys to less than all of the sons of Yaakov, he must take an oath that he does not retain anything belonging to Yaakov; since the distribution is to less than all of Yaakov's sons, Levi is not deemed to be in the role of a guardian.[42] If any of the sons of Yaakov are minors, beth din will appoint a guardian for them and the guardian will request that Levi take an oath in all instances.

If the guardian dies and his heirs find that the books and records of the guardian show that the guardian is owed money he has

40. Beth din must in each case devise the exact language and form of the oath.

41. "A father of the fatherless, and a judge of the widows, Is God in His holy habitation" (Psalms 68:6).

42. Levi must take an oath only if it is independently known that Yaakov gave him the money. If it is not independently known, Levi is believed without an oath because of *migo* (see Glossary). Levi could have remained silent and have kept the money because no one knew that Yaakov gave him the money. Since (*migo*) he did not keep silent, he is believed when he states that the money was to be given only to some of the sons.

expended on behalf of the minor, such books are not in and of themselves sufficient to base a claim by the heirs of the guardian against the assets of the minor. However, had the guardian been alive, he would have been believed.

Removal of the guardian

If there is a rumor that David, the guardian, is eating and drinking beyond his means or way of life and spending more on things than he used to do and perhaps beyond his known means, beth din should examine him to see if he is spending the assets of the orphans on himself. Beth din may impose an oath upon the guardian that he did not steal anything belonging to the minor. There is a difference depending upon whether the guardian was appointed by the father or by beth din. If he is appointed by beth din, if it turns out that it is possible that the guardian may be spending the moneys of the minors on himself, then he is removed as guardian and another guardian is named in his place. However, if David, the guardian, was appointed by the father, Yaakov, he is not removed on the basis of a rumor, and all doubts are resolved in his favor.[43] However, if it was shown to beth din by witnesses that the guardian has been using assets of the minors, he is to be removed even if he was appointed by the father. Beth din has broad discretion whether to remove the guardian.[44] Opinions differ as to whether it is necessary for the guardian to be present when beth din receives testimony from witnesses regarding the conduct of the guardian. If beth din finds that the guardian stole or used for himself assets belonging to the minor, the guardian must make restitution to the minor.

If the guardian when appointed has all of the virtuous qualities that are required and then changes his ways and no longer has these moral qualities, he is to be removed as a guardian. Beth din is the final arbiter as to whether he should be removed. Beth din may impose an

43. There is an opinion that even if beth din appointed the guardian, he cannot be removed unless there are witnesses to prove that the guardian used the assets of the minor.

44. There is an opinion that it makes no difference whether the guardian was appointed by beth din or by the father; the procedure is the same in both situations and the guardian is not removed unless there is clear proof that he misused the funds of his wards.

oath upon the guardian that he did not steal or use any assets belonging to the minor for himself. If beth din finds that the guardian stole or used for himself assets belonging to the minor, the guardian must make restitution to the minor. However, if the guardian was appointed by the father and at the time of his appointment was not honest or virtuous, and the father knew of his conduct and nevertheless appointed him, the guardian is not removed on the basis of not being honest, unless he stole from the minor.

If a guardian is removed he must take an oath that he did not use assets of the estate, and failing to take such oath he must compensate the estate for an amount that beth din shall assess.

Unofficial guardians

Assume that the orphaned minor resides with a person (Shlomo), male or female (other than a guardian), whether by invitation or by moving in with the person. Such a person (Shlomo), assumes the role of an unofficial guardian. There is a difference of opinion whether he has the role of a guardian appointed by the father or appointed by beth din when he completes his role as guardian. The difference is whether he has to take an oath of his accounting. This may now be academic, since as was stated dealing with the completion of the role of guardian, the current practice is for the guardian to take an oath in all situations.

The authority of the unofficial guardian to spend, invest, and deal with the assets of the minor is limited to transactions approved by beth din. If he acted without their authorization he will be liable for losses incurred.

If the unofficial guardian is the mother of the minor, the result is the same as in the prior paragraph.

If the unofficial guardian spends his own money on the minor he will be reimbursed from the assets of the minor unless he states that he is supporting the minor as an act of charity.

Part III

LAWS OF THE UNPAID BAILEE

Chapter 291

THE RESPONSIBILITIES OF THE UNPAID BAILEE

INTRODUCTION

Commencing with this chapter and continuing to the end of this volume and most of Volume IX,[1] the *Shulhan Aruch Hoshen haMishpat* deals with the laws of bailments. The bailment situation, that is, one person lawfully holding an object of personal property[2] belonging to another person, is a common situation. I have called the holding of the object for another person "guarding" the object.[3] All businesses and individuals that lease objects are part of this situation; the person who borrows his friend's pen to write a few words is in this situation. The person who guards a friend's belongings while his friend goes

1. The reference to Volume IX has no relationship to the volumes of the *Shulhan Aruch* of Rabbi Yosef Karo. The entire *Shulhan Aruch* is usually printed in ten large volumes; the last three volumes devoted to civil law are entitled *Hoshen haMishpat*. The chapter numbers of this work follow the chapter numbers of Rabbi Karo's *Shulhan Aruch, Hoshen haMishpat*. But the volume numbers are my own.

2. The lease of real estate is also the topic of bailments, but appear in Volume IX, Chapter 312.

3. It is referred to in some translations as "keeping" the object, or "watching" the object, or "holding" the object. I have used the term "guard" to include all of these meanings.

away for a few minutes is in such a situation. All those entities that are in the warehousing business are in that situation. An auction house that holds objects for sellers is in that situation. These are only a few of the myriad of examples.

The "owner" (the bailor) of the object is designated as such, except that when he lends the object to a borrower, he is designated as "the lender." The person who holds the owner's object is the "bailee," except that when he borrows the object from a lender, he is designated as the "borrower." The person who is asked to become a bailee but has not yet become a bailee is designated as "the second person." The article of personal property that is being guarded by the bailee is the "object."

Although this chapter and all of the chapters until the end of this volume deal with the unpaid bailee, I have included in this opening chapter some of the laws of the other bailees to show the interrelationship of the four classes of bailees.

In *halachah*, bailees are divided into four classes: (1) the unpaid bailee; (2) the paid bailee; (3) the lessee; and (4) the borrower. In all four classes, the owner has entrusted an object to the person who is now holding it legally.

There is a general principle in *halachah* that in matters regarding their money, the parties may make any stipulations that do not contravene the *halachah*.[4] May the parties stipulate that an unpaid bailee has greater liability or less liability than the *halachah* imposes on this class of bailee?

At what moment does one become a bailee? What is the responsibility of the bailee? When is he liable and when not liable to the owner for loss or damage to the object? What if a bailee who is not permitted to use the object does use it? What if there is a deviation in the use of the object by the borrower or lessee from the purpose for which the object was borrowed or leased? What if the owner or lender is employed by the bailee when the bailee is entrusted with the object? If a purchaser of an object leaves the object with the seller for temporary safekeeping, is the seller a bailee?

Assume that the bailee cannot return the object and has a claim

4. An example of where the parties may *not* stipulate how to spend their money is in the case of paying interest on a loan. There is no exception to this *halachah*. Neither the lender nor the borrower may stipulate interest into a loan.

that will exonerate him from liability for the nonreturn; how does he raise and prove his defense? What if there are no witnesses? When does the bailee take "the oath of the bailees"?[5] Rabbi Yosef Karo discusses this topic here and also in chapter 294.

What is the proper standard of care required of an unpaid bailee? What are some examples in *halachah* of such care? It should be remembered that when the *halachah* was historically established there were no banks with safe deposit boxes, nor burglar alarms, nor locks on doors or other devices to withstand the sophisticated burglar of today. What are some examples of negligent care? How is the value of the object determined and how are the damages assessed if the bailee is negligent in his care of the object? There are some standards that do vary with time and some that persist in the *halachah* through the ages.

How and when does the role of the bailee terminate? What is the relationship between the owner and the bailee after the relationship has terminated and the object is still in the possession of the bailee?

May a bailee, without the authorization of the owner, ask a second person, whether compensated or not compensated, to become the bailee in his place? What are the rights and liabilities of each party if the original bailee gives the object to a second bailee? Does it matter whether the second bailee is a member of the family of the original bailee? There are many paragraphs in *Shulhan Aruch* that discuss this question and I have set forth a separate section on this point, although it is often discussed as part of the negligent conduct of the bailee.

This chapter has been arranged in the following sequence: the classes of bailees including laws from chapter 302 that deal with the fact that whether the owner and/or bailee is a man or a woman makes no difference. Once the various classes of bailees has been set forth, there is then discussed the situations in which the bailee is liable to the owner for loss or damage to the object entrusted to the bailee; these differ from one class of bailee to another. There is an omnibus exception to the liability of the bailee and this is set forth in the section dealing with the owner of the object working for the bailee. May the parties stipulate that the liabilities of the bailee shall be otherwise than the *halachah* provides? Assume that the owner

5. See Volume III, page 126.

pleads that the bailee is liable to him. How can the bailee defeat this claim and prove nonliability? If the bailee is liable for his conduct there must be an assessment of the monetary value of the object and the time of the valuation of any loss, so that the bailee will know the extent of his liability to the owner; the manner of payment of the damages is included in the same section. Once these rights and liabilities have been set forth, the chapter shows how a person enters the role of a bailee, the standard of care required of a bailee, and what constitutes negligence on the part of a bailee (including the situation where the bailee was negligent but the loss came about from *force majeure*). As a corollary of this last topic of what constitutes negligence, there is discussed the situation where the original bailee gives the object to a third person to guard. Is this negligence? The chapter concludes with sections on how the owner/bailee relationship terminates, and the liabilities of the bailee if the object is left with him after such termination. I have moved the laws of chapter 293 of *Shulhan Aruch* dealing with the termination of the owner/bailee relationship to this chapter since the laws there also deal with this topic.

TEXT

Classes of bailees

All that is said in these chapters regarding bailees apply whether the owner and/or the bailee is a man or a woman or a minor. There is an exception: If the wife holds objects belonging to her husband and breaks it through her negligence, she is not liable to him. The reason is for the stability of the home. However, if she intentionally breaks his things she is liable. A person should not in the first instance accept an object to guard for a woman/owner who is married because there is the possibility that it was taken by her from her husband without his permission. But if a bailee did accept an object from a married woman he should return it to her when the time for the return of the object has arrived.

The following four classes of bailees are named in the Introduction above.

(1) **The unpaid bailee.** In the case of the unpaid bailee, the owner

asks the bailee to guard something for him. A typical case might be a passenger in an airline waiting room who wishes to go to the restroom asks someone whom he knows or whom he just met to guard his suitcase for him. There are certain expectations that the owner has when he entrusts the unpaid bailee to guard the suitcase, such as he will not walk away and leave the suitcase unguarded. The unpaid bailee on the other hand cannot be expected to safeguard the suitcase if an armed robber demands that he hand over the suitcase or be shot. In the situation of the unpaid bailee, the owner is the sole benefited party and the unpaid bailee receives no benefit.

(2) **The paid bailee**. The owner, instead of asking the unpaid bailee to guard the suitcase, can check the suitcase with a clerk who is an employee of the airport and to whom the owner pays an agreed-upon fee. The owner's expectations are now higher than they were in class (1) where the bailee is unpaid. Here the bailee is getting paid and has greater responsibilities. Both the owner and the paid bailee receive benefit; the owner in that his object is being guarded, and the bailee in that he is being paid.

(3) **The lessee**. A person (the lessee/bailee) wants to rent a car for a week and he goes to a car-rental agency and rents a car and pays (or will pay) the agreed-upon weekly rental. Both the owner and the lessee receive benefit; the owner/lessor by receiving a fee and the lessee the use of the car.[6]

(4) **The borrower**. A person would like to type a letter but does not own a typewriter. He goes to a friend's house and borrows the friend's typewriter, without any fee involved. The borrower is the sole beneficiary of the transaction; the owner receives no benefit. The borrower has more responsibility than in the three prior classes.

Liabilities of the bailees

(Although there are four classes of bailees, the *halachah* classifies the aforesaid four classes of bailees into three classes. Classes (2) and (3), the paid bailee and the lessee, have some of the same responsibilities and liabilities.)

6. The benefits are just the opposite in types (2) and (3). In type (2) the bailee receives a fee, and in type (3) the lessor/bailor receives the fee. In type (2) the object is held by the person receiving the fee, and in type (3) the object is held by the person paying the fee.

In general, the responsibilities and liabilities of the four classes of bailees revolve around six factors that come into play when it is not possible for the bailee to return the object to the owner; the four classes of bailees are analyzed below against these six factors. (i) The object was lost through the negligence of the bailee. (ii) The object was lost by or stolen from the bailee. (iii) The object was lost by *force majeure* (an event sometimes referred to as an act of God and beyond the control of the bailee to prevent).[7](iv) The object "died" while being used in the natural course of events.[8] (v) The object cannot be returned for any reason after the bailee made unauthorized use of the object.[9] (vi) The object cannot be returned for any reason but the owner was working for the bailee, even in an unrelated job, when the bailee or the borrower took possession of the object. The same rules apply even if the bailor was not working for the bailee at the actual time when the object was lost even by the negligence of the bailee. There is an exception to the broad principle of exonerating the bailee; if the bailee intentionally damaged or destroyed the object, he will be liable even if the bailor was working for him when he took possession of the object. (See the next section.)

In all the situations the nonreturn of the object intact is due to the object being lost, stolen, damaged, destroyed, or to *force majeure*. The bailee's keeping the object for himself, or denying that the object was given to him or that he returned the object, or similar reasons are not covered in this section.

(1) **The unpaid bailee**:

(i) He is liable for the nonreturn of the object if due to his negligence, it was lost, damaged, or destroyed. This is close to

7. For example, a fire broke out and he cannot rescue the object; or a robber threatened to harm him if he did not surrender the object. Robbery differs from theft (the object was stolen from him). In the former the bailee is threatened and he is not in danger; in the latter the bailee is not aware that the object is being stolen and his safety is not threatened.

8. For example, an automobile is being driven and the engine fails to work. Or a horse dies while pulling a plow; or a computer fails to function.

9. The bailee is considered to be like a robber and the object is deemed to have passed to the ownership of the bailee for purposes of liability when he made unauthorized use of the object; he is liable for its return no matter what the circumstances of its loss. See Chapter 292.

destroying the object willfully (for which he is liable) since the owner is relying upon him for the minimal protection of the object.

(ii) He is not liable for the nonreturn of the object if it was lost by him in a non-negligent manner, or if it was stolen from him.[10]

(iii) He is not liable for the nonreturn of the object if it was lost through *force majeure*.

(iv) He is liable for its nonreturn if the object "dies" while the bailee uses the object, since an unpaid bailee has no right to use the object.[11] (See (v).

(v) He is liable for the nonreturn of the object no matter what the reason, if he uses it, since any use by an unpaid bailee is unauthorized.

(vi) The bailee is not liable to the owner for not returning the object to him if the owner was present and working for the bailee (even in an unrelated job) when the bailee took possession of the object. This is true even if the owner was not working for the bailee at the actual time when the object was lost, even by the negligence of the bailee. However, the bailee is liable if he intentionally damages or destroys the object.

(2) **The paid bailee**:

(i) He is liable for the nonreturn of the object if due to his negligence, it was lost, damaged, or destroyed. This is close to destroying the object willfully (for which he is liable) since the owner is relying upon him for more than the minimal protection of the object.

(ii) He is liable if the object was lost by him or if it was stolen from him. This holds true even if he guarded the object in a normal manner and was not negligent.

(iii) He is not liable for the nonreturn of the object if it was lost through *force majeure*.

(iv) He is liable for its nonreturn if the object "dies" while the bailee uses the object, since a paid bailee has no right to use the object. (See (v).)

10. The two situations, the theft of the object from the bailee and the loss of the object, are not alike. In the case of the theft it is almost *force majeure*; in the case of loss it almost borders on negligence. Yet both situations free the unpaid bailee from liability.

11. He is not liable in this situation if he can return the object in the manner in which he received it.

(v) He is liable for the nonreturn of the object no matter what the reason, if he uses it, since any use by a paid bailee is unauthorized.[12]

(vi) The bailee is not liable to the owner for not returning the object to him if the owner was present and working for the bailee (even in an unrelated job) when the bailee took possession of the object. This is true even if the owner was not working for the bailee at the actual time when the object was lost even by the negligence of the bailee. However, the bailee is liable if he intentionally damages or destroys the object.

(3) **The lessee:**

(i) He is liable for the nonreturn of the object if due to his negligence, it was lost, damaged, or destroyed. This is close to destroying the object willfully (for which he is liable) since the owner is relying upon him for more than the minimal protection of the object.

(ii) He is liable if the object was lost by him or if it was stolen from him. This holds true even if he guarded the object in a normal manner and was not negligent.

(iii) He is not liable for the nonreturn of the object if it was lost through *force majeure.*

(iv) and (v) He is not liable for its nonreturn if the object "dies" while the bailee uses the object in the manner that lessees use that particular object; the purpose of leasing the object was to use it.[13]

(vi) The bailee is not liable to the owner for not returning the object to him if the owner was present and working for the bailee (even in an unrelated job) when the bailee took possession of the object. This is true even if the owner was not working for the bailee at the actual time when the object was lost even by the negligence of the bailee. However, the bailee is liable if he intentionally damages or destroys the object.

(4) **The borrower:**

(i) He is liable for the nonreturn of the object if due to his negligence, it was lost, damaged, or destroyed. This is close to destroying the object willfully (for which he is liable) since the owner is relying upon him for the maximum protection of the object.

---

12. See prior note.

13. If he uses the object in a manner other than for what he leased the object, he may be liable. See Volume IX, Chapters 308 and 309.

(ii) He is liable if the object was lost by him or if it was stolen from him. This holds true even if he guarded the object in a normal manner and was not negligent.

(iii) He is liable for the nonreturn of the object even if it was lost through *force majeure*.

(iv) and (v) He is not liable for its nonreturn if the object "dies" while the borrower uses the object in the manner that borrowers use that particular object; the purpose of borrowing the object was to use it.[14] The lender realizes that the borrower will use his object.

(vi) The borrower is not liable to the lender for not returning the object to him if the lender was present and working for the borrower when the borrower took possession of the object. This is true even if the lender was not working for the borrower at the actual time when the object was lost even by the negligence of the borrower. However, the borrower is liable if he intentionally damages or destroys the object.

The bailee hires the owner

It has been stated in all four classes of bailees under factor (vi) "The bailee is not liable to the owner for not returning the object to him if the owner was present and working for the bailee (even in an unrelated job) when the bailee took possession of the object. This is true even if the owner was not working for the bailee at the actual time when the object was lost even by the negligence of the bailee. However, the bailee is liable if he intentionally damages or destroys the object."

The owner entrusts an object with any of the four classes of bailees. The bailee hires or borrows the services of the owner together with the delivery of the object to the bailee or the owner was already in the employ of the bailee as a paid employ or his services were borrowed. The bailee has no liabilities to the owner even if the bailee is negligent in how he guards the object. (The bailee is liable if he intentionally damages or destroys the object.) But if the bailee first became a bailee of the object and thereafter hired or borrowed the services of the owner, the bailee is liable the same as any other bailee;

14. See prior note.

he must pay for the loss even if the owner was present when the loss occurred. Conversely, if the owner was hired or borrowed when the object was delivered to the bailee, the bailee is free of liability even if the owner is not present when the loss of the object occurs.[15]

Stipulations regarding liability

It was stated above in the section dealing with the liabilities of the bailees that each had specific liabilities. But as is stated many times in this work, the parties may stipulate among themselves to vary the terms of the usual liabilities, if to do so does not violate a Torah command.[16] Thus the unpaid bailee may take upon himself the liabilities of a borrower that are the highest degree of liability and the borrower and lender may agree that the borrower will not be liable in any event even if he is negligent with the borrowed object. All such stipulations will be binding upon the parties, whether or not there were witnesses present when the stipulations were made. If the stipulations are made prior to or contemporaneously with the commencement of the role, they may be oral, without the necessity of a *kinyan*[17] being performed.[18] If made after the bailee has commenced his role as a bailee they are binding only if a *kinyan* is performed.[19]

15. See Volume IX, Chapter 305.

16. See note 4 above.

17. The *kinyan* is performed by the bailee handing his handkerchief to the owner and the owner handing his own handkerchief to the bailee. See Glossary; see Volume VI, Chapter 195.

18. Although the stipulations are oral statements, they are binding as personal obligations taken upon themselves and the consideration is the personal pleasure that the parties have in the trust that they place in each other and the public esteem that will flow from such displays of trust. See Volume II, page 147.

19. An interesting question arises if the unpaid bailee stipulates that he will have the liabilities of a paid bailee. The unpaid bailee is not liable if the object is stolen while the paid bailee is liable; the paid bailee is not liable if the object was lost through *force majeure*. The object was lost and the bailee pleads that it was lost through *force majeure*. The owner demands that the bailee take an oath (see the next section, "Proving the nonliability of the bailee") that the object was lost through *force majeure*. The bailee responds that he will take the oath of an unpaid bailee and that his stipulation that he would pay if the object was stolen only applies if there are

Proving the nonliability of the bailee

As seen in the prior sections, each of the four classes of bailees is sometimes free of liability although he cannot return intact the object that was entrusted to him or which he hired or borrowed. As is discussed in Chapter 297, the bailee may raise a defense that he never received the object from the owner, or that he returned it to the owner, and also be relieved of liability. He may be required to take an oath similar to the "oath of objects" to be free of liability.

The unpaid bailee is not liable if the object was lost or stolen from him, if it was lost by *force majeure* or an act of God, or if the owner was employed by the bailee at the time that the object was delivered to the bailee. He may be required to take the "oath of bailees" to be free of liability. This is discussed in Chapter 294.

The paid bailee is not liable if the object was lost by *force majeure* or an act of God, or if the owner was employed by the bailee at the time that the object was delivered to the bailee.

The lessee is not liable if the object was lost by *force majeure* or an act of God, or if the owner was employed by the bailee at the time that the object was delivered to the bailee, or if the object was damaged while being used in the manner for which it was leased.

The borrower is not liable if the object was damaged while being used in the manner for which it was borrowed or if the lender was employed by the borrower at the time that the object was delivered to the borrower.

In all situations where the bailee or borrower can free himself of liability, he will win the lawsuit brought by the owner or lender if he can bring witnesses who testify in support of his plea of lack of liability. If he cannot produce witnesses, then the bailee or the borrower will be found not liable in any of the aforesaid situations if he takes "the oath of the bailees" as set forth in Chapter 294.[20]

If the unpaid bailee pleads that he is not liable because the object was stolen from him, and then witnesses testify that the bailee stole the object, according to Torah law, he must pay the owner the double

---

witnesses that it was stolen. There are opinions both ways as to whether the bailee must take the oath demanded by the owner or may take the oath of an unpaid bailee. The latest holdings are that he must take the oath of a paid bailee.

20. Also see Volume III, page 126.

penalty paid by a thief.[21] However, the beth din system at the current time does not have jurisdiction to enforce payments of penalties.[22] Therefore, if the bailee pleads that the object was lost and witnesses testify that it was stolen by the bailee, he does not pay the double penalty.

Valuing and paying for the lost object

Assume that the object is damaged while in the custody of the bailee. It was worth $100 when the damage occurred. It is now worth $30. The bailee must return the object and add $70.[23]

Assume that the unpaid bailee is found to be liable to the owner for the loss or damage of the object because the bailee was negligent. Assume that the value of the object fluctuates between the time that the object is entrusted to the bailee and the time when the loss occurs. The bailee makes payment for the value of the object at the time when the loss occurs,[24] in this case the time when he was negligent that resulted in the loss of the object. (In the case of a paid bailee or a lessee, it is valued at the time that the object was lost or stolen or when the bailee was negligent. In the case of a borrower, it is valued whenever the loss occurs since he is always liable, except if the borrowed object dies while in use.)

The bailee is not liable for an amount of money greater than that which he was told the object was worth. If the owner understates the value of the object or the type of object it is, the liability of the bailee is limited to that value.[25] Assume that the owner informs the unpaid

21. See Volume I, pages 10 and 16.

22. See Volume I, page 16, and Volume IX, Chapters 348 and 352.

23. Similarly, in the cases of tort where the defendant damaged an object of the plaintiff/owner, the tort-feaser pays the difference as he does in the case of the bailee. However, in cases of robbery or theft, the law is different and the robber or the thief would have to pay $100 and keep the damaged object.

24. In the case of a robber who is not able to restore the object that he robbed, he makes payment in accordance with the value of the object when it was robbed. As soon as he robs the object, the owner loses jurisdiction over the object and he cannot sell it or donate it to charity. But in the case of the bailee it is still under the jurisdiction of the owner and he can sell it or donate it to charity.

25. Or the value of that type of object on the date that the loss occurs as stated in the prior paragraph.

bailee[26] that the contents of the package that the bailee agreed to guard contains bars of silver when in reality it contains bars of gold. If the bailee is negligent and the package is lost, the bailee must pay for the value of bars of silver valued at the time that the bailee's negligence caused the package to be lost.[27] However, if the bailee intentionally causes the loss, he has to pay for the value of the bars of gold, if the owner can prove that they were of gold.[28]

If the second person undertakes the role of a bailee under a mistake of fact, then he is not liable if there is a loss. An example given in the codes is as follows: The owner asks Ruven to travel to a foreign place and to take a load of books for him to the other place and agrees to pay Ruven a set fee. The only method of travel to that place is through an area frequented by robbers who take merchandise by force. All those who travel that route try to avoid the robbers or try to hide as much of the merchandise as they can. The robbers seize the books. The owner pleads that Ruven was negligent in not taking precautions to avoid the robbers. Ruven pleads that he was not aware of the perils of that route and that the owner should have told him about the perils and if he had told him, that Ruven would not have undertaken the trip. It was held that the owner was negligent in not advising Ruven of the perils and Ruven was not liable to the owner for the loss of the books.

Similarly, if the owner advises the bailee that the guarding of the object is relatively simple and it turns out that it is difficult to guard the item, the bailee is not liable for loss.

---

26. In the case of a borrower who borrows bars of silver and they are really bars of gold, and the bars are stolen or lost or even if lost through *force majeure*, he too must pay only for bars of silver. (For example, the borrower wants to impress his guests and borrows the bars from the lender.) This holds true even if the borrower knows that the bars are of gold. The same holds true for a finder of the bars that are silver-plated and he lost them in a situation where he is liable to the loser of the bars. He need pay the loser only for bars of silver. In the case of a thief or a robber, he must pay for bars of gold.

27. The bailee can plead that if he had known the true nature of the package he would not have undertaken to guard it.

28. Assume that the owner did not tell the bailee what the contents of the package were and the package was intentionally destroyed by the bailee. The owner pleads with certainty that the package contained gold bars and the bailee pleads that he is not certain what was in the package. The owner takes an oath and is paid for gold bars.

There is one opinion that holds that payment may be made by the bailee paying in cash or in kind or by transferring real estate for that value to the owner. These payments in kind may be made even if the bailee has cash. If the payment is made by transferring real estate it must be made from the highest quality land of the bailee.[29] There is another opinion that if the bailee possesses cash or real estate he is not permitted to pay in kind. I think that in our times, the latter opinion should be followed.

Taking up the role of the bailee

The unpaid bailee is not liable for the care of the object, nor for the "oath of the bailees," nor for feeding an animal if it is the object that is left with him, until he assumes the role of an unpaid bailee.

According to most opinions,[30] all that is required to establish the legal relationship of owner and bailee is a simple meeting of the minds as seen through the discussion between the owner and a second person to make the second person an unpaid bailee, or sometimes as seen through their actions.

The owner usually initiates the transaction by asking a second person to guard the object,[31] such as "Guard this for me," or other words to that effect, and the second person states, "I will guard the object," or words to that effect, and the owner departs. At that moment the second person becomes an unpaid bailee, since the words of the second person indicates his intent to accept the offer of the owner to become a bailee and that he undertakes to guard the object.

There are situations where the agreement of the offer and acceptance between the parties is not that clear-cut. The codes give many examples and sometimes with conflicting results. I set forth some of these fact patterns and the results as seen in the codes and cases. In essence, each case must be judged by beth din to determine if the second person accepted to be a bailee. If he did and there is a loss resulting from his negligence, he is liable; if he did not and there is a loss, he is not liable.

Some examples:

29. By transferring *idith* land. See Glossary, *bainanith*.
30. See second opinion below.
31. Any personal property.

The owner asks the second person to guard his object. The second person replies, "Leave the object in front of me," or other words to that effect.[32] Held: he is a bailee, since the words "leave the object in front of me" indicates that "I accept to guard the object."

The owner asks the second person to guard his object. The second person replies, "Leave it down in front of you," or "Leave it," or "The place is before you," or other words to the effect that fail to show that without doubt he undertook to be a bailee. Held: he is not a bailee.[33] There is an opinion that this holds true only if the conversation takes place in the market or in the courtyard of the second person.[34] But if the conversation takes place on a highway and the second person is continuing on the highway and the owner is not going on the highway, he is a bailee. Also, if the place that he instructs the owner to place the object is unguarded, and the owner is about to depart, the second person becomes an unpaid bailee even without explicit words to that effect.[35]

The owner states to the second person "Keep your eyes on the object" and the second person replies "Leave the object in front of me." Held: he is not a bailee.

---

32. Such as "Leave it with *me*" or such other words from which beth din can determine evinces an intention on behalf of the second person to undertake to guard the object.

33. Although the second person does not become a bailee, he is liable if he or his property caused damage to the object.

34. There is an opinion that even if the conversation takes place in a public place the second person becomes a bailee. Otherwise, why did he tell the owner "Leave the object in front of you," or "Leave it," or "The place is before you"? If the second person did not intend to become a bailee, the owner does not need his permission to leave the object in a public place. Therefore, we attribute intent to the second person to become a bailee.

35. The following case decided by R. Asher ben Yechiel (Asheri, Toledo, Spain, 1250–1324, Responsum Chapter 24, response 2) is cited by all of the subsequent codes: Ruven was about to depart on a journey and Shimon asked Ruven to deliver a pair of shoes to someone at Ruven's destination. Ruven, without taking the shoes himself, instructed Shimon to put the shoes on the donkey that Ruven was taking with him, and Shimon put the shoes on the bundles that the donkey was carrying. Ruven did not tie the shoes to the bundles but left them there as Shimon had placed them. Ruven departed and walked alongside the donkey and along the way stopped to use the toilet facilities. The shoes were lost. It was held that Ruven was an unpaid bailee and responsible for the shoes since he was negligent in not tying the shoes to the bundles on the donkey and Shimon did not accompany Ruven on the journey.

The owner places the object in front of the second person without saying anything. The second person says, "Leave the object in front of me." Held: He is not a bailee.

The owner places the objects in front of the second person without saying anything. The second person states, "I will guard the object." Held: he is a bailee.

The owner asks the second person for permission to bring his animal or his merchandise into the second person's courtyard. The second person replies, "O.K." or "The courtyard is before you."[36] Held: not only is the second person not a bailee; he is not even liable if the second person's animal damages the merchandise.[37] There is also a dissenting opinion that the second person is liable for damages inflicted on the merchandise by the animals of the second person, but not for loss caused in any other manner, since the second person is not a bailee; this latter opinion is not usually followed.

The owner asks the second person if he can bring his merchandise into the house of the second person and he is told "O.K." Held: the second person is a bailee.[38]

36. According to the second view expressed at the end of this section, since placing the object within the property of the second person could constitute an act of acquisition if the second person were purchasing the object, it is a sufficient act to create the relationship. The property of the second person acts to acquire the bailee relationship.

37. It is presumed that when the second person said "O.K.," he meant that the owner could bring in his merchandise but would guard them himself. All that the second person has undertaken is to permit the owner to place his object on his outdoor property without compensation. The second person has not undertaken to guard the object without explicitly so stating. If the second person states that the owner will pay a fee and does so, the second person is still not deemed to be a bailee since the fee is deemed to be rent for the place and no part of the fee for the guarding the object. Furthermore, the second person is not responsible if his animal injures or damages the object that the owner left on the second person's real estate.

38. This case differs from the case in the prior paragraph where permission was sought to enter into a courtyard and in this paragraph permission is sought to enter into the house of the second person. There is an obvious difference between permitting the owner to enter the outdoor yard of the second party and to enter into his house. In the former case there are probably many people who enter into the yard and the owner is being given permission to guard his own object in the second person's outdoor yard. But no one can enter the house without permission, and such latter's permission is tantamount to the second party agreeing to become a bailee to guard the object.

The owner asks the second person if he can bring his merchandise into the house of the second person. The second person replies, "The house is open to you," or "The house is before you." Held: He is not a bailee.

The owner asks the second person if he can bring his merchandise into the house of the second person. The second person designates a place or corner or room in the house. Held: he is not a bailee.

There is a *second opinion* that holds that mere agreement is not sufficient to establish the relationship of owner/bailee. According to this opinion, the second person does not become an unpaid bailee unless there is also performed an act to the object that would have been an act of acquisition had the object been sold from the owner to the second person.

There are times when a person's property or even parts of the public street acquire an object that one purchases on behalf of the purchaser. The same would hold true in making the second person an unpaid bailee. (The acts of acquisition of personal property are discussed in Volume VI, Chapters 197 through 203.)

Ruven purchased from Shimon by an act of *kinyan*[39] an object that is in Shimon's premises; Ruven did not take possession of the object, nor did he pay for the object; the object remained in Shimon's possession. Shimon is deemed to be a paid bailee of the object. But if Shimon received the money or is willing to give Ruven the object before being paid, Shimon is not even deemed to be an unpaid bailee regarding the object that is now owned by Ruven.

Similarly, Shimon gave a gift to Ruven by handing it to Levi, and Ruven does not have possession of the object.[40] If Ruven is a minor, Levi is an unpaid bailee for Ruven regarding the gift, whether or not Ruven is present or even knows of the gift. If Ruven has reached adulthood,[41] knows of the gift, and is within the city or in a place that it is possible for him to take possession of the gift, Levi is not even an unpaid bailee for Ruven; if Ruven is not aware of the gift or Ruven is too far away to pick up the gift, Levi is an unpaid bailee for Ruven. In all of these situations, Levi can refuse to accept the gift for Ruven.

---

39. See Volume VI, Chapter 195; see Glossary.

40. See Volume VII, Chapter 243.

41. 13 years and 1 day for a male and 12 years and 1 day for a female.

Standard of care required of a bailee

The standard of care required of the bailee depends upon the object that is entrusted to him. Every community will have its own standards depending upon the climate and standards of refrigeration of perishable objects, the types and amount of thieves and burglars, the types of safes and other things of that nature. Much of what is said here is obviated by owners of personal property storing their possessions in vaults, at home, or in banks. When a person spends time in a hotel or motel there are usually notices in each room that the hotel has safe deposit boxes to store valuables.

Beth din in each community must adopt standards that are in conformity with the habits of the community and the type of object that is entrusted to the bailee. The fact that the bailee treated the object entrusted to him in the same manner as he treats his own object is not a defense if the object gets lost or damaged, unless his standard for his own objects measures up to the community standard.

A great deal of the laws in the codes deal with entrusting clothing or cash to bailees, and I have included only those two types of objects. What follows are some of the laws that go back to Talmudic times regarding these specific objects entrusted by the owner to the bailee. All the rules are applicable only if the parties between themselves do not agree otherwise. The owner and the bailee can set their own standards of proper guarding of the object by the bailee.

Clothing should not be stored in trunks since mice find their way in and destroy the clothing. Rather it should be hung in a closet out of the reach of mice.[42] This may not apply if the trunk is placed near water, since mice will not eat the garments if there is water to drink. Garments containing furs or skins must be stored in cool places; otherwise, they will spoil from the moisture in the walls of the closet.

Moneys (moneys were then always coins and not paper money) have special rules to protect against rust and other spoilage and against theft.[43] The bailee should bury them in the ground at least a

42. There is an opinion that this applies only if the trunk contained some food resulting in food particles still being in the trunk.

43. What is said regarding moneys also applies to jewelry, precious stones, gold pieces, and similar objects.

tefach[44] deep, and where thieves abound who are adept at finding things buried in the ground, they should be buried into the walls of a house. Certain exceptions are made if the money is entrusted to the bailee on the eve of the Sabbath or a Holy Day or immediately at the conclusion of these days, when the bailee does not have time to hide the money. The aforesaid Talmudic requirements were changed during the Middle Ages and the standard became what a reasonable person would do with his own money, he could do with the money he was guarding as a bailee. If the bailee received the money to deliver it to another place, he was required to hold the moneys tied up in his hand and if there was a long journey, the bailee had to sew the money into his garment or to put it into a money pouch that he kept under his clothing. All these things had to be done in such a manner that pickpockets could not get to the money.

Negligent conduct by the unpaid bailee

The unpaid bailee is liable to the owner if a loss occurs through his negligence. Each community should set its own standards depending upon the time and place of the bailment.

The owner and the bailee can agree among themselves to the type of guarding that the bailee should follow (and the extent of his liability). Absent such agreement, the following are some of the rules as laid down in the Talmud and the subsequent codes and responsa literature.

If the bailee hides the object so well that he cannot locate it when the owner demands it back, this is deemed negligence and the bailee is immediately responsible to compensate the owner for the loss of the object. The owner is not required to wait until the bailee finds the object. Each plea of "I do not know where the object is" is deemed to be a confession of negligence and is equivalent to "I destroyed the object," in which case he is liable even if the owner was present and working for the bailee when he received the object.

Another situation: If a bailee does not know whether the object is lost through his negligence or through *force majeure*, he must pay the owner since he cannot take the oath that will absolve him from

44. About 3.5 inches. See Glossary.

liability. He can take the oath of bailees to free himself of liability only if he can swear with certainty that he was not negligent.

The bailee realizes that someone is stealing the object or faces a robber and if he cries out the thief or the robber will flee since others will come to his defense. He fails to cry out without being threatened that he will be injured if he cries out, he is negligent of not having cried out. If he is threatened, he is not negligent if he fails to cry out. The unpaid bailee is liable if there were people available who could have come to his aid without any expense to him. If there were people who would come to his aid but insisted upon being paid, the unpaid bailee is not required to offer them compensation and if they then refuse to help him, he is not liable for not having made compensation to the others.[45]

There is a well-known topic in Talmudic law and that also appears in all of the codes, commentaries, and responsa literature known in its original as *techilosah bepeshia v'sofoh b'ones*. That is, the bailee was at the outset negligent in how he guarded the object, but the object was lost through *force majeure*. Is the bailee liable? The Talmud after much discussion concludes that the bailee is liable (with a few exceptions as seen below) if there can be shown some casual connection between the negligence and the *force majeure*. That is, if not for the negligence the *force majeure* would probably not have caused the loss. The concept can best be illustrated by a few examples:

The bailee hid the object in a picket of reeds, a place where it would be difficult for thieves to find it, but it was a place where there were many fires. The object was stolen from the hiding place. The bailee was found liable, for had he hid the object in another place, the thief may not have found the object to steal it.

The bailee guarded the animal that was entrusted to him in a place that was safe from wild animals such as lions and wolves but was frequented by thieves. The animal was devoured by wolves. The bailee was liable[46] because if he had guarded it in a place that was safe from

45. If the bailee is a paid bailee he will be liable for not hiring the other people to help him save the object from the robbers and thieves. The bailee will be reimbursed for the expense. See Volume IX, Chapter 303.

46. The converse is also true. The place is safe from thieves but is frequented by wild animals. The animal was stolen. The bailee is liable.

thieves, then it would also probably have been safe from wild animals.[47]

However, if the event would have occurred regardless of the precautions taken, then the bailee is not liable even if he acted negligently in the first instance. For example, the bailee is guarding the animal in a place frequented by both wild animals and thieves. The animal dies a natural death. There is no liability since there is no causal connection between the negligence and the death of the animal.[48]

The bailee entrusts the object to a third person

The owner entrusted the object to the bailee, who in turn entrusts the object to a third person. The object is lost or damaged while in the possession of the third person. There are now three parties to the transaction, the owner, the bailee, and the third person. What are their respective rights?

The *halachah* is now established that if the bailee entrusts the object to a third person to guard and the object is lost, stolen, or damaged, the bailee is liable. The reason given is that the owner can state that he believes the bailee should the bailee take an oath to relieve himself of liability, while the owner does not trust any other person to take an oath of nonliability.

Not only is the bailee liable to the owner if he was a paid bailee who entrusted the object to an unpaid bailee whose liability is more restricted than that of a paid bailee, but he is liable to the owner even if the first bailee is an unpaid bailee and he entrusts the object to a third person whom he pays. This third person is therefore a paid bailee and has additional liabilities that the bailee did not have.[49] This holds true even if the third person enjoys a reputation that he is more trustworthy than the bailee. Therefore, if the object was lost or stolen or damaged in the presence of witnesses so that the bailee is not

47. The codes containing many other cases dealing with a bailee who guards animals since raising animals was part of the economic lives of the people.

48. However, if the animal had been stolen and died a natural death in the possession of the thief, he is liable for the cost of the animal to the owner.

49. See above that an unpaid bailee is only liable for negligence but not if the object was lost or stolen, while the paid bailee is liable not only for negligence but also when the object is lost or stolen.

called upon to take an oath, the bailee is not liable since there is no oath involved. Similarly, if the bailee was present when the object was lost or stolen or damaged and the bailee can testify to facts that show no liability to the owner, the bailee is not liable. The owner cannot raise the plea of the bailee only being believed by him since it is the bailee who is taking the oath of nonliability.

If the bailee entrusted the object to the third person in the presence and knowledge of the owner and the owner did not protest, then the bailee is not liable if the object was lost, stolen, or damaged in the possession of the third person. Therefore, if the owner was accustomed to entrust this third person, then the bailee is not liable to the owner if the object was lost, stolen, or damaged while in the possession of the third person. This hold true only if the third person does not have less liability than the bailee. If the third person does not have the money to pay the owner, the bailee is still liable to him.

When the owner entrusts the bailee with the object to be guarded in the home of the bailee, it is assumed that the wife, sons who are of age, and other members of the household of the bailee will also be engaged in the guarding of the object; this is not included in the laws at the beginning of this section providing for liability. But if the bailee entrusted the object to minor children or to others in the house but who do not reside with the bailee, the bailee is liable for loss. However, if it can be shown that the owner knows that the bailee never guards the object by himself but always entrusts the object to another person, the owner cannot be heard to plead that the bailee is liable for loss of the object.

There are two reported cases in the Talmud that appear in all of the codes: The owner entrusted the bailee with moneys to guard. The bailee entrusted the moneys to his mother, who hid the moneys but not too well, and the moneys were stolen. It was held that the bailee is not liable because he entrusted the moneys to a member of his household. This case also involved the situation where the bailee did not inform his mother that the moneys were not his since the bailee felt that the mother would take better care of the money if she thought it belonged to her son. The mother had no liability to the owner since she was not told that the money belonged to the owner and not to her son. The bailee was required to take an oath that the money that he gave to his mother that was stolen from her was indeed the money entrusted to him by the owner, and the mother was required to swear that she hid the moneys from view. If they both took the oaths they are free of liability to the owner. However, if the bailee advised his wife and the members of his household that the money he is entrusting to them belongs to the owner, and they did not guard the object as they should have, they are liable to the owner and the bailee is not liable. If the wife or the other members of the household who are liable to the owner do not have money to compensate the owner, there are opinions both ways whether the bailee is liable to the owner.

The other case: The owner of hops entrusted the hops to the bailee, who also had hops of his own. The bailee instructed his servant to place some hops into the beer, pointing to his own hops. The servant placed some of the owner's entrusted hops into the beer. When the owner sued to recover the value of the hops, it was held that the servant was not liable since his master the bailee did not tell him to put these hops in and not the others. The servant might have thought that the bailee pointed to certain hops only to make things easier for him but it did not matter which hops he put into the beer. The bailee is not liable since he told the servant to place "some of these hops into the beer." The bailee pays to the owner the benefit of the owner's hops in his beer. Thus if the beer turned sour and the bailee has no benefit, he pays nothing to the owner. The bailee must take an oath that all of these facts are true.

Termination of the role of the bailee

At the time that the bailee is entrusted with the object by the owner, they may stipulate the length of the term of the bailment, the time and place where the object should be returned to the owner, and any other agreements they may have regarding the return of the object. All such agreements will be binding on both parties.[50]

Assume that there is no agreement between the parties regarding the termination of the role of the bailee and how and where to return the object to the owner. There are two ways to look at the situation: (1) from the perspective of the owner or (2) from the perspective of the bailee.

(1) The owner may at any time, even before the agreed-upon time

50. For example, a car rental company may permit the lessee to return the car in another city if that is convenient for the lessee.

of termination, request that the bailee return the object and terminate the bailee's role.[51] He may not do this in the case of the lessee or the borrower.[52] The owner cannot demand that the bailee return the object to a place other than the place where the object was entrusted to the bailee. If the object was entrusted to the bailee in Tel Aviv, the owner cannot demand its return in Jerusalem. The owner cannot make such demand even if he offers to pay the expenses of the bailee to make such delivery. This holds true even if the object that was deposited was money and the bailee has other money in Jerusalem to give to the owner in place of the money that he is holding in Tel Aviv. However, if the bailee brought the object to Jerusalem, the owner can demand its return there. On the other hand, even if the bailee brought the object to Jerusalem, the owner can demand that the object be returned in Tel Aviv.

(2) Assume that the time of termination has not yet arrived. There is an opinion that the bailee may terminate his role the same as any employee may resign his employment at any time. There is another opinion that he is not similar to an employee and thus he may not resign his role as a bailee. The bailee may return the object to the owner wherever he may find him (or the owner's wife if the object is returned to the home of the owner), except if the place stated by the bailee is too remote and is desert-like. If the bailee forced the owner to receive the object back, it is a valid return of the object.

The bailee informs the owner that he is ready to return the object to the place where it was entrusted to him, and the owner is not there to receive it; the bailee has no further liabilities regarding the object. However, if a borrower has not returned the object to the owner, he has the liabilities of a paid bailee. All bailees are liable if the object is lost because of their negligence that occurs after the time of termination of the bailee's role if the bailee did not offer to return the object.

The bailee is about to depart the community, for example, for an

51. If the bailee is a paid bailee, then the owner must pay to him the moneys that the bailee earned.

52. In the situation of the lessee he may terminate the lease before the time agreed upon his paying the rent until such time except in the case of a leased house if there is no one to live in the house and the owner is concerned to leave the house vacant. In the situation of the borrower, he may return the object at any time.

overseas trip, and he wants to return the object to the owner. The owner is himself away overseas. The bailee may deliver the object to beth din and be absolved from further liability. To hold otherwise would make the bailee a prisoner when he must quickly depart. Beth din will entrust the object to a trustworthy person. The bailee may not entrust the object to such other person, and if he does, he has the same liabilities as above stated regarding a bailee who entrusts the object to a third person.

If the bailee gave the object to another person to deliver it to the owner, whether it was the desire of the bailee to so deliver the object or even if it was the request of the owner[53] to so deliver the object to him, the bailee is liable until the object is returned to the owner. The bailee can recall the object from the agent until it is delivered to the owner, unless the bailee has been designated a fraudulent person by beth din in the interim.

53. The fact that it was the owner who requested that the object be returned by that messenger does not make that person an agent of the owner.

Chapter 292

UNAUTHORIZED USE OF THE OBJECT BY THE BAILEE

INTRODUCTION

The unpaid bailee is entrusted with an object to guard, not to use.[1] In Chapter 291 it was stated in discussing the liabilities of the unpaid bailee: "He is liable for the nonreturn of the object no matter what the reason, if he uses it, since any use by an unpaid bailee is unauthorized." The object may be resting in a place designated by the owner or it may be resting in a place selected by the bailee with the right of the bailee to move the object to another place.

This chapter discusses the unauthorized use of the object by the unpaid bailee. The Torah in discussing an unpaid bailee states, "If a man delivers unto his neighbor money or things to be looked after, and it is claimed that it has been stolen from the house of the man [the bailee]; if the thief be found he shall pay double. If the thief shall not be found, then the master of the house [the bailee] shall place himself unto God, if he has not put forth his hands to the goods of his

1. Of the four bailees, only the lessee and the borrower may use the object, for it was leased or borrowed to be used. Neither the unpaid bailee nor the paid bailee may use the object that is entrusted to them.

neighbor."[2] The Mishna, in discussing this law, states, "If a person intends to make use of a bailment, Beth Shammai maintains that he is immediately responsible for the object. Beth Hillel maintains that he is not responsible until he actually makes use of the object."[3] The law as it appears in Maimonides states, "If a bailee makes unauthorized use of an object entrusted to him, either himself or via his son or a slave or his agent, he is deemed a robber and is held responsible for all *force majeure* damage, and the robbed object is deemed to be in his custody similar to that of all robbers. He is not held responsible for the object until he actually uses it, and not for mere intent alone. Once he has made use of it, he is held responsible. Even if his use does not depreciate the value of the object, but he merely moves the object from one place to another on his premises to make use of it, he becomes responsible for the object, because unauthorized use does not require depreciation."[4] Rabbi Yosef Karo calls this chapter "One Must Not Make Unauthorized Use Of A Bailment, And What If One Did."

The bailee, when he makes unauthorized use of the object, either takes up the object with the view to keeping it, or just to use it and return it. Even when he takes up the object without authorization, just to use it, the use may depreciate the object, such as using an automobile where there is wear and tear on the tires and motor. Or there is no depreciation of the object, such as standing on a ladder that has been entrusted to the bailee. There is also another concept similar to that of the bailee making unauthorized use of the object: the concept of the person who "borrows" an object from an owner without the consent of the owner. The text commences with the general prohibition and the distinctions between these two concepts.

What if the bailee, after making an unauthorized use of the object, decides to return it to its place? Is he restored to being an unpaid bailee with limited liabilities? Or, once he leaves that status is he unable to reenter that status and, instead, remains absolutely liable the same as a robber of an object?

There is a section of examples of what is considered unauthorized use and what movement is permitted of the entrusted object. There is

2. Exodus 22:6–7.
3. Mishna, *Baba Metzia*, 43b.
4. Maimonides, *Laws of Robbery and Lost Property*, chapter 3, law 11.

a special section of unauthorized use of money. Actually, the earlier codes speak of coins, which was the major method of paying for objects. There was no paper money or checks or other method of payment. I have substituted the concept of money instead of coins. Most times coins were interchangeable one for the other and thus the bailee could return coins other than the ones that were entrusted to him. Also, the bailee had the right under some conditions to use the money entrusted to him.

There are times when the bailee is threatened by a robber or other person who employs force to give up the entrusted object or be harmed. This is similar to unauthorized use of the object of the owner although here it may sometimes be justified. What are the rights of the bailee and the owner in such circumstances? What if the money he is holding is for the redemption of captives, the highest form of spending money?

Another aspect of unauthorized use of the owner's object occurs when the bailee commingles the owner's objects with his own, such as when money or produce of the owner is commingling with money or produce of the bailee. This is discussed in the section dealing with commingling of the object.

Once Rabbi Karo discusses the spoilage and shrinkage of commingled objects, he discusses the responsibility of a bailee regarding spoilage and shrinkage of the owner's objects even when there is no commingling. I discuss these laws in the section called "Spoilage and shrinkage of the objects."

TEXT

The prohibition against unauthorized use of the object by the bailee

The Torah prohibits the unpaid bailee (or the paid bailee) from unauthorized use of the object that was entrusted to him by the owner.

The mere intent, whether or not verbalized, to make unauthorized use of the object does not impose any additional liability upon the unpaid bailee. This is true even if he declared his intent to witnesses. His intent, coupled with some action on his part, may cause him to be liable in all events of damage to the object, including *force majeure*. This extention of his intent will place him into one of two categories, that of a bailee who makes unauthorized use of the object entrusted to him, or that of a borrower without authority of the owner.

The bailee intends to make an unauthorized use of the bailment, which use will probably result in a depreciation of the value of the object. As soon as he pulls or lifts the object,[5] he is transformed into a robber of the object, regardless of the fact that he intends only temporary use of the object and that he intends to return the object after its use. He is a robber although he never actually made use of the object after he lifted it or pulled it. Actual depreciation is not required once he intends to use it in a manner that might depreciate it. Thus intent to use it in a manner that might depreciate it coupled with a lifting or pulling of the object makes the bailee into a robber.

The bailee intends to use the object in a manner that will *not* depreciate the object. He does not become the equivalent of a borrower without authority (which is also equivalent to being a robber) until he actually uses the object, as distinguished from merely lifting it or pulling it to himself.

The bailee is liable even if he personally did not perform the unauthorized act; he is liable even if the act was performed by his agent. There is an opinion that the bailee is liable if the act to make the bailee liable was performed by the agent only if the agent was not aware that the object was entrusted to the bailee, or the agent is not mentally competent,[6] or the agent does not have the money to pay the owner.[7]

5. See Volume VI, Chapter 198, "Acquisition Of Personalty: By Lifting, Pulling, Or Delivery." An object cannot be transferred from one's ownership to that of another until an act of acquisition is performed on the object. The robber or thief also is not liable until he performs such an act. Once the robber or the bailee without authorization or the borrower without authorization performs such an act of acquisition, he becomes the custodian and is liable for anything that happens to the object.

6. Such as being mentally deficient or still a minor.

7. Ordinarily, a principal is not responsible for violations committed by his agent; the agent is responsible for his own violations. He should not have followed illegal

Restoring the object to its place

Assume that the bailee makes unauthorized use of the object and there is no depreciation, or that there is depreciation and he restores it and wants to pay for the depreciation. The object is thereafter stolen, or lost, or damaged or lost through *force majeure*. Is the unpaid bailee liable? Under ordinary circumstances the unpaid bailee is not responsible for such loss. In the situation being discussed here, he is liable as soon as he lifts or pulls the object to use it in a manner that would depreciate the object. Does his returning the object to the place where it was stored reinstate him in the same position he was in before he lifted or pulled the object?

The majority opinion is that once he has become a robber of the object, his replacing the object does not reinstate him to a role of an unpaid bailee and continues his unlimited liability for the object. There is also a strong dissent that once he replaces the object he is reinstated to his role as an unpaid bailee and has the limited liabilities of an unpaid bailee.

Acts constituting unauthorized use

The Talmud and codes give examples of acts constituting unauthorized use and the extent of the liability of the bailee when there is an unauthorized use of the object, which can be achieved only if the object is lifted or pulled, and those situations where there is some taking of part of the object but there is not a lifting or a pulling of the entire object. There are situations where even in the latter case the bailee will bear full liability for the loss or damage to the object.

There are times when the owner will designate a place or the bailee will designate a place for the object to remain to which the owner agrees. The object cannot be moved from that place (except as shown in this section). There may be times when no specific place is designated for keeping the object except that the unpaid bailee may not be negligent.

The owner entrusts the bailee with a barrel of wine that is set down in a special place in the bailee's wine cellar. The bailee tips the barrel

orders, but should rather have obeyed the laws of the Torah. This situation is an exception based on an interpretation of a verse in the Torah.

without moving, lifting, or pulling it from its spot where it rested and removes a quart of wine. If the barrel breaks after the bailee takes the wine from the barrel, the bailee is not liable for the breakage, but is responsible to pay the owner for a quart of wine.[8] The bailee is liable only for the part of the object that he actually took; the balance still belongs to the owner who bears the responsibility for all loss except for the negligence of the unpaid balance. However, if the balance of the wine in the barrel turns sour, the bailee is liable for the price of wine for the entire barrel.[9] This may not apply to other types of beverage such as whiskeys or juices.

The owner entrusts the bailee with a barrel of wine that is set down in a special place in the bailee's wine cellar. The bailee lifts[10] the barrel to take a quart of wine.[11] The bailee is liable for all loss that will thereafter occur to the barrel of wine even if he does not actually take the quart of wine.[12]

The bailee takes the entrusted barrel of wine not to drink from it or to use it and the bailee moves the barrel to a place other than where it is left. If the barrel was moved for the sake of the barrel, such as to keep it away from heat, and the barrel breaks while the bailee is handling it or afterward when it was returned to its place or a new place, the bailee has no liability. However, if he moves the barrel for his own purposes, such as to stand on it, the bailee is liable if the barrel breaks at any time. If he moves the barrel to get to the space on which the barrel stood, the bailee is liable if the barrel was then lost or damaged through his negligence but not if through *force majeure*.

---

8. Since he did not move or lift or pull the barrel from its spot he is not guilty of unauthorized use.

9. The wine would not have turned sour if the barrel was full. It was only because the barrel was opened and air came in that the balance of the wine soured.

10. Or pulls it into his domain. See Volume VI, Chapter 198.

11. There is an opinion that the bailee is liable in this case only if he intended to take the wine for his own benefit. However, if he took the wine to spill out he is not liable for the entire barrel but rather only for the wine that he spilled.

12. The bailee is liable since he lifted the object with the intent to cause some depreciation to the barrel of wine by taking some of the wine. At that moment he is liable for the entire object since he is now deemed to have robbed the wine from the owner.

Acts constituting unauthorized use of money

The owner may instruct the bailee that he may not use the money that is entrusted to him. Should the bailee use the money or refuse to return the money to the owner when demanded of him, he is a robber and responsible for the return of the money. Or the owner may permit the bailee to invest the money or otherwise use the money entrusted to him. The bailee may be deemed a borrower or a paid bailee depending upon the circumstances. Absent any agreement, the following laws prevail.

The owner entrusted money[13] with a money changer or a shopkeeper or a person who lends money on interest.[14] If it is contained in a purse that is not sealed nor tied with a peculiar knot, the bailee is permitted to use the money.[15] Since the bailee may use the money, he has the status of a paid bailee regarding the money even before he actually uses the money. If the owner demands the money back, the bailee may give him other money in an equal amount. If the money was lost or stolen or lost or damaged because of the negligence of the bailee, he is liable to the owner; he is not liable if the money was lost through *force majeure*. Once the bailee uses the money he has the status of a borrower and is liable under all circumstances. This last law holds true even if the bailee restored the money to the purse, he is liable as a borrower until he restores the money to the owner. All of the profits made by the bailee belong to the bailee. If the bailee does share the profits with the owner, it is not considered interest to the owner. When the owner makes a demand for the return of the money and tells the bailee that he needs the money to invest it and the bailee does not give the money back to the owner, the bailee is liable for the loss of profits that the owner sustained by not having the money returned to him.[16] The bailee may tell the owner that the money is

13. This does not apply to bars of silver or ingots that are not readily acceptable as money. It all depends upon the community.

14. This refers to a person who lends money to a non-Jew.

15. It is known by all that money lenders, money lenders on interest, and shopkeepers are always looking to borrow money. He is permitted to use the money since it is assumed that if the owner did not want the money changer or shopkeeper to use the money, he would have tied the money up in a peculiar manner.

16. The burden of proof will be on the owner to prove his loss of profits. There is also a dissent that holds that loss of profits is not collectable.

invested and if the bailee wants to participate in the investment, for loss or for gain, the owner may agree or may wait until the bailee completes his investment. If the bailee advises people that he has invested the money for the owner and if there is a profit, such profits belong to the owner.

If the money was entrusted to the money changer or shopkeeper or a money lender on interest, and the money is contained in a purse that is sealed or tied in a peculiar way, the bailee is not permitted to use the money. If therefore the money was lost through his negligence, he is liable; if lost or stolen or lost through *force majeure*, he is not liable.

The owner entrusted a bailee who is not a money lender, a lender on interest, or a shopkeeper with a purse of money. The bailee may not use the money. Therefore the unpaid bailee, if he placed the money in a suitable secure place,[17] is not liable for any loss unless there was a loss due to the negligence of the bailee. The nonmoney-lender bailee lifted the purse to take out one coin or other money, a part of the object that is not attached to the other part of the object. The majority view is that the bailee assumes full liability for the entire purse and contents of the money if they are later lost or stolen or lost through *force majeure*. There is a strong dissent that holds that there is some doubt as to the accuracy of the majority holding: perhaps the bailee is liable only for the money that he took from the purse or perhaps he is liable for the entire purse.

The bailee relinquishes the object to save himself

The bailee is properly guarding a valuable object. The bailee is accosted by robbers who demand the object be given to them. If the robbers would probably not have accosted the bailee except that he was guarding the valuable object, he is not liable to the owner for having surrendered the object to the robbers. However, if the bailee is wealthy enough that robbers would seek him out to rob even if he was not guarding this particular valuable object, the bailee is liable to the owner for having saved himself with someone else's object.

If the money that the bailee surrenders to the robber was from a

17. See Chapter 291.

general fund for the poor or from a fund to ransom captives,[18] and he had no other money to rescue himself,[19] he is not liable to the fund for redeeming captives.[20] The same applies if the bailee is negligent with moneys from these funds and they were lost; he is not liable.[21] However, if the fund was earmarked to redeem specific captives or specific poor of the community, then the bailee is liable to the fund if he was negligent with the moneys and a loss ensued.

Commingling the object with the bailee's objects

The bailee must not commingle the object with his own objects of the same type which objects are subject to shrinkage or other common types of loss.[22] For example, the owner gives the bailee a specific amount of produce. The bailee may not commingle the owner's produce with his own produce. If he does and there is some loss in the total produce, he is responsible for a proportionate amount of the loss such as shrinkage, if the loss is the normal type of loss through shrinkage or spoilage.[23] But if the loss exceeds the normal amount of loss, the bailee takes an oath as to the balance, that he did not act negligently in guarding the object, and returns the balance. In this latter situation they share the loss proportionately. If the bailee does not agree to take the oath he must reimburse the owner for the loss. If the bailee was taking for his own needs from the commingled batch, and he does not recall how much he took for himself, he calculates the amount of shrinkage according to a scale that the

18. The captives spoken of here are those who were captured by non-Jews to torture and murder them, or else to hold them for money ransom.

19. He has no other money of his own in the place where the demand is made by the robbers; although he has money of his own in another place, it is deemed that he has no money of his own. The bailee need not thereafter reimburse the charity fund from the money he has in another place.

20. He redeemed himself, which is the purpose of this fund.

21. According to the Torah law a bailee is only liable to persons or entities that may make claims against the bailee. See Exodus 22:6, which speaks of a *man* delivering an object to the bailee.

22. When the bailee uses the commingled objects he may make unauthorized use of the objects of the owner.

23. For example, the owner entrusted the bailee with ten objects and the bailee had five of his own; three objects are lost. The owner lost two objects and the bailee lost one object.

community develops. The amount of shrinkage will vary from community to community depending upon the climate and the time of the year.

Assume that the amount of the owner's produce was not measured when entrusted to the bailee, who commingled it with his own. The bailee is negligent in not measuring it before commingling it, and therefore must pay for any loss. If the owner pleads that there were 100 bushels and the bailee pleads that he does not know, the bailee must give the owner 100 bushels without the owner having to take an oath. The law is the same in all situations where the bailee admits liability due to his negligence but does not know the amount of his liability; if the owner pleads that he knows the amount and the bailee does not know, the bailee pays the amount demanded by the owner. This is true if it can be shown that the bailee did receive an amount in keeping with what the owner pleads, and that the owner would be in possession of such a amount. This topic is more fully discussed in Chapter 298.

The bailee agrees to transport the owner's money, without any warranty to the owner as to their safe arrival. The bailee commingles it with his own in one sack or wallet;[24] the results are as stated above in this section. If some of the money was lost, the loss is shared proportionately. This is so because all of the money is indistinguishable one from the other. If the bailee transports rings made of gold (instead of money) and the bailee commingled the rings with his own rings, the result is different.[25] If one of the commingled rings was lost, the bailee can successfully plead that the ring that was lost was the owner's ring.[26] This is so in spite of the fact that the container contained more rings belonging to the bailee than to the owner. If the rings were placed into separate wallets or containers and the containers were commingled so that it is not known which belongs to whom, this is the same as rings. If one container is lost and the bailee pleads that it was the owner's, the loss is borne by the owner.

---

24. The laws of this sentence apply if the money or objects were placed all in one wallet or sack or box without any separate compartments to prevent true commingling.

25. The rings are different, although it is not known which rings were lost.

26. In the case of money there is really no objection on behalf of the owner that it will be commingled with the owner's since all money is interchangeable. The same applies also to produce that ordinarily is interchangeable. The loss is borne proportionately.

The bailee, with a waiver of warranty by the owners against him, is entrusted with objects such as rings from two owners and he commingles their objects with his own in a single bag. Some of the rings were lost or stolen. The loss is apportioned between the owners and the bailee does not bear any part of the loss.

Spoilage and shrinkage of the objects

The bailee may not touch the objects of the owner even if they keep shrinking in volume, provided that they are shrinking not greater than the normal annual shrinkage. If the shrinkage is greater than normal the bailee must notify the owner if he is available to be notified.[27] If the owner cannot be notified, the bailee should apply to beth din for an order to sell the objects under the supervision of beth din.

Should the objects, such as produce, honey, or wine, become spoiled, rotten, or sour, the bailee should notify the owner. If the owner cannot be notified, the bailee should apply to beth din for an order to sell the objects under the supervision of beth din.

A similar situation arises when the objects consist of leavened matter that is prohibited to be used during and after the Passover Holy Days. The bailee is authorized to sell it and keep the proceeds for the owner. Nowadays the bailee has another option available to him, such as selling the ownership of the leaven to a non-Jew through the auspices of a rabbi. In case a bailee is confronted with such a situation, he should consult a rabbi who is familiar with the laws of Passover.

A similar situation arises when the bailee has information that the government is about to seize the objects. He may not take any action because the owner may also have heard the rumor and come to retrieve his objects.

When a bailee sells the objects pursuant to the order of beth din he may not buy the objects at the sale because of suspicion. The money realized at the sale remains with the bailee and he may use it. As soon as he obtains the money he is deemed a paid bailee regarding the

27. The codes speak of notifying the owner if he is in the city, and if he is not in the city the bailee should make his application to beth din for an order of sale. With global communications so common, being in the city is no longer the criteria, but rather if the owner can be located.

moneys even if he has not used them. As soon as he uses them he is deemed a borrower regarding the moneys.

There are times, however, that the bailee must do something to the objects to keep them from spoiling. For example, if the object entrusted to the bailee is a Torah scroll, he must unroll it once in 12 months. If he happens to read it while he is unrolling it, he is not guilty of using the Torah scroll without authorization. He is not permitted to open it to read from it for his own use; if he does he is considered to have made unauthorized use of the Torah and becomes liable for any loss no matter the reason for the loss, including *force majeure*. Similar rules apply to other books and scrolls of the owner. Just as one may not read from them for his own use, so he may not copy therefrom. There is an exception to the last law in the case of a scholar who does not have a copy of this particular book, since it is assumed that the owner entrusted the scholar with the book so that he would be able to read and copy from the book. As a corollary to this last law, if certain books are unavailable to the scholars, beth din may compel the owners to loan the books to the school to study and copy them. Another example given in the codes: If the owner entrusted the bailee with a woolen garment, the bailee must dust it once in 30 days. Similar care must be given to all objects entrusted to the bailee. When possible, the owner should be contacted by the bailee before he commences such care.

Chapter 293

THE RETURN OF THE ENTRUSTED OBJECT

The matters discussed in this chapter of the *Shulhan Aruch* are discussed in Chapter 291 of this book, which deals with all facets of the return of the entrusted objects. Therefore they are not repeated here.

Chapter 294

THE BAILEE DENIES LIABILITY

INTRODUCTION

Beginning with this chapter and continuing to the end of the laws dealing with the unpaid bailee (chapter 301), Rabbi Yosef Karo deals mostly with laws of pleading and related matters. In this work these chapters form the end of this volume. I have rearranged some of the material as it appears in *Shulhan Aruch Hoshen haMishpat* as follows: Chapter 294: the bailee denies liability because of what happened to the object entrusted to him; Chapter 295: the bailee desires to pay the owner for the object that he is not returning and the ramifications of such decision; Chapter 296: miscellaneous pleas of liability or non-liability and other disputes between the owner and the bailee other than the pleas entered by the bailee in Chapter 294 and Chapter 297; Chapter 297: the bailee's plea of nonliability because he was never entrusted with the object or he returned it to the owner; Chapter 298: dispute as to the quantity of the object; Chapter 299: which of two alleged owners is entitled to the object; Chapter 300: which of two owners entrusted the bailee with the larger amount of cash; Chapter 301: classes of owners or objects excluded from the laws of owner/bailee; Chapter 302: The role of women and minors in the laws of owner/bailee (these laws have been moved to Chapter 291).

The owner requests from the unpaid bailee that he return the object that was entrusted to the bailee. There are several possibilities. (1) The bailee returns the object and the matter is closed. (2) Or the bailee may state that the object was lost or stolen or lost through *force majeure* and the bailee is not liable to the owner for the loss of the object. In such event the bailee must produce witnesses that the object was lost or stolen as alleged, or he must take an oath to substantiate his allegation. (3) Or the bailee will pay the owner for the object that the bailee alleges was lost or stolen. As stated below, this chapter does not discuss the possibilities when (4) the bailee states that the object was never entrusted to him or (5) that he had returned the object to the owner.

Under (2) the bailee does not have the option of producing witnesses or taking the oath. If there are witnesses, they must be produced to testify as to the loss. This chapter discusses when the witnesses must be produced and when the bailee may swear and be absolved of liability.

The parties may by agreement provide that the bailee need not take an oath in the event that the object is not returned to the owner. The text begins with this possibility. This is followed by a discussion of the production of witnesses followed by the laws of the oaths to be taken by the bailee to free himself of liability. The chapter includes a discussion of the situation where the bailee alleges that the object was stolen and the thief is found.

The best evidence is the testimony of two witnesses who witnessed the event. Lacking such witnesses, beth din may have to rely on presumptions or on oaths taken by one of the parties to the lawsuit. In this chapter beth din will rely on the oath of the bailee to relieve him of responsibility if there is no competent testimony. This chapter concludes with the laws of the contents of the oath, and the oaths that are attendant to the first (or second) oath.

It is stated in Chapter 291:

> [E]ach of the four types of bailees is sometimes free of liability although he cannot return the object intact that was entrusted to him or which he hired or borrowed. As is discussed in Chapter 297, the bailee may raise a defense that he never received the object from the owner, or that he returned it to the owner and also be relieved of liability. He may be required to take an oath similar to the "oath of objects" to be free of liability.

The unpaid bailee is not liable if the object was lost or stolen from him, if it was lost by *force majeure*, an act of God, or if the owner was employed by the bailee at the time that the object was delivered to the bailee. He may be required to take the "oath of bailees" to be free of liability. This is discussed in Chapter 294.

There are thus two different types of pleas of nonliability of the unpaid bailee: (1) that he does not have the object belonging to the owner (bailor) because he never was entrusted with it or he returned it to the owner, or (2) that he is free from liability because the object was lost, stolen, or lost through *force majeure*. In each of these types the bailee may under certain circumstances be required to take an oath to be free of liability, an oath similar to the "oath of objects" in type (1) and the "oath of bailees" in type (2).

Rabbi Yosef Karo discusses in this chapter of *Shulhan Aruch Hoshen haMishpat* both of these types of pleas by the bailee to prove nonliability. He also discusses the first type in chapter 297; I have moved the laws of this chapter dealing with the first type of plea to Chapter 297. Only the second type of plea is discussed in this chapter; this involves the oath of bailees.

There are times when the unpaid bailee is free of liability for loss or damage of the object entrusted to him. This is set forth below, as it appears in Chapter 291. He may have to take the oath of bailees; this too is set forth below, (immediately after the statements from Chapter 291) as it appears in Volume III, Chapter 87.

In Chapter 291 it is stated:

(1) **The unpaid bailee:**

(i) He is liable for the nonreturn of the object if, due to his negligence, it was lost, damaged, or destroyed. This is close to destroying the object willfully since the owner is relying upon him for the minimal protection of the object.

(ii)He is not liable for the nonreturn of the object if it was lost by him in a non-negligent manner, or if it was stolen from him.[1]

(iii) He is not liable for the nonreturn of the object if it was lost through *force majeure*.

---

1. The two situations, the theft of the object from the bailee and the loss of the object, are not alike. In the case of the theft it is almost *force majeure*; in the case of loss it almost borders on negligence. Yet both situations free the unpaid bailee from liability.

(iv) He is liable for its nonreturn if the object "dies" while the bailee uses the object, since an unpaid bailee has no right to use the object.[2] (See (v).)

(v) He is liable for the nonreturn of the object no matter what the reason, if he uses it, since any use by an unpaid bailee is unauthorized.

(vi) The bailee is not liable to the owner for not returning the object to him if the owner was present and working for the bailee (even in an unrelated job) when the bailee took possession of the object. This is true even if the owner was not working for the bailee at the actual time when the object was lost even by the negligence of the bailee. However, the bailee is liable if he intentionally damages or destroys the object.

In Volume III, Chapter 87, it is stated:

3. The oath of the bailees.
   a. Oath taken by one of the four types of bailees to free himself of liability.
   b. Oath taken by the defendant/bailee.
   c. The plea of the plaintiff/bailor need not be certain.
   d. The defendant may elect to take an oath that the bailment was lost in a manner that would relieve the bailee/defendant from liability.
   e. If the defendant takes the oath, the complaint of the bailor/plaintiff will be dismissed. If he does not take the oath, he will have to pay for the object entrusted to him.
   f. Chapters 291–347.[3]

The two concepts, nonliability of the bailee and the oath of bailees, are interconnected. Very often when the bailee asserts nonliability because he fits into the categories set forth in Chapter 291, he will prove such nonliability by taking the oath of bailees set forth in this chapter.

This chapter discusses when he may take the oath instead of producing witnesses who testify as to the facts, when he may not, and what the result is of his taking the oath.

2. He is liable in this situation if he cannot return the object in the manner in which he received it.

3. See Volume III, page 126.

TEXT

Agreement of the parties

The owner and the bailee may by agreement decide that the allegation of the bailee that the object was lost or stolen will be believed and the matter will be at an end. That is, when the owner requests that the bailee return the object, if the bailee alleges that the object was lost or stolen, or lost through *force majeure*, the bailee will be believed as if he had produced witnesses to that effect or as if he had taken an oath to that effect.

There are opinions both ways as to whether the agreement is to absolve the bailee from taking an oath, where witnesses are unavailable, but he has to produce witnesses who saw the event of the alleged theft or loss of the object.

Production of witnesses

Absent an agreement such as that set forth above, if the bailee has a plea of nonliability he must prove his allegations. If there are witnesses, he must produce the witnesses; failing to produce them, he is not permitted to free himself of liability by taking an oath. The bailee does not have the option of producing witnesses to the event of the loss or of taking an oath. If there are witnesses he must produce them. If he fails to produce the witnesses he must pay the bailee for the object.

By witnesses are meant qualified persons who saw the event. The fact that there were people in the vicinity of where the loss took place does not necessarily mean that there will be witnesses. The people may have been unaware that the object was being stolen from the bailee.

Assume that there were witnesses who saw that a thief seized a garment from a bailee. The bailee pleads that the garment that was seized was entrusted to him by the owner to guard as an unpaid bailee. The witnesses describe the garment as being an overcoat, made of wool and blue in color. That describes the garment that the owner entrusted to the bailee. But there are many blue wool overcoats, and the witnesses cannot state that the garment that was stolen was the owner's overcoat. The owner does not know if the overcoat described by the witnesses is his overcoat or one that looks like his overcoat. The bailee wins the lawsuit brought by the owner without even having to take an oath.

The thief is discovered

The object is stolen from the unpaid bailee[4] without any negligence on his part. Sometime later, but before the bailee produced witnesses to show it was stolen or before the bailee takes his oath, it becomes known who the thief is. The bailee although he is not liable to the owner for the loss of the object, must bring legal action against the thief to recover the object or its value on behalf of the owner. The bailee is not given the option of taking the oath of bailees and avoiding bringing action against the thief. If the bailee endeavors to obtain a judgment against the thief and to enforce collection of the judgment against the thief, and fails to obtain recovery on behalf of the owner, the bailee's responsibility is at an end, and he has no liability to the owner if he takes an oath that he was not negligent with the object.[5]

Assume that the bailee has already brought witnesses to absolve him of liability, or in an appropriate case the bailee takes the oath of bailees and is free of liability to the owner. Then the thief is discovered. The unpaid bailee has the option of not taking any action against the thief; the paid bailee must take legal action against the thief.[6] The paid bailee does not have the option of refunding the payment he received from the owner and pleading that he is now an unpaid bailee and need not pursue the thief. If the paid bailee fails to take such action and if beth din estimates that the paid bailee would have been successful, he must make payment to the owner.

The thief restores the object to the unpaid bailee. The object is then lost as a result of the negligence of the bailee. There are opinions both

4. The law is the same if the bailee is a paid bailee and the object was robbed by armed robbers, which is the equivalent of being *force majeure*: the paid bailee is not liable in such event for the loss of the object.

5. In the case of the paid bailee the oath is that he was not negligent, nor was it lost or stolen from him, nor did he use the object without authorization. But rather it was taken from him by *force majeure*.

6. The paid bailee was paid to guard the object and his guarding was cut short by the theft. He is still under the employ of the owner until he restores the object or its equivalent or is free of liability. Since he can restore the equivalent, he must do so.

ways as to whether the bailee is liable to the owner for the loss resulting from his negligence. If the role as bailee terminated when the object was first stolen from him, then he is not liable; if the role as bailee was not terminated, then he is now liable for his negligence. The latter view seems to be the preferred view.

The codes cite a case that may be analogous to the law of the last paragraph. Ruven, a lender of money on interest to non-Jews, loaned money to a Gentile who always made his payments on time, and the loan was considered a safe loan. Shimon, a broker, was employed by Levi to find a good loan. Shimon approached Ruven to sell the loan to Levi, the loan was assigned to Levi, and Levi paid Shimon a brokerage fee. It turned out that the Gentile did not make his payments when due and Levi requested that Shimon approach his friend the governor to ask him to intervene to have the Gentile pay the loan. Shimon refused to go see the governor. One view holds that the position of Shimon is similar to that of the bailee in the last paragraph to whom the object was restored and his role as a bailee had been terminated and he is not liable; similarly the role of Shimon as a broker had terminated and he has no obligation to go to the governor. The other view holds that the position of Shimon is similar to the bailee in the last paragraph to whom the object was restored and his role as a bailee had not been terminated; similarly, the role of Shimon as a broker had not been terminated and he has the obligation to intervene with the governor.

The unpaid bailee's oath

The owner requests that the unpaid bailee return the object to the owner. It does not matter whether the object was entrusted to the bailee in the presence of witnesses or without witnesses being present. The bailee pleads[7] that the object was stolen from him.[8] There was no witnesses to the theft. The Torah describes the oaths of the bailee that he may take and be absolved of liability. How one takes an oath is described in Volume III, page 144.

7. These pleas are an admission that the object was entrusted to the bailee and was not returned to the owner.

8. Or he pleads any other pleading that would absolve him of liability, such as the object was lost, or was lost or destroyed as a result of *force majuere*.

There are three oaths involved:

1. The bailee takes an oath that the object is not in his possession because it was stolen.[9]
2. The bailee takes an oath that he was not negligent in causing the loss of the object.[10]
3. The bailee takes an oath that he did not make unauthorized use of the object.

There are two opinions as to which oaths are provided for in the Torah and which oaths are revolved upon the bailee since he is taking certain oaths anyway.[11]

According to the first opinion, the Torah requires the bailee to take an oath that the object was stolen, which is the same as (1) above. Oaths (2) and (3) are revolved upon the bailee.

According to the second opinion, the Torah requires the bailee to take oaths (1) and (2). Oath (3) is revolved on the bailee.

There are practical differences resulting from these two opinions.

According to the first opinion, assume that there are witnesses that the object was stolen. Since the bailee is not required to take this oath (1), he does not have to take oaths (2) and (3), which revolve onto oath (1). Since there is no oath (1), there are not oaths (2) and (3) to be taken by the bailee.

According to the second opinion, assuming that there are witnesses that the object was stolen, the bailee will still have to take oath (2). Since he has to take this oath, oath (3) will be revolved upon him. Assuming that there are witnesses that the object was stolen and that he was not negligent, he is absolved from taking oaths (1) and (2). Since he does not take these oaths, he does not take oath (3).

9. This prevents the situation where the bailee claims that the object was stolen when in reality he still has the object in his possession.

10. The paid bailee takes this oath that he was not negligent in bringing about the loss of the object, nor was it lost by him, nor was it stolen from him. In all of these situations he would be liable to the owner.

11. See Volume III, Chapter 94. Laws of Resolving Oaths.

Chapter 295

BAILEE DESIRES TO PAY RATHER THAN TAKE AN OATH

INTRODUCTION

As was stated in Chapter 294, there are times when the bailee has no choice but to either take the bailee's oath or to pay the owner for the loss or damage to the object. From this it may seem that the bailee has the choice of paying and not taking the oath. There are many reasons why the bailee may want to pay and not to take the oath. He may on principle have an aversion to taking oaths. However, he may want to keep the object and pay for it instead of shopping for it, especially if it is unique or hard to come by. Therefore laws are in place to permit the bailee to avoid the oath when it is clear that his motives in not taking the oath are beyond question.

TEXT

Procedure when the bailee wants to pay and not take an oath

The owner requests that the bailee return the object to him. The bailee advises the owner that the object is lost and that he does not want to be relieved of paying for the object, which he can do by taking the bailee's oath as set forth in Chapter 294.

Assume that the object is (1) of the type that is readily available and may be easily purchased by the bailee; and (2) is of uniform quality, he pays for the object and is free of any oaths. If one of these two criteria is lacking he goes through the procedure of the next paragraph.

However, if the object is unique or a type that is not readily available in the marketplace, the procedure is different. The unpaid bailee takes an oath instituted by the Rabbis[1] of the Talmud similar to the oath (1) listed in the section entitled "The bailee's oath" in Chapter 294, which is the oath that the bailee does not have the object in his possession, which oath includes a statement how it came to be out of his possession.[2] The bailee then makes payment for the object. If there is a dispute between the owner and the bailee as to the value of the object, the bailee takes an oath as to its value, according to the standards set forth in Chapter 291.[3] Although the bailee must take oath (1) he is absolved from taking oath (2), that he was not negligent, and oath (3), that he did not make unauthorized use of the object.[4] There is authority that the owner can require the bailee to take oath (1) even if he has already accepted payment of the object from the bailee.

1. This oath is administered as if it were a Torah oath by the bailee holding a sacred object while taking the oath. The procedure of taking the oath is described in Volume III, at page 144.

2. The same procedure applies to the other three types of bailees, the paid bailee, the lessee, or the borrower. Each of them, if they do not want to plead that they are not liable for payment because of a reason that would absolve them from payment, may decide to pay but still have to take this oath that the object is not in their possession, which then will include in the oath declaring how it came to be out of their possession.

3. The amount to be paid is discussed in Chapter 291 in the section called "Valuing and paying for the object."

4. If a person is wary of taking an oath because of uncertainty as to the facts, oaths (2) and (3) are more critical since he may have been inadvertently guilty of the matters spoken of in these two oaths.

Chapter 296

MISCELLANEOUS PLEAS OF THE OWNER AND THE BAILEE

INTRODUCTION

There are times when the owner and bailee disagree as to the terms of entrusting the object to the bailee by the owner. This has nothing to do whether there was ever a bailment, as when the bailee says he never received the object, as stated in Chapter 297, or if the bailee pleads that he is not liable to the owner because of an event that frees him of liability, as is stated in Chapter 294. It also does not have anything to do with the situation where the bailee wishes to pay for the lost object, as described in Chapter 295.

This chapter discusses such things as whether the second person ever became a bailee, if there were conditions to the terms of the bailee's liabilities, whether the object returned is the object that the owner entrusted to the bailee, the condition of the object that is returned, the quantity of the object that is returned, and other related types of differences.

TEXT

Did the bailee take up the role of a bailee?

It is stated previously:

"The unpaid bailee is not liable for the care of the object, nor for the 'oath of the bailees,' nor for feeding an animal if it is the object that is left with him, until he assumes the role of an unpaid bailee." The owner pleads that the second person assumed the role of a bailee. The second person pleads that he never assumed such role. It is also stated in Chapter 291, "The owner asks the second person to guard his object." The second person replies "Leave it down in front of you," or "Leave it," or "The place is before you," or other words to the effect that fail to show that without doubt he undertook to be a bailee. Held: he is not a bailee. The owner pleads that he said "Leave the object in front of me," which would make him an unpaid bailee, while the second person states that he said, "Leave it down in front of you," which would not make him a bailee. The second person takes a *hesseth*[1] oath that he did not accept to be a bailee and there is also revolved upon him to take an oath that he did not use the object without authority, and that he did not cause the loss of the object to be destroyed, nor did he destroy it in such a manner that he would be liable to the owner.

Were there stipulations regarding liability?

It is stated in Chapter 291:

It was stated above in the section dealing with the liabilities of the bailees that each had specific liabilities. But as is stated many times in this work the parties may stipulate among themselves to vary the terms of the usual liabilities, if to do so does not violate a Torah command.[2] Thus the unpaid bailee may take upon himself the liabilities of a borrower that are the highest degree of liability and the borrower and lender may agree that the borrower will not be liable in any event even if he is negligent with the borrowed object. All such stipulations will be binding upon the parties, whether or not there were witnesses present when the stipulations were made. If the stipulations are made prior to

1. See Volume III, Chapter 87; see Glossary.

2. The parties cannot stipulate that a loan will bear interest even if both agree, since there is a Torah command not to take nor to pay interest.

or contemporaneously with the commencement of the role, they may be oral, without the necessity of a *kinyan*[3] being performed.[4] If made after the bailee has commenced his role as a bailee they are binding only if a *kinyan* is performed.[5]

There are times when the owner will plead that there were stipulations increasing the scope of liability of the bailee; there are times when the bailee will plead that there were stipulations decreasing the scope of the liability of the bailee.

The owner pleads that there were stipulations regarding the liability of the bailee and the bailee pleads that there were no stipulations that would increase his liability in the situation. The bailee takes the regular oath of a bailee[6] and there is revolved upon him an oath that there were no stipulations.

The bailee admits that he was negligent, but pleads that there were stipulations exonerating him for negligence. The owner pleads that there were no such stipulations. There were witnesses present when the object was entrusted to the bailee by the owner but they do not know if there were any stipulations. The bailee is believed in this situation.[7] The bailee is required to take an oath that he did not use

---

3. The *kinyan* is performed by the bailee handing his handkerchief to the owner and the owner handing his own handkerchief to the bailee. See Glossary; see Volume VI, Chapter 195.

4. Although the stipulations are oral statements they are binding as personal obligations taken upon themselves and the consideration is the personal pleasure that the parties have in the trust that they place in each other and the public esteem that will flow from such displays of trust. See Volume II, page 147.

5. An interesting question arises if the unpaid bailee stipulates that he will have the liabilities of a paid bailee. The unpaid bailee is not liable if the object is stolen while the paid bailee is liable; the paid bailee is not liable if the object was lost through *force majeure*. The object was lost and the bailee pleads that it was lost through *force majeure*. The owner demands that the bailee take an oath (see the next section, "Proof of nonliability") that the object was lost through *force majeure* and the bailee responds that he will take the oath of an unpaid bailee and that his stipulation that he would pay if the object was stolen only applies if there are witnesses that it was stolen. There are opinions both ways if the bailee must take the oath demanded by the owner or may take the oath of an unpaid bailee. The latest holdings are that he must take the oath of a paid bailee.

6. See Chapter 294, "The bailee's oath."

7. The bailee is believed since he could have pleaded that he was not negligent and that the object was lost through *force majeure*.

the object without authority and that it is not in his possession, and there was such a stipulation as he had pleaded. If the owner produces witnesses who testify that they know that the bailee had assumed the role of being a bailee and that the bailee was negligent with the object, then the bailee is not permitted to plead that there was a stipulation decreasing his liability.

Owner pleads that the object returned is not his

The owner requests that the bailee return the object to him and the bailee proffers an object to the owner.

The owner claims:

(1) That the object is not the one he entrusted to the bailee; the bailee pleads that this is indeed the object that he entrusted to the bailee.

(2) That the object was not broken when he entrusted the object to the bailee and now it is broken; the bailee pleads that the object was broken when entrusted to him.

(3) That the object was new when he entrusted it to the bailee and it has now been used; the bailee pleads that the object entrusted to him was not new.

(4) That 100 bushes of wheat were entrusted to the bailee and there are now only 50 bushels of wheat there; the bailee pleads that the wheat that he is returning is the wheat that was entrusted to him.

(5) That there were 100 bushels of wheat entrusted to the bailee and now barley is being returned to him; the bailee pleads that he was entrusted with 100 bushels of barley.

In all of these five situations described in the prior paragraph, and in all cases of disagreements between parties the best evidence is that of the witnesses. Lacking witnesses the bailee takes a *hesseth*[8] oath that the facts are as he stated. The oath of the bailee is accepted as full evidence of the true facts by beth din. In (5) the bailee need not return the barley.[9]

---

8. See Volume III, Chapter 87; see Glossary.

9. The theory is that by pleading for wheat and not accepting the barley, the owner waived any rights to the return of the barley.

The owner pleads that there were 100 bushels of wheat entrusted to the bailee and the bailee pleads that there were only 60 bushels of wheat entrusted to him. The bailee takes a Torah oath[10] of partial admission and if he does he wins the lawsuit.[11]

---

10. See Volume III, Chapter 88.

11. In the case of the owner pleading that there were 100 bushels and the bailee stating that there were only 60 bushels, this is a case of a partial admission and the bailee should take a Torah oath of the defendant who pleads that he owes part of the debt being claimed. However, in case (4) above, the bailee proffers the object without stating how much he is returning, and therefore the situation of a partial admission is not present. See Volume III, page 138.

Chapter 297

BAILEE'S DENIAL OF HAVING THE ENTRUSTED OBJECT IN HIS POSSESSION

INTRODUCTION

Chapter 294 contains laws dealing with the bailee attempting to absolve himself from liability as a bailee since his conduct did not warrant him being liable for loss or damage to the owner's object. Chapter 296 contains laws when the parties disagree as to the terms of the entrustment of the object to the bailee or when he returns the object to the owner. Chapter 297 discusses the laws when the second person states that he was never a bailee of the owner regarding the object, or if he was, he already returned the object to the owner and was therefore not any longer a bailee of the owner. The person who claims he is not or was never the bailee is designated as the "second person," except where it is acknowledged that he is or was a bailee of the object for the owner.

What if there are witnesses who saw the initial entrustment or who now testify that the second person has in his possession the object or something that looks like the object of the owner?

The object spoken of in this chapter is not money, that is, that the second person is holding money intact for safekeeping for the owner. If the alleged bailment consists of money, there may be a special law applicable, as stated in Volume III, page 124. In every other instance and sometimes even if the object is coins, the laws of this chapter regarding oaths will prevail.[1]

TEXT

The second person denies that he was or is the bailee of the object

The owner pleads that the second person is the bailee of a particular object belonging to the owner and now the second person refuses to return the object to the owner.The second party denies that the owner ever entrusted him with the object to guard.If there were no witnesses present when the owner alleges he entrusted the object to the second person, the second person takes a *hesseth* oath[2] holding a sacred object as one does who takes an oath prescribed in the Torah,[3] that he was never a bailee for the owner of the object. He may take the oath even if there are witnesses to testify that they recognize that the object is now in the possession of the second person, or even if the owner identifies the object as his, provided as stated in the prior sentence, there were no witnesses present when the alleged entrustment to the

1. *The oath of objects (Shevu'oth haPikadon).* Actually this is the oath arising from a bailment. I have called this oath the oath of objects since it deals with objects and/or money the plaintiff alleges is in the hands of the defendant and the defendant denies the plaintiff's plea by stating that he does not have the plaintiff's object or money in his possession.The plaintiff pleads that it was lost by the plaintiff and found by the defendant; or it arises out of wages due to the plaintiff by the defendant; or that the defendant obtained the money or object by loan, by holding it as a bailment, by having stolen the object or money from the plaintiff, or by other similar reason. (In *halachah* it is called the "oath of bailments," but I call it the "oath of objects" so that it not become confused with the oath of bailees.) In the latter case, the bailee/ defendant does not deny that he had at one time the bailment in his hands; instead he has a reason why he is not liable for its loss, according to rules enunciated in Chapters 291–347.The bailee has to take an oath to be relieved of liability; and those oaths are called the "oaths of the bailees."

2. See Volume III, Chapter 87; see Glossary.

3. See Volume III, page 141.

second person took place.[4] This is true even if the object is not the type of object that the second person could afford to have in his possession.

The owner pleads in beth din that the second person is the bailee of a particular object belonging to the owner and now the owner refuses to return the object to the owner. The second person admits that he was a bailee of the object but that he returned the object to the owner. Whether or not there were witnesses present[5] when the owner alleges he entrusted the object to the second person, the second person takes a *hesseth* oath[6] holding a sacred object, as one does who takes an oath prescribed in the Torah,[7] that he returned the object to the owner. He may take the oath even if there are witnesses to testify that they recognize that the object is now in the possession of the second person, or even if the owner identifies the object as his, provided there were no witnesses present when the alleged entrustment to the second person took place.[8] This is true even if the object is not the type of object that the second person could afford to have in his possession or known to have in his possession. He may take such oath even if the owner has a written instrument attesting to the bailment.[9] In the situation where the owner holds a written instrument attesting to the bailment and the bailee pleads that he returned the object to the owner, if there are witnesses that the bailee was negligent with the object, he may not take the oath that he returned the object to the owner.

However, if (1) there were witnesses present when the owner entrusted the object to the bailee and (2) there are witnesses who

4. The second person may plead that he purchased the object from the owner or from a third person.

5. The reason is that even if a bailee is entrusted with the object by the owner in the presence of witnesses, the object may be returned by the bailee to the owner without witnesses being present.

6. See note 2.

7. See note 3.

8. If not for these witnesses, the second person may plead that he purchased the object from the owner or from a third person.

9. The bailee may logically state that the written instrument being left with the owner does not prove anything since the bailee could have admitted the bailment and yet have pleaded that the object was lost through *force majeure*.

recognize[10] and saw the object in the possession of the bailee before the lawsuit started in beth din, the bailee is liable to the owner for the nonreturn of the object and may not plead that he returned the object to the owner. There is much that is said in the codes and commentaries as to the degree of proof necessary by the witnesses to establish that the object is the one entrusted to the bailee by the owner. In the end it is determined by beth din in each case and there cannot be hard and fast rules in such situations. The laws of this paragraph hold true in the event that the bailee dies and the owner makes claim against the heirs for the return of the object. If the witnesses do not have access to the premises of the heirs, the heirs can be compelled to bring the object to beth din so that the witnesses can examine the object there to see if this is the object that the owner entrusted to the heirs.

A case that appears in the codes: The owner entrusted a quantity of sesame to a bailee. When the owner demanded the return of the sesame, the bailee responded that he had already returned the sesame to the owner. The owner replied that the sesame is now in the same barrel of the owner in which he placed the sesame when he entrusted it to the bailee and the sesame is still there. The bailee pleaded that the sesame now in the barrel is the bailee's. The bailee, taking a *hesseth* oath as above stated, won the lawsuit, since it was possible that the sesame was the bailee's.

It may[11] be that if the object consisted of money that the bailee takes a Torah oath.[12]

There is an opinion that if the bailee has one witness to testify that he returned the object to the owner that he is relieved of having to take the oath.

False denial of the bailment

The owner of the object pleads that he gave the second person an object to guard as a bailee and the second person denies ever having

10. There is much that is said in the codes and commentaries as to the degree of proof necessary by the witnesses to establish that the object is the one entrusted to the bailee by the owner. In the end it all is determined by beth din in each case and there cannot be hard and fast rules in such situations.

11. I have found no source for this statement except that Jacob Tur (1270–1340) in his code speaks of the bailee taking a Torah oath in these circumstances. Perhaps this is what he had in mind.

12. See note 1 above.

received the object from the owner. Or the second person admits having been a bailee of the object but pleads that the object was returned to the owner. Witnesses testify that the second person was lying and either he was a bailee or that he never returned the object to the owner, according to the facts of the case. The second person is immediately branded a robber, and is liable for anything that may happen to the object, including loss through *force majeure*, and he is branded a perjurer and is henceforth disqualified to testify or take oaths in beth din. This is true if the witnesses testify that the object was in the possession of the second person and he knew it at the time when he pleaded that he did not have the object in his possession. However, if the witnesses do not testify to the fact that the object was in his possession when he pleaded that it was not in his possession, he is not branded a liar nor a perjurer, even if they testify that the object was in his possession after he denied its possession.[13]

13. Perhaps the object was not in his possession when he testified that it was not and the object was delivered to him later.

Chapter 298

THE BAILEE PLEADS THAT HE IS NOT AWARE OF THE VALUE OF THE OBJECT

INTRODUCTION

The bailee admits that he was negligent with the object entrusted to him, but he pleads that he does not know what the value of the object was and thus does not know how much he owes to the owner of the object. The owner pleads that he does know how much is due to him. What is the result? What if the owner also does not know the value of the object entrusted to the bailee?

TEXT

The bailee pleads he does not know the extent of his liability

The bailee admits that he was negligent with the object entrusted to him and owes money to the owner, but he does not know the value of the object. The owner pleads that he does know the value of the lost object. The example given is that the owner entrusted the bailee with a purse full of gold coins and the coins were lost through the negligence of the bailee. The owner pleads that 200 gold coins were in the purse and the bailee admits that there were gold coins in the purse but he does not know how many. This is a case of the owner pleading a sum certain and the bailee making a partial admission and having to take an oath[1] to absolve himself from liability as to the balance; since he cannot take the oath not knowing the truth, he must pay the amount pleaded by the owner. The owner will collect the value of 200 gold coins without having to take an oath; provided that beth din believes that the owner would have 200 gold coins in his ownership, and further provided that the object alleged to be in the purse is the object or thing that one keeps in a purse. There is a strong dissent that holds that the owner must take an oath before he will be able to collect the value of 200 gold coins.[2]

The bailee, instead of admitting that the purse contained gold coins and he does not know how many, pleads that he does not know what was in the purse. There are opinions both ways if the bailee has to pay if the owner takes an oath of what the purse contained. One view holds that this is not a case of admission and the bailee takes an oath that he does not know what was in the purse and does not pay anything, while the other view holds that the owner takes an oath and collects the amount included in his oath.

The bailee could have prevented all of these laws by having the owner show him what is in the purse and having a receipt written and signed by the parties with each side keeping one copy, and if possible signed by independent witnesses.

The bailee can ask beth din to proclaim a ban on those who take from others more than they are entitled to take.[3]

The owner is not sure how much was entrusted to the bailee

If neither the owner nor the bailee know what was in the purse, the bailee has no liability to the owner even if the purse was lost through the negligence of the bailee.

1. See Volume III, Chapter 88.

2. The dissent holds that there is no way that the bailee can know what the contents of a closed purse are and he is not negligent in not knowing.

3. See Volume II, page 246, regarding proclaiming bans.

However, if the owner does not know what was entrusted to the bailee because of some cogent reason, then the bailee takes an oath that he does not know the contents of the purse and is free of liability. The example given[4] is that of a person dying and part of his estate consists of a purse filled with some objects. The son Ruven inherits the purse and entrusts it to the bailee to guard. The bailee is negligent and should be liable to Ruven for the value of what was lost. Ruven admits that he does not know what the contents of the purse were, perhaps diamonds. The bailee also does not know what was in the purse that was lost through his negligence. The bailee has no liability, for perhaps the purse contained pieces of glass. The bailee is not required to take an oath to be free of liability. The owner can have beth din proclaim a ban on all those who have property belonging to others and do not return it. The bailee takes an oath that the purse is not in his possession, and is free of liability. He also includes in his oath that the value of the objects in the purse could not have exceeded a set sum and he pays that sum. If he does not even know such minimal sum he takes the oath to that effect and pays nothing to the owner.

4. The example given of an heir who inherits the purse is meant to convey the situation where someone might not know what the contents of a purse are. The person who put the objects into the purse would be expected to know what the contents of the purse are.

Chapter 299

TWO OWNERS ENTRUSTING ONE OBJECT WITH THE BAILEE

INTRODUCTION

Assume that the object has two owners, Ruven and Shimon, who together entrust the bailee with an object. One of the owners comes by himself to retrieve the entire object or what he claims is his half. Must the bailee give the object to that owner?

TEXT

The instructions of the owners are binding on the bailee

Ruven and Shimon jointly own an object that they entrust to the bailee to guard for them. At that time they may give instructions to the bailee regarding the return of the object, such as he should not return the entire object or any part of the object unless both Ruven and Shimon come for it together, or unless Ruven comes alone with a note from Shimon, or Shimon comes alone with a note from Ruven, or if either Ruven or Shimon comes alone, or only if Ruven comes alone, or only if Shimon comes alone, or by any instructions they give to the bailee.

One owner comes to retrieve the object from the bailee

Assume no instructions have been given to the bailee when the joint owners entrusted him with the object. Ruven[1] comes to the bailee to retrieve the entire object or even only one-half or even less than one-half of an object that is divisible. The bailee must not give the entire object or even part of the object to Ruven unless Shimon is present with him. This is true if Shimon is not available to come to the bailee as for example Shimon is out of the city or he has no knowledge of the fact that Ruven is going to the bailee to retrieve the object. But if Shimon is available and knows that Ruven is going to retrieve the object and fails to accompany him, or fails to notify the bailee that the bailee should not release the object to Ruven when he comes alone, the bailee may release the entire object or any part of the object that Ruven requests to Ruven. Ruven is acting as an agent for Shimon for Shimon's part of the object.

With modern methods of communication, the bailee should try to ascertain if Shimon is aware of what Ruven is doing.

If one of the owners sues the bailee regarding the object, he may do so by himself and it is no defense to the bailee that the other owner did not join in the lawsuit.[2]

1. The same would hold true if Shimon comes to the bailee.
2. See also Volume VI, page 19.

Chapter 300

TWO CLAIMS MADE AGAINST THE BAILEE, ONE OBVIOUSLY FALSE

INTRODUCTION

There are two types of situations regarding claims discussed in this chapter where in each situation one claim is obviously false. For example, two people come to beth din and each claims that he alone entrusted the bailee with money and the bailee does not remember who is telling the truth and who is lying. Or else they both entrusted the bailee with money, one with $200 and the other with $100, and he does not remember or never knew who gave him the $200 and who gave him the $100, and now each one claims that he is the one who gave him the $200. What is to be done in these circumstances? When are the parties required to take an oath to win the lawsuit that is brought? There are times that the things entrusted by the two entrustors are objects of personal property rather than money. Are the laws the same? What if the objects entrusted are animals?

TEXT

The bailee should know what it is that he is entrusted with and by whom

The bailee, to protect himself, should always know who is giving him what to guard. The best practice for all involved is to have a memorandum signed by all of the parties to the entrustment of the object and preferably to have the memorandum witnessed by two witnesses. In the event that there is a dispute, as discussed in this chapter, the memorandum can be presented to beth din to save both the bailee and the honest entrustor with the loss that follows because of one entrustor's dishonesty or because someone actually forgot the facts. This applies whether they entrusted the bailee with money or purses containing money or vessels or animals or other objects.

If the bailee does not have a memorandum, he is considered negligent regarding his dealing with the entrustors, and he pays for his negligence.

The bailee is one party to the entrustment (the depositing of the object with the bailee); the two entrustors (depositors) of the money or the objects entrusted to the bailee are Ruven and Shimon.

One entrustor and two claimants

Someone, either Ruven or Shimon, entrusted the bailee with $100. Ruven and Shimon each claims that he is the one who entrusted the $100 to the bailee; the bailee knows that it is one of them, but does not remember who. He thus knows that one is telling the truth and one is lying. The bailee has to pay each one $100. That is provided that each takes an oath that the money is due to him.[1]

However, if neither Ruven nor Shimon makes the demand for the $100, and the bailee comes forward to plead, "One of you entrusted

1. The reason that they take an oath is that one of them is obviously not telling the truth. Otherwise, the bailee is confronted with a situation where each makes a claim and he admits part of the claim which would obligate him to take an oath of partial admission. (See Volume III, Chapter 88.) Since he is not able to take the oath not knowing the facts, he would have to pay the balance without the claimant having to take an oath. But since one is not telling the truth, Ruven and Shimon cannot collect from the bailee without each of them taking an oath.

me with $100 and I do know not know who it was," the $100 should be kept by him for safekeeping forever, or better yet should be given to beth din to keep until the coming of Elijah the prophet,[2] or until they decide what should be done, or until Ruven and Shimon reach some agreement. The result is the same if Ruven and Shimon each pleads that he does not remember if he entrusted the bailee with $100.

But if the bailee tells the son of Ruven and the son of Shimon that one of their fathers entrusted him with $100 and he does not remember who, he must give each son $100 to fulfill his religious obligation.[3]

Two entrustors, each claiming the larger deposit

Ruven and Shimon each simultaneously entrusted money to the bailee, one entrusting him with a purse containing $100 and the other entrusting him with a purse containing $200. The bailee does not know who entrusted him with the purse with the larger amount and who with the purse with the smaller amount. Each claims that he is the one who entrusted the $200. Ruven and Shimon each takes an oath that he is the one who entrusted the $200 and the bailee pays each one $200.

However, if neither Ruven nor Shimon makes a demand for the moneys and the bailee comes forward to plead, "One of you entrusted me with a purse containing $100 and one with a purse containing $200, and I do not know which is which," the bailee should give each one $200 to fulfill his religious obligation, although he does not have a legal obligation to do so. His legal obligation is to give each one $100 and keep the remaining $100 for safekeeping forever, better yet, the remaining $100 should be given to beth din to keep until the coming of Elijah the prophet, or until Ruven and Shimon reach an agreement as what should be done with the $100. The result is the same if Ruven and Shimon each pleads that he does not remember if he entrusted the bailee with $200 or $100.

2. In Volume II, at page 174 it is stated: "There is a concept in *halachah* known as 'setting the matter aside until the prophet Elijah appears.' The prophet Elijah is the harbinger of the coming of the Messiah. When matters that the beth din cannot decide because they cannot ascertain the facts, such matters are held in abeyance, with neither party to the dispute obtaining judgment."

3. In *halachah* it is called to fulfill one's obligation to Heaven.

Two entrustors entrusting one purse to the bailee

Ruven and Shimon put moneys into one purse, one having put in $100 and the other $200, and the purse with its $300 contents is entrusted to the bailee for safekeeping.[4] Each entrustor demands the purse and the $200 from the bailee, each claiming that he should be getting $200 from the purse. The bailee gives $100 to Ruven and $100 to Shimon; the remaining $100 should be kept by him for safekeeping forever. Better yet, the remaining $100 should be given to beth din to keep until the coming of Elijah the prophet, or until Ruven and Shimon reach an agreement as what should be done with the $100, or until either Ruven or Shimon admits that he only put $100 into the purse. The bailee can claim that he did not pay attention as to who put in $200 and who $100 since they seemed to trust each other by placing the moneys into one purse. He does not have to pay more than the $300 even to fulfill his obligations to Heaven.[5]

Personal property of different sizes entrusted to the bailee

Ruven and Shimon each simultaneously entrusted the bailee with two vessels, one larger and one smaller, and the bailee does not remember who entrusted him with the larger vessel and who with the smaller vessel; Ruven and Shimon each claims that his is the larger vessel. Ruven and Shimon each takes an oath that the larger vessel is his. Ruven (or Shimon) gets the larger vessel and the bailee pays to Shimon (or Ruven) the money to purchase a larger vessel and the smaller vessel is retained by the bailee. The best way to decide who gets the vessel and who the money is by drawing lots.

However, if Ruven and Shimon entrusted the vessels in one package then one of them (either Ruven or Shimon) will be given the smaller vessel, and the other will be given money to purchase a smaller vessel. The remaining larger vessel should be kept by the bailee for safekeeping forever or better yet should be given to beth din

---

4. There are authorities that the laws of this section and the laws of the prior section are identical if the moneys were in two purses and the purses were simultaneously entrusted to the bailee, it is as if there is only one purse.

5. There is an opinion that even under these circumstances, he should give each claimant $200 to fulfill his obligations to Heaven.

to keep until the coming of Elijah the prophet, or until Ruven and Shimon reach an agreement as what should be done with the larger vessel, or until either Ruven or Shimon admits that the larger vessel is not his.

Animals of different sizes entrusted to the bailee

All of the laws regarding money and vessels apply equally well to animals. Ruven and Shimon each simultaneously entrusted the bailee with an animal, or one entrusted him with a large animal and one with a small animal, or one entrusted him with two animals and one with only one animal. One of the animals died and the bailee does not know whose animal died. Ruven and Shimon each pleads that the live animal is his or that the larger animal is his or that he entrusted two animals. Ruven and Shimon must each take an oath as to the truth of his pleading and the bailee has to give each one a live animal or its equivalent or one large animal each or two animals, respectively.

However, if they placed their animals in the bailee's herd without his observing which animal belonged to whom, the bailee tells them to take the dead animal and the live animal and divide it as they see fit.

Chapter 301

MATTERS NOT INCLUDED IN THE LAWS OF BAILEES

INTRODUCTION

This is the last substantive chapter dealing with the laws of the unpaid bailee.[1] There are certain persons and entities that are not included in the laws of bailees, as there are certain objects that are also excluded from the laws of bailees. These are the topics of this chapter.

In discussing the unpaid bailee, the Torah states: "If a man delivers to his neighbor money or objects to keep, and it is stolen out of the man's [bailee's] house."[2]

The Talmud[3] interprets the words "money or objects" to teach that it applies only to movable property, such as money or objects that have intrinsic value. This excludes the applicability of the laws of bailees to real property and slaves[4] who are often likened in ownership to real property in certain laws of the Torah. This also excludes the applicability to notes of indebtedness that have no intrinsic value except to represent money owed.

---

1. Actually, there is another chapter in *Shulhan Aruch*, chapter 302, but I have included the material from that chapter in Chapter 291.

2. Exodus 22:6.

3. *Baba Metziah* 57b.

4. See Volume VI, Chapter 196, and footnotes thereto.

The Talmud[5] interprets the word "neighbor" to exclude the applicability of these laws to things belonging to the Holy Temple or to non-Jews.

The Talmud[6] interprets the words "to keep" to exclude the applicability of these laws to poor persons or charities. The words "to keep" also exclude those cases where the object is given to the bailee to destroy or to tear.

Rabbi Yosef Karo calls this chapter "Laws of Bailees Concerning Slaves, Real Property, The Holy Temple and of Poor Persons."

The text will show how these matters are excluded from the laws of bailees.

TEXT

Nonapplicability of the laws of bailees to certain classes of objects

All that is said in this chapter can be changed by agreement between the parties.[7] Thus, although there may not be any liability on the part of the bailee in these cases, the parties may agree that there will be liability if there is a loss of the object.

The laws of bailees do not apply in two situations: (i) depending upon what the objects are, or (ii) depending upon who is the owner of the object.

(i) The laws of bailees generally do not apply to the following classes of objects that are entrusted by the owners to a bailee: real estate,[8] slaves, and notes of indebtedness. If the bailee is guarding things attached to the soil they are the same as guarding real estate.[9]

(ii) The laws of bailees generally do not apply to objects owned by a non-Jew nor to objects owned by the Holy Temple in Jerusalem, may it be rebuilt speedily in our days.

---

5. See note 3.
6. *Baba Kamma* 93a.
7. The agreement must be made binding by a *kinyan*. See Volume II, Chapter 60, and Volume VI, Chapter 195; see Glossary, *kinyan*.
8. However, see Volume IX, Chapter 312, regarding leasing of real estate.
9. This includes grains ready to be harvested.

There is a difference of opinion among the leading codes as to what extent the laws of bailees do not apply to these objects or these entities.

The first opinion holds that the laws do not apply at all and there is no liability on any bailee, whether unpaid or paid, or a lessee or a borrower, if he, in guarding any of the objects in class (i) above or any object owned by anyone in class (ii) above if the objects are lost or destroyed, even if his negligence caused their loss. Since there is no liability on the part of the bailee, there are no oaths that they have to take in these situations. However, the Rabbis instituted an oath of the bailees where the object belonging to the Holy Temple was claimed to be lost or stolen. The reason is so that people will not think that the laws regarding the Holy Temple are less stringent than those of individuals. (In those situations where the paid bailee has no liability, he will not be paid for guarding these objects if they were lost or destroyed.)

The second opinion holds that the laws do not apply at all and there is no liability on any bailee, whether unpaid or paid, or a lessee or a borrower, if he, in guarding any of the objects in class (i) above, or any object owned by anyone in class (ii) above if the objects are lost or destroyed, except if the bailee's negligence caused their loss. The bailee is thus required to take an oath that it was not his negligence that caused the loss of the object.

According to both opinions if the bailee caused the loss intentionally he is liable. There is therefore authority that if the bailee entrusted the object to a second bailee, he is liable if the object is lost since this is the equivalent of intentionally destroying the object.

Moneys belonging to the poor

If the bailee is entrusted with money belonging to poor persons or money collected for the redemption of hostages and he was negligent in guarding the money and it was lost, he has no liability. This applies only if the money has not been segregated for specific poor persons or to redeem a specific hostage. If the money was so designated, the bailee must make restitution if they were lost through his negligence, and if they were lost not through his negligence he must take the oath of bailees.[10]

10. There are many customs regarding the distribution of moneys to the poor. It is suggested that the local custom be followed to ascertain if these moneys are to be

The money of orphans is treated the same as money of other private people, and the bailee is liable the same as for any other person; however, the bailee may not use the money, although there are circumstances where he may use money entrusted to him.[11]

Moneys belonging to non-Jews

Moneys entrusted by a non-Jew to a Jewish bailee do not come under the laws of bailees, and the bailee is not liable for any loss according to the first opinion above and is liable for negligence according to the second opinion above stated. If a non-Jew converted after entrusting the object to the bailee, he is treated the same as a non-Jew for the purposes of this chapter. He is treated as a Jew for the purposes of this chapter if he was converted prior to entrusting the object to the bailee.

The exclusion of entrusted objects not intended to be guarded

The bailee is not liable if the objects were given to him to destroy or to tear; he is not liable if they are lost, although the owner did not state that he would not be liable if he destroyed or tore them. This is true only if the object was entrusted to the bailee originally to tear or to destroy. But if the object was originally entrusted to him to guard and afterward the owner told the bailee to tear or destroy the object, he is not absolved from liability unless the owner specifically told him that he would be so absolved if he destroyed or tore the object.

---

treated as moneys in the hands of a bailee regarding liability to the poor of the community.

11. See Chapter 292.

Chapter 302

PERSONS INCLUDED IN THE LAWS OF BAILEES

The matters discussed in this chapter in *Shulhan Aruch Hoshen haMishpat* have been included in Chapter 291 of this book, which deals with many facets of the laws of bailees.

GLOSSARY

agov: The literal translation means "along with." Personal property may only be acquired by certain acts of acquisition, such as lifting the object acquired (see Volume V, Chapter 189). If a person acquires realty by one of the methods by which real estate is acquired, if the parties have agreed, then the personal property may be acquired "along with" the realty, although a separate act of acquisition has not been made for the personal property.

aleatory instrument: An aleatory contract is one in which the promise by one of the parties is conditioned upon a fortuitous event, which he wishes will never come about, and he anticipates with confidence that it will never come about. It is usually hazardous for the party making the promise. Such a promise is known as *asmachtah* and is generally unenforceable. Also see Volume VI, Chapter 207.

along with: See *agov*.

apotiki: There are three types of mortgages in *halachah*: Type 1 is called in Hebrew *apotiki stam*, or unspecified security interest. It does not mean that the security interest does not attach to a specific realty. It means that it is not limited to that specific realty. Type 2 is called in Hebrew *apotiki m'furash*, or specified security interest. This can be enforced only against the specific realty and against no other realty. Type 3 is called in Hebrew *mashkanta* or user's security interest. The creditor has the use of the secured realty until the debt is paid, by the debtor paying money to the creditor and/or by the creditor making a profit from the operation of the realty and giving the debtor credit for the profits. Sometimes the *mashkanta* is for a specific period of time after which the realty returns to the debtor and the debt is deemed paid in full. In this work a *mashkanta* is termed as a mortgagee-in-possession type of mortgage.

apotiki stam: See *apotiki.*

area: A cubit equals 21 inches (see *cubit*). All the measurements are based on this assumption. Also there are 43,560 square feet in an acre. The areas given below can be used for all the square footage measurements in this work:

1 square cubit = 3.06 square feet

beth kab = 416.6 square cubits; 1,275 square feet; 0.029 acre

beth seah = 6 *beth kab*; 2,500 square cubits; 7,650 square feet; 0.175 acre

beth kor = 30 *beth seah*; 75,000 square cubits; 229,500 square feet; 5.26 acres.

arrur: A person who is *arrur* is cursed. It may apply to the curses that the Torah sets forth in several places (Leviticus 26 and Deuteronomy 27). It may apply to persons whom the Rabbis have cursed because of unbecoming conduct: for example, a person agreeing to buy or sell something, money changing hands, but legal title not having been transferred as required by Volume 5, Chapter 189. The person who reneges on the deal is cursed by the Rabbis.

asmachtah: See *aleatory instrument.* Also see Volume VI, Chapter 207.

assignee: The person to whom an assignment has been made. The assignor assigns his interest to the assignee. Often he may be called the grantee.

assignment: The transfer by the assignor to the assignee of all or part of his rights to some kind of property, usually intangible property such as rights in a lease, mortgage, contract of sale, or a partnership.

assignor: A person who assigns or transfers property or rights to another person, the assignee.

attachment: There are two kinds of attachment mentioned in this work: (1) The goods or real estate of a party is seized before an action is started so that the owner of the attached property who is outside of the jurisdiction of the beth bin will submit to its jurisdiction. It may also be held so that if the plaintiff is successful and obtains a judgment against the defendant, there will be property already seized on which he can make a levy. (2) The taking of the defendant's property after the plaintiff has won the lawsuit and has a judgment against the defendant.

authentication (of a document): A document on which beth din affixes a statement that they have examined the document and have examined the signatures of the witnesses and have ascertained that the document is genuine.

avairah: A transgression. There are 613 commandments in the Torah, 248 positive commandments and 365 negative commandments. If one does not fulfill a positive commandment or violates a negative commandment, he has committed an *avairah*.

bailee: The person to whom goods are delivered to take care of the goods.

bailment: The goods that are delivered by the bailor to the bailee.

bailor: The person who delivers the bailment to the bailee.

bainanith: Real estate is classified into three categories, as follows: Assuming that a debtor owned three types of realty classified as to quality—*idith*, the highest quality, *bainanith*, the medium quality, and *ziburith*, the lowest quality. They are classified according to production per acre. The highest quality costs more for each acre than does the medium quality, which in turn costs more than the same acreage of the lowest quality land. For the same price one will obtain a smaller area of highest-quality land than he would if he purchased the medium quality, and the greatest area for the same price would be purchased if one were to purchase the lowest-quality land. For example, for $100 one could purchase one acre of *idith*, or two acres of *bainanith*, or three acres of *ziburith*. The rules of collection are as follows: if the judgment arose from a tort, then the judgment creditor may insist on being paid from *idith*. If the judgment arose from a loan or other credit transaction, then the judgment creditor may insist on being paid from *bainanith*. If the judgment arose from a *kethubah* claim, then the wife can be paid out of *ziburith*. Of course, the debtor may always pay in money and the options are no longer available to the judgment creditor. In the case of the lender creditor, if he was given a security interest in either of *idith, bainanith,* or *ziburith* he could insist on having enforcement from the land on which he held a security interest or from some field of *bainanith*.

bearer: The person in possession of an instrument or any other document of title or security endorsed in blank.

bearer instrument: An instrument is payable to bearer when by its terms it is payable to (a) bearer or the order of bearer; or (b) a specified person or bearer, or any other indication that does not purport to designate a specific payee.

bedikah: An examination. In laws of evidence it means that the witness was examined as to matters that do not deal directly with the guilt or innocence of a defendant in a criminal matter, or to the proving of a case by a party to a litigation. It concerns itself with collateral matters. For example, if the witness to a homicide had testified to all of the facts of the homicide, he would be questioned as to the color of the clothes worn by the slayer or the victim. The examination regarding the facts of the event are known as *drishah* and *hakirah*.

berrurin: There are two interpretations given in the Talmud in defining instruments of *berrurin*. One definition is the instrument whereby parties to a dispute agree to submit the dispute to arbitration, by each selecting one arbitrator and the two selected arbitrators selecting a third arbitrator. The instrument naming the arbitrators selected is an instrument of *berrurin*. Another definition is the instrument containing a record of the pleadings of the parties.

beth din: A duly constituted court that has jurisdiction over certain cases. Nowadays, the jurisdiction of the beth din is almost exclusively limited to the judging of commercial cases.

beth kor: An area of land equal to 5.26 acres (see *Area*).

borrower: The person or firm that is borrowing the money from the lender.

commodatary: The person to whom property is loaned gratuitously by the owner for the sole benefit of the borrower. This term has been used for a person who borrows things to distinguish him from the borrower who borrows money.

credence agreement: An agreement containing clauses wherein any party thereto agrees that if the other party presents the instrument, then it shall be given credence without any proof being presented. For example, the note of indebtedness may state that the seller, upon presenting the note of indebtedness, shall be believed that he delivered the goods agreed to be shipped to the buyer without having to present any other proof of delivery, or a lender being believed to state that a loan has not been paid in circumstances where he would have had to present proof to win the case.

credence clause: The clause in the credence agreement that states who shall be believed and to what extent and to which matters.

creditor: The person to whom money is owed by another person who is the debtor. In this work the creditor is usually the lender.

critically ill: For the purposes of the *halachah* a person is critically ill if it is assumed that he will die from the existing illness. His statements are made in contemplation of his immediate death. See also *gifts causa mortis*.

cubit: A linear measure equaling between 18.8 and 23 inches. I have used 21 inches as the equivalent of a cubit or *amah*. See *tefach*.

debtor: The person owing the money to the creditor. In this work the debtor is usually the borrower.

dina d'malchuta dina: The literal translation is "the law of the land is the law." A Jew is required to follow the laws of the land in which he resides, for example, in matters of criminal law, taxes, and real estate. This is discussed in Chapter 369.

draftsman: A person who draws or frames a legal instrument such as an instrument of indebtedness, deeds, wills, mortgages, and so forth.

drishah and hakirah: Examinations of witnesses that go to the essence of the act to which they are testifying. In a criminal case, it may mean questioning the witness as to the time and place of the crime, the facts constituting the crime, and any other details the judges deem significant. In civil cases it would consist of the facts of the transaction, for example, in the case of a loan, the terms of repayment agreed upon, and if there was a note of indebtedness executed, the facts of the note.

easement: A right enjoyed by one person to use the property of another. For example, Ruven has the dominant estate and Shimon has the subservient estate. An easement may be Ruven's right to travel by foot, by animal, or by vehicle over Shimon's land. It may be the right for light thus preventing Shimon from using his property to block Ruven's light. It may be a right for support of a structure on Ruven's land, or the right to a flow of water or air.

If it is a positive easement, it gives the holder the right to use the property of another. If it is a negative easement it restricts the right of the other in his use of his property. The easement does not confer a property right on the dominant estate.

An easement may be obtained by grant from the subservient estate to the dominate estate, or it may be obtained by use (prescription). An easement may be lost by nonuse or by abandonment.

effecting a lien: When the realty of the borrower becomes subject to a lien in favor of the lender. The lien puts the lender in the first position to take the property, even if the borrower has sold the realty subject to the lien to a third-party purchaser. The lien is usually effected if there is a note of indebtedness or a note of admission. The lien takes effect from the time the loan is reduced to writing and signed by the two subscribing witnesses, or from the time that a *kinyan* has been made. A promissory note and an oral loan do not effect a lien. There is a difference of opinion among the authorities if the basis of the lien is of Torah origin and covered all of the property of the debtor, real and personal, or whether the lien is of Rabbinic origin and the decree was to cover only real property, or perhaps a combination of the foregoing. In all events, the law is now that the lien extends to the real property of the debtor in his hands at the time the lien was created, either by the *kinyan* or by the delivery to the creditor of the note of indebtedness. The lien does not exist in any of the other categories of loans, not even of the written note executed by the debtor, if it does not have two witnesses who signed it. Since it is not witnessed in writing by two witnesses, there is no note of indebtedness to deliver to the creditor in the presence of witnesses. It does not extend to a loan witnessed by two eligible witnesses but not reduced to writing as a note of indebtedness. The lien does not extend to personal property, since it would then be impossible to sell anything, for the purchaser would always be fearful that there might be some lien of which he may not know. The parties may by agreement insert into the note of indebtedness that the lien extends to after-acquired property. Any such real property sold or given away or levied upon by third parties for loans that arose after the note of indebtedness loan are subject to the superior lien of the note of indebtedness loan. The theory is that if there is a note of indebtedness loan, then the news of such debt will be publicized and all will be aware of the note of indebtedness loan and the lien it has created. The indexing of such notes of indebtedness loans will facilitate such awareness. There are several ways in which the law presumes that there will be an awareness among the population that a lien has been established on the debtor's realty. The witnesses who witness the delivery of the note to the creditor establish such a lien. There is also an opinion that the witnesses, by merely signing the note, establish such a lien. This opinion is usually not followed unless there are also witnesses to the delivery. And a *kinyan*, whereby the debtor receives the handkerchief from the creditor, establishes the lien. At the time of the making of the *kinyan*, the debtor accepts the lien on his realty. For example, the lender loaned money to the borrower on January 1, 1990, with repayment to be made on March 1, 1990. The loan was evidenced by a duly executed promissory note, and thus it effected a lien on all of the realty owned by the borrower on the date of the making of the loan. On January 1 the borrower owned a piece of real property known as parcel A. On February 1, 1990, the borrower sold parcel A to purchaser. On March 1, 1990, the borrower did not have money to repay the loan. The lender may trace the realty to the purchaser and demand repayment of the loan from the purchaser or else parcel A will be sold to satisfy the loan.

eruv: A symbolic act to permit a person to do something that may not otherwise be done on the Sabbath. As used in this work in Volume 5, Chapter 161, it enables the residents of a housing complex to carry their things in and out of their own apartment to other parts of the complex. This is done by the residents contributing to the purchase of a loaf of bread, which, together with another edible, are placed in one of the apartments. Thus the entire complex is "mixed" into one domain.

escrow: Property delivered by the depositor or depositors (the escrower) to the escrowee to be held by him until the occurrence of a certain event or contingency or performance of a condition. The property may consist of personal property or intangible things such as instruments of indebtedness or securities or money or anything the parties wish to deposit with the escrowee.

escrowee: The person who is holding the escrowed property.

escrower: The person who has given property to the escrowee to hold.

execute (or **execution**): When a document is signed by the witnesses or the debtor.

force majeure: Usually an act that takes place without human intervention, such as a storm, earthquake, lightning, or other natural events. It may also refer to unforeseen events that are not ordinary, such as war intervening or a ferry not running, or a labor strike, and so forth.

gabbai: A functionary, usually of a synagogue. He coordinates the services to be sure that certain persons will lead the services, read from the Torah, receive the honor of opening the Holy Ark, and so on. The *gabbai* may function outside of the synagogue, as, for example, a *gabbai zedakah*. He is the person who distributes money, food, and clothing to the needy. There may also be a *gabbai* in charge of collecting funds for a community or a synagogue.

gifts causa mortis: A gift given by a person on his deathbed in contemplation of death, with the intent that the gift is to take effect if the donor does not recover and the donor dies of that illness.

grantee: The person who receives a thing, whether a gift or property, resulting from a sale to him. The grantee is the person named in the deed as the person to whom the ownership of the thing, usually real estate, is transferred.

grantor: The person who gives a thing by gift or by sale to the person who receives the thing. The grantor is the person named in the deed who is transferring ownership.

guarantor: One who becomes secondarily liable for another's debt or performance, in contrast to a strict surety, who is primarily liable with the principal debtor. To undertake collaterally to answer for the payment of another's debt or the performance of another's duty, liability, or obligation.

hakhchashah: One of two ways witnesses may be contradicted by other witnesses. The other way is by *hazamah*. In the case of *hakhchashah*, the witness contradicts the testimony of another witness bearing on the facts of the lawsuit or trial. Thus, if witness A says there was a loan made by Ruven to Shimon in a certain amount of money on a certain date and time, and witness B testifies that the transaction was not a loan, but the money was in payment for an item that Shimon sold to Ruven, this is *hakhchashah*. Such witnesses may be called contradicted witnesses.

halachah: The status of the law at a given time. What may have been the *halachah* at a certain point in time may change because of the Rabbis' decrees. *Halachah* may vary in different communities. A Jewish community in Spain is more apt to follow the holdings of Rabbi Yosef Karo, whereas a Jewish community in Russia is more apt to follow the holdings of Rabbi Moshe Isserles.

halizah: A ceremony performed in lieu of a *yibbum*. If a husband dies without any children or issue of children surviving, then his wife, according to Torah law, is to be married to the deceased husband's brother (Deuteronomy 25:5–10). This is known as *yibbum*. If the widow or the brother does not want to conclude the ceremony of *yibbum*, then they perform the ceremony of *halizah*, also described in Deuteronomy 25. After this, the widow is free to marry whomever she wants.

hanahah: A benefit that flows to a person. It may be something tangible or intangible, such as psychological benefit, as when someone relies upon the person.

hazakah: A method of acquiring real estate. It is perfected by the buyer (or donee) (1) in the presence of the seller (or donor), (2) doing an act to the realty or the building that he is acquiring, an act that (3) results in an improvement to the realty or the building. As soon as the act of *hazakah* is completed on even a small fraction of the realty, the buyer is the owner of the entire realty.

The term *hazakah* has another meaning that is more frequently used. It means a presumption that beth din will rely upon absent other proof.

hazamah: A method whereby a witness is refuted. (I have called such a witness a refuted witness as opposed to the witness who has been contradicted by *hakhchashah*, therefore a contradicted witness.) In *hazamah*, the second pair of witnesses do not testify as to the event at all. They testify that the earlier pair of witnesses could not have witnessed the event, since at the time they say they saw the event, they were with the second pair of witnesses in a place where it was not possible to witness the event. For example, the first pair of witnesses testifies that they saw a car driven by the defendant strike a pedestrian, who is the plaintiff in the action, on January 10, 1992, at 10:00 A.M. at the corner of Broadway and 42nd Street in New York City. The second pair of witnesses testifies that on January 10, 1992, at 10:00 A.M. the first pair of witnesses was with the second pair of witnesses in London, England. The second pair of witnesses does not testify as to the occurrence on January 10, 1992. For all they know, the defendant's car could very well have struck the plaintiff at that time and place. They testify only as to the untrustworthiness of the first pair of witnesses. The *halachah* is that the latest pair of witnesses is always believed in the case of *hazamah*.

herem: A state of excommunication. In a religious sense, a person is in *herem* for conduct unbecoming a Jew. In a civil sense, it means that the ban proclaimed against a person is not coming forth to testify as to certain conduct of which he is suspected, or a general *herem* to seek out persons who may be familiar with certain information. A plaintiff may ask beth din to proclaim a *herem* against anyone who has knowledge about a certain occurrence but does not come forth to testify. The plaintiff knows that there were witnesses when he was struck by defendant's automobile, but he does not know who they are.

heresh: A person who cannot speak or hear. In *halachah* it is assumed that such a person is usually not educable and thus generally does not have the status of a person who has reached majority regarding legal actions taken by him or being able to witness occurrences and then act as a witness.

hesseth oath: A post-Mishnaic oath instituted by the Rabbis of the Talmud. It is usually administered when the plaintiff has put forward a plea that he cannot prove and he is entitled to have the defendant take a *hesseth* oath to deny the claim of the plaintiff. The theory is that the plaintiff will not bring to litigation an unfounded lawsuit.

holder: The person who has in his possession an instrument or security or other intangible property.

Holy Day: In the Jewish calendar there are differences among Holy Days. Certain Holy Days prohibit all work, whereas other Holy Days permit some work. All the Holy Days have certain rituals attached to them, some applying to all or most of the Holy Days and some unique to certain Holy Days. The Holy Days are described in Volume I, Chapter 5, notes 3 and 4.

idith: See *bainanith*, above.

instrument: A written document such as a contract or note of indebtedness, a negotiable instrument, or security.

instrument of trust: See *note of trust.*

ir hanadachas: A city whose majority of inhabitants have been accused of idolatry and have been judged by the Great Sanhedrin and convicted of idolatry. The procedure to be followed with such a city is described in Deuteronomy 13:13–19.

joint and several liability: When one of at least two persons who are liable may be sued separately for the entire liability or the creditor may join all those who are liable in the lawsuit.

kethubah: A document in which the groom undertakes certain obligations to his bride. Besides general obligations of support, he undertakes to pay her the sum stipulated in the *kethubah* in the event that he divorces her. In the event of his death, his estate will pay the widow the same sum. The wife cannot waive the *kethubah*. The *kethubah* places a lien on all of the real estate, even if the real estate is sold, until the death of the wife if she predeceases the husband.

kinyan: One of the methods by which property may be acquired, as is shown in Volume VI, Chapter 195. A *kinyan* also acts to bind a person to his promise. In the case of a sale, the purchaser hands to the seller his handkerchief, which the seller holds for a moment. This symbolic trade of the handkerchief, and the money to be paid, are in exchange for the sold article. Similarly, the person who undertakes to perform an act, such as repaying a loan and liening his real property for the promise to repay, takes from the obligee a handkerchief and in exchange for receiving the handkerchief obligates himself to perform the act agreed upon. A *kinyan* may act as an instruction to the witnesses to the *kinyan* that the debtor acquiesces to a note of indebtedness being drawn, executed by the witnesses, and delivered to the creditor.

lender: The person or firm that lends the money to the borrower.

lender's oath: The lender who is holding collateral security that he alleges was lost or destroyed without his negligence must take an oath that he does not have possession or control over the collateral.

lien clause: A clause in an instrument that is subscribed by at least two witnesses and given to the lender in the presence of witnesses that creates a lien on the real property of the borrower. Thus, if the borrower owned real estate at the time the loan was made, all of the real estate then owned by him is subject to the lien of the lender. If the borrower thereafter sold any such real estate and the borrower does not have the means to pay the lender, the lender may make a levy on the real estate the borrower sold. The absence of a lien clause does not mean that the real estate of the borrower is free of the lien, since it is presumed that the lien clause was inadvertently omitted and the instrument will be treated as if the lien clause was in the instrument.

There is also a lien clause in favor of a purchaser of real estate. If the seller warranted good title to the real estate that he sold, then all of the remaining real estate owned by the seller at the time of the sale is liened to the purchaser, and if the purchaser loses the real estate to someone who had superior title to the seller, then the purchaser may sue the seller on the warranty of title, and if the seller does not have any money to pay the purchaser, the purchaser may levy on the purchasers who bought the real estate the seller owned at the time of the sale to the first purchaser. For example, on January 1, 1992 seller sold parcel A to purchaser A, and at the time seller warranted title to purchaser A. When the sale was made, seller also owned parcel B. On February 1, 1992, seller sold parcel B to purchaser B. On March 1, 1992, Mr. X. sued purchaser A to recover parcel A because it really belonged to him and never belonged to seller. Mr. X. won the lawsuit and purchaser A lost parcel A to Mr. X. Purchaser A sues seller on the warranty given on January 1, 1992, and wins the lawsuit against seller. Seller now has no assets to pay purchaser A. Purchaser A may levy on the property that seller sold to purchaser B on February 1, 1992.

liened property: Real estate is owned by the borrower at the time he borrows money and there is an executed note of indebtedness. All of the real estate owned by the borrower at that time has a lien placed on the real estate by virtue of the execution and delivery of the note of indebtedness to the lender.

lifnim mishurath hadin: When a person acts over and above what the *halachah* demands of him. Thus, if the *halachah* permits a person to renege on a certain contract, but he insists on honoring his commitment, he may be acting *lifnim mishurath hadin*. See *"Lifnim Mishrath Hadin"* by the author in *Annual Volume of the Council of Young Israel Rabbis in Israel*, Volume 2 (Jerusalem, 1988).

loan: The money loaned may fit into one of the following four categories:

(1) A loan made without any witnesses being present and without any writing evidencing the loan. This is designated as an oral loan.

(2) A loan made with two or more witnesses present and without any writing evidencing the loan. This is designated as an oral loan.

(3) A loan made with or without any witnesses being present, which loan was evidenced by a writing signed by the borrower and/or by one witness. This is designated as an oral loan. The writing signed under this category shall be designated as a promissory note, as distinguished from a note of indebtedness, which is category 4.

(4) A loan made with at least two witnesses being present who signed a writing evidencing the loan. The writing is then delivered to the lender in the presence of two witnesses who need not be the witnesses who signed the writing. This is designated as a loan with a writing. This writing shall be designated as a note of indebtedness.

Whether the borrower does or does not sign the note of indebtedness is of no legal significance.

ma'ah: A coin whose weight is the equivalent of 16 barleycorns.

ma'amad sheloshton: Literally, "the three persons standing." Ordinarily, as is seen in Volume II, Chapter 66, an instrument can be assigned only with a writing and transfer of the instrument being assigned. However, if the creditor, the borrower, and a third person are all present together, the lender may instruct the borrower to pay the debt to the third person and the debt is deemed transferred. See Volume IV, Chapter 126.

maneh: A weight of gold or silver. If a *perutah*, the smallest coin, is equivalent to a U.S. penny, a *maneh* is worth $192.

mashkanta: See *apotiki*.

migo: Literally, "since." A person who makes a plea is believed, since he could have presented another stronger plea that would have been believed. For example, the lender sues the borrower on an oral loan the lender is not able to prove. The borrower pleads payment. He is believed "since" he could have pleaded that the loan never took place and the lender could not have proved otherwise.

mikveh: A pool or bath of ritually clean water used to immerse people or utensils that are ritually unclean because of contact with the dead, or through an unclean flux from the body, such as a menstruant.

minyan: A quorum consisting of ten adult Jewish males, required for certain religious acts.

Mishnah: From the time of Moses until the end of the second century C.E., the Oral Law that Moses received on Mount Sinai from God was handed down orally from generation to generation. Due to the Roman persecutions in Israel beginning in 66 C.E., it became increasingly difficult to orally transmit the Oral Law. Rabbi Judah the Prince and his academy organized the Oral Law into sixty-three books. Each book contains many chapters, and each chapter contains many paragraphs of law relating to the subject matter of that particular book. Each paragraph is called a *mishnah*, and the entire body of these books is called The *Mishnah*. (The plural of *Mishnah* is *Mishnayoth*.)

mi'un: A disaffirmance. According to Torah law the father of a minor daughter has the right to betroth her to a husband. The Rabbis added certain situations where the mother or adult brothers of a minor girl whose father had died might betroth her to a husband. In the cases enacted by the Rabbis, the enactment provided that the girl upon her reaching her majority could disaffirm the marriage.

moches: A tax collector. Very often he would collect taxes beyond the amount authorized by legitimate government authorities.

moda'ah: A notification of duress. The seller of a piece of realty notifies witnesses that the sale he is about to make is under duress, and that at the first opportunity he intends to take legal steps to undo the sale.

moment: The amount of time it takes to state three words: "welcome my teacher." There are authorities who hold that it is the time that it takes to utter four words: "welcome rabbi and teacher." The actual term used in *halachah* is "the time of an utterance." This is a very short time, perhaps a second or two.

mortgage: A security of a particular property, usually real estate, for the payment of a debt. For example, the lender will not lend money to the borrower unless the borrower gives the lender a security interest in the real estate that the borrower owns. If the borrower does not pay off the loan, the lender may levy on the real estate on which he has the mortgage, the security interest. In this example, the borrower is the mortgagor, and the lender is the mortgagee.

mortgagee: The person who holds a mortgage on the property of the owner, who is the mortgagor. When a bank lends money for a person to purchase a home, the bank takes a mortgage on that home and the bank is the mortgagee. The homeowner who borrowed the money and gave the mortgage on his home is the mortgagor.

mortgagee in possession: The lender loaned money to the borrower and demands a security interest in the real estate of the owner. The lender is the mortgagee. The owner gives the mortgagee permission to enter upon the land on which the mortgagee holds the mortgage and the mortgagee may remain on the land until the land has given profits to the mortgagee to pay off the loan, at which time the mortgagee will leave the real estate and return it to the owner and the owner will not owe any more money to the lender. Or else the parties may agree that the lender will take possession of the mortgaged real estate for a specified time and at the end of the time the loan will be considered as fully repaid and the owner/borrower will retake possession of his land. The number of years must approximate the amount of time it would take to pay off the loan from the profits of the land. Some years the lender may make a larger profit from the land, but there may be some years of drought and the lender may lose from his operation of the real estate.

mortgagor: The owner of the property who has borrowed money from the mortgagee and who gives the mortgage on his property to the mortgagee.

nichsai melog: The real estate that a wife brings into the marriage (the dowry) may be used by the husband, and all income belongs to the husband. Such real estate may be under the stewardship of the husband in one of two ways. In either case he keeps all the profits of the real estate. According to the method known as *nichsai tzon barzel* (iron sheep property), the husband guarantees to the wife that the property will be returned to her upon divorce or upon his death at the same value it had on the day he took possession, regardless of whether he makes a profit or loses money during the operation of the property. Alternatively, the property may be delivered to the husband as *nichsai melog* (milking property), in which case the husband does not guarantee the value of the property when it is returned to the wife, upon divorce or death of the husband. In the case of *nichsai melog*, all losses and gains in the value of the property are the wife's. In both *nichsai tzon barzel* and *nichsai melog* the husband enjoys the profits of the property. The right to have the husband enjoy the profits of the wife's property is one of four obligations of the wife. These are enumerated on page 164 of Volume II.

nichsai tzon barzel: See *nichsai melog.*

niddui: A light form of *herem* (excommunication). The person under a *niddui* is given the opportunity to clear himself, usually within a period of thirty days, and failing that he may be given another thirty days. If he fails to cease the conduct that had placed him under the *niddui*, he is placed in *herem.*

Nissan: A month in the Jewish calendar corresponding to March/April. The festival of Passover occurs in this month.

note of admission: A note written after the borrower has admitted in the presence of two persons that he owes money to the lender. The note must be signed by the witnesses who heard the admission.

note of confession: A person does not owe any money to a certain person. Yet in the presence of at least two witnesses he admits that he owes that certain person a specified sum and he instructs the witnesses to write a note stating that he confesses that he owes the certain person money and he authorizes the witnesses to deliver the note of confession to that certain person.

note of indebtedness: A note signed by two witnesses evidencing the loan and delivered to the lender in the presence of two witnesses who need not be the same as the witnesses who signed the note. See *Loan*, item 4.

note of indebtedness loan: A loan that is evidenced by a note of indebtedness.

note of trust: A note of indebtedness that was completed and signed by the subscribing witnesses and given to the lender to hold in trust until such time as he will actually lend the money to the borrower. The loan was not yet made when the note of trust was written and delivered to the lender.

notification of duress: See *moda'ah*.

obligee: The person to whom an obligation or performance of an act is owed. If Ruven owes money to Shimon, Ruven is the obligor and Shimon is the obligee, or the promisee.

obligor: A person who owes money to another person, or owes performance of an act for the benefit of another person. The promissor.

onen: A person who is a mourner for one of his kinsmen, during the day of death; according to Torah law on the day of death alone and, according to Rabbinic law, the following night also. If the kinsman's body remained unburied, he was an onen until burial.

operative clause: The part of the instrument, no matter what type, that intends to create or transfer rights, by which the main object of the instrument is carried into effect.

oral loan: A loan that is not by a note of indebtedness.

payee: The person to whom an instrument is made payable, for example, a person named in the check as the person to whom it shall be paid.

payor: The person who will make the payment that is due on an instrument, for example, the person who writes a check to the payee.

perutah: The smallest copper coin mentioned in Rabbinic literature. If a thing is not worth at least a *perutah*, it is for many legal purposes deemed to be worthless.

pitka d'latotah: An authorization from beth din for one to curse a person who will violate a ban that is about to be pronounced. See Volume II, Chapter 71.

postdated note: An instrument that bears a date after the date in which the transaction actually occurred. For example, a loan was made on January 1, 1992, and the note of indebtedness is dated February 1, 1992.

predated note: An instrument that bears a date before the date on which the transaction actually occurred. For example, the loan was made on February 1, 1992, and the note of indebtedness is dated January 1, 1992.

promissory note: A writing signed by the borrower and/or only one witness evidencing the loan. See *Loan*, item 3.

rasha: A wicked person. He may be called wicked because of his conduct to his fellow man and/or his conduct in violating laws of the Torah that relate to man's relationship to God. The person becomes a *rasha* if he persists after being warned to cease such conduct. Generally there must be at least two witnesses who have testified before a beth din as to his conduct.

realty: Real property owned by the seller or borrower, as distinguished from personalty, which is any property owned by the seller other than real property.

reducing the loan to writing: Writing down evidence of the transaction that occurred. Most often it will refer to writing the note of indebtedness, a note of admission, or promissory note.

release: The abandonment or giving up of a right, claim, or privilege by the person in whom it exists to the person against whom it might have been demanded. For example, a borrower owes money to a lender and the lender releases the repayment of the loan.

rules of construction: The rules used by a beth din to determine the sense or real meaning of obscure or ambiguous terms in an instrument. The beth din will look to extraneous, connected circumstances and try to ascertain the aim and purpose of the terms.

scribe: The person who writes the document. Nowadays this will usually be a lawyer for one of the parties.

semichah: The laying on of hands. *Semichah* was the act whereby a person was ordained by an already ordained person. *Semichah* traces its origins to Moses laying his hands upon Joshua and Joshua thereby becoming ordained. Thereafter, the *semichah* was given by the person who had *semichah*, in the presence of at least two other persons authorizing the person to be ordained to judge matters of ritual and/or matters of civil law. All members of the Great Sanhedrin and the Lesser Sanhedrin had to be ordained. The members of the beth din did not ordinarily have to be ordained to judge most monetary cases. The granting of *semichah* lapsed in the middle of the fourth century C.E.

set-off: A claim, by the defendant, in a specified amount of money as a defense to the whole or part of the claim made against him by the plaintiff. This amount, which the defendant claims is due from the plaintiff, may be set up as a defense against the claim of the plaintiff or may be sued upon as a counterclaim or in a separate lawsuit.

shemitah: The seventh year. The years in the Jewish calendar are divided into groups of seven. The number of the year determines which tithes and other agricultural dues will be given to the priests, the Levites, and the poor. The seventh year of each cycle, the *shemitah* year, marked a period when the fields would lie fallow and the poor could take whatever aftergrowth there was in the fields. At the termination of the *shemitah* year, debts were usually forgiven, unless there was a procedure to keep the debt alive. See Volume II, Chapter 67.

shikul hadath: A concept permitting the judge on a case to weigh the precedents. There may be a dispute among the Rabbis of the *Mishnah* or of the Talmud, and the *halachah* is not specifically decided. The authorities have thereafter accepted one view, and this would be the *shikul hadath* of the case. If the judge or the beth din decides in accordance with the view not generally accepted, it would be a violation of *shikul hadath*.

shoodah dedaini: A concept giving the judge or the beth din that is deciding the case wide discretion to decide in the direction that the evidence and testimony are inclined, although there is no fully competent testimony or proof.

shotah: A mentally deficient person. The *halachah* views him as a person who is not responsible for his acts, nor can he take care of himself.

simtah: An area that is part of a public street, yet is off to a side and is not frequently used. Because it is not frequently used the community by general usage permits passersby to use the area as if it were their private property for temporarily placing objects there and for acquiring personal property in special situations (see Volume VI, Chapter 198).

sinar: Either a belt or other garment that women wore to protect their modesty.

stay of enforcement (of a judgment): Suspension of proceedings in a lawsuit, which may be temporary until something permanent has been ordered. The beth din has the right to suspend proceedings, including the suspension of permitting a party who has a judgment to enforce payment of the judgment until further order of the beth din.

subscribing witness: A witness, other than the borrower, who signs a writing evidencing the borrowing.

surety: One bound with his principal for the payment of a sum of money or for the performance of some duty or promise and who is entitled to be indemnified by someone who ought to have paid or performed if payment or performance be enforced against him. One who undertakes to pay money or to do any other act in event that his principal fails therein.

takkanah: A decree made by the Rabbis.

tallit: A prayer shawl used by men during morning prayers. There was a time when men wore the *tallit* and *tefilin* during the entire daylight hours.

tefach: A measure that I have calculated for the purposes of this work to be about 3.7 inches. The Talmud and *halachah* use certain measurements. The exact equivalents to metric or United States measurements can only be guessed at by scientists and great Rabbinic authorities. There is a difference of opinion regarding the *amah* or cubit. It has been estimated that an *amah* is between 18.8 inches and 23 inches. I have taken the mid-point of about 21 inches to equal a cubit. A *tefach* is one-sixth of a cubit and is therefore 3.5 inches. I have, however, used 3.7 inches because most authorities, for purposes other than civil law, use this measurement as the measure of a *tefach*. When three *tefachim* (the plural of *tefach*) are mentioned, I have used 11 inches, and I have used 37 inches for ten *tefachim*.

tefachim: The plural of *tefach*.

tefilin: Two black leather boxes containing Scriptural passages that are bound by black leather straps on the left hand and head and worn for morning services except on the Sabbath and Holy Days. In foregone times they were worn during the entire daylight hours. There are still some people nowadays who wear them all day.

tereifah: The Mishnah in *Hullin*, chapter 3, enumerates eighteen defects discovered in an animal after it has been slaughtered according to Jewish ritual law. If an animal contains any of these defects it is *tereifah* and forbidden to be eaten by a Jew.

The eighteen *tereifoth* (plural of *tereifah*) are (1) the gullet was pierced; (2) the windpipe was severed; (3) the membrane of the brain was pierced; (4) the heart was pierced as far as the chamber; (5) the spine was broken and the spinal cord was cut; (6) the liver was gone and nothing remained; (7) the lung was pierced; (8) part of the lung was missing; (9) the abomasum (the food is passed by an animal into four stomachs, the fourth of which is the abomasum) was pierced; (10) the gallbladder was pierced; (11) the intestines were pierced; (12) the rumen (first stomach) was pierced; (13) the greater part of the outer covering over the stomachs was pierced; (14) the omasum (the third stomach) was pierced; (15) the reticulum (the second stomach) was pierced; (16) the animal had fallen from a roof and was immediately slaughtered before it stood up; (17) most of the ribs were fractured; and (18) the animal was clawed by a wild animal.

testator: A person who writes a will or the person who has died leaving a will.

tracing the assets: If the borrower does not have assets to repay the loan, the lender may recover from the purchaser the realty that the purchaser purchased from the borrower. Usually this will only apply to realty that was owned by the borrower at the time when he borrowed the money.

unsold property: Any property in the hands of the debtor at the time when the creditor comes to collect his debt.

waiver: The voluntary, intentional relinquishment of a known right.

warranty: A promise that certain facts are true as they are represented to be and that they will remain so. In sales it may be a warranty that the seller is the owner and has the right to sell the property without any restriction and is sold without any other person having any rights in the property.

witness: A person who is eligible to be a witness in accordance with Volume I, Chapters 33, 34, and 35. The witnesses may not be related to each other or to any of the parties.

witness of delivery: A witness who sees the note being delivered to the lender.

zedek: Justice or righteousness.

ziburith: See *bainanith*.

zommemim: Refuted witnesses. When witnesses have been refuted by *hazamah*, they become *zommemim*.

INDEX

About the Author

Emanuel Quint is a rabbi and lawyer and a co-founder (with Rabbi Adin Steinsaltz) of the Jerusalem Institute of Jewish Law, where he is dean and *rosh kollel*. With Professor Neil Hecht he wrote *Jewish Jurisprudence* which bears the approbation of the late Rabbi Joseph Soleveitchik. He was one of the founders and a trustee of Touro College, which named him an honorary Doctor of Laws, was president of the Young Israel Council in Israel, head of the beth din of the Young Israel Rabbis in Israel, a member of the board of trustees of Jerusalem College of Technology, and was a senior partner of the New York law firm of Quint, Marx, and Chill. Rabbi Quint and his wife Rena have four children, and live in Jerusalem.